AIR WAR
SOUTH ATLANTIC

Jeffrey Ethell and Alfred Price

SIDGWICK & JACKSON
LONDON

First published in 1983 in Great Britain
by Sidgwick and Jackson Limited

Copyright © Jeffrey Ethell and Alfred Price

ISBN 0-283-99035-X

Typeset by Tellgate Ltd, Shaftesbury, Dorset
Printed in Great Britain by
The Garden City Press Limited, Letchworth,
Hertfordshire SG6 1JS
for Sidgwick and Jackson Limited
1 Tavistock Chambers, Bloomsbury Way
London WC1A 2SG

Contents

List of Maps

Photo Acknowledgements

The authors and publishers are grateful to the following for providing and/or granting permission to reproduce the illustrations between pages 164 and 165:

1, Royal Navy; 2, FAA; 3, RAF; 4, Royal Navy; 5 and 6, RAF; 7, Royal Navy; 8, Press Association; 9 and 10, Col Carlos Corino's private collection; 11, Lt Thomas's private collection; 12 and 13, Armada Argentina/Dr Scheina's private collection; 14, Dr Scheina's private collection; 15, Royal Navy; 16, 17 and 18, Cdr Eduardo Alimonda's private collection; 19, Jeffrey Ethell's private collection; 20, Royal Navy; 21 and 22, RAF; 23, British Aerospace; 24, Wing Cdr Emmerson's private collection; 25, Chief Technician Fred Welsh's private collection; 26, Sqn Ldr Mel James; 27, Alfred Price's private collection; 28, Flt Lt W.J. Perrins' private collection; 29, British Aerospace; 30, RAF; 31, 32, 33, 34 and 35, FAA; 36, Royal Navy; 37 and 38, Lt Cdr Ward's private collection; 39, Lt Cdr Rupert Nichol/Rex Features; 40, Royal Navy; 41, Cdr West's private collection; 42, Lt Cdr Rupert Nichol/Rex Features; 43, Foto Luce/Lt Cdr Philippi's private collection; 44, Lt Cdr Morell's private collection; 45, Lt Cdr Rupert Nichol/Rex Features; 46, Royal Navy; 47, Alfred Price's private collection; 48, Sub-Lt Dibb's private collection; 49, FAA; 50, Jeffrey Ethell's private collection; 51, FAA; 52, Jeffrey Ethell's private collection; 53, Sub-Lt Dibb's private collection; 54, Royal Navy; 55, Cdr Eduardo Alimonda's private collection; 56, Alfred Price's private collection; 57, Flt Sgt Knights' private collection; 58, RAF; 59, FAA; 60, Royal Navy; 61, Capt. Pentreath's private collection; 62, British Aerospace; 63, RAF; 64, Royal Navy; 65, Wing Cdr Squire's private collection; 66, 67 and 68, Royal Navy; 69, P. Holdgate; 70, Lt Cdr Clark's private collection; 71, Capt. Drennan's private collection; 72, RAF.

Acknowledgements

This book would not have been possible without the generous assistance of numerous members of the Royal Navy, the Army and the Royal Air Force, and the Argentine Navy and Air Force.

At the Ministry of Defence in London the three services' public relations directorates afforded considerable help. Captain Ian Sutherland, the Royal Navy Director of Public Relations, gave his support to the project and Ted Knowle of his staff and Michael Hill at Northwood provided several useful interviews. At Yeovilton Lieutenant Commander Jan Larcombe arranged interviews with several Sea Harrier pilots. For the Army Brigadier David Ramsbottom and his staff gave a lot of help, especially Jerry Baldwin. Brigadier Jebens of the Army Air Corps made possible the interviews with several of his helicopter pilots and crewmen. For the Royal Air Force Air Commodore Richard Miller and Michael Pentreath gave considerable assistance and encouragement. At Headquarters Strike Command Graeme Hammond and Tony Talbot arranged every interview requested within their area of responsibility, as did Paul Chesterfield and Keith Ansell at Headquarters Support Command. On the stations the press liaison officers worked hard to meet requests, and the authors are grateful to Flight Lieutenant John Blenkiron at Wittering, Flight Lieutenant Fogarty at Waddington, Flight Lieutenant Brooks at Marham, Flight Lieutenant Wood at Odiham, and Terry Heffanen at Boscombe Down.

The Argentine Embassy in Washington DC was likewise a considerable source of assistance. In the Air Attaché's office Brigadiers Ricardo Peña and Marcelo Bonino, and Comodoro Ruben Corradetti, made possible the research visit to air force bases in Argentina. In the Naval Attaché's office Capitán de fragata Eduardo Alimonda made possible a similar visit to naval air stations; Capitán de fragata Basilio Pertiné, his successor, assisted in answering many questions which arose after the visit. In Argentina itself Vicecomodoro Ricardo Di Liscia and Saul Haedo of the Air Force High Command served as escorts during visits to units which fought in the conflict; Capitán de fragata Crivellini did the same for the naval air stations.

Once the interviews in Argentina had been completed there remained the problem of translating them accurately into English; Castilian as spoken there differs in many respects from the Spanish used elsewhere, and the expertise of Efrain Ortiz at the National Air and Space Museum in Washington DC was invaluable in transcribing the interview tapes quickly. Susanna Donnally and Mike Goodwin also gave much valuable assistance.

Dr Robert Scheina and Colin Smith both made available information from their own research into Argentine air operations during the conflict. Larry Webb copied many of the photographs used in this book.

Last, but by no means least, the authors wish to express their gratitude to those involved with the conflict who made available their stories. Some have asked not to be named, and the authors respect their wish to remain anonymous; the others are listed as The Witnesses.

The Witnesses

ABBREVIATIONS:

RN Royal Navy
RAF Royal Air Force
AAC Army Air Corps
FAA Fuerza Aérea Argentine (Argentine Air Force)
AA Aeronaval Argentina (Argentine Naval Air Arm)

Teniente Hugo Argonaraz, FAA, Pucará pilot, Grupo 3
Capitán Alberto Baigorri, FAA, Canberra pilot, Grupo 2
Flight Lieutenant Ted Ball, RAF, Sea Harrier pilot, No. 800 Sqn
Capitán Guillermo Ballesteros, FAA, Mirage pilot, Grupo 8
Flight Lieutenant Paul Barton, RAF, Sea Harrier pilot, No. 801 Sqn
Captain Ben Bathurst, RN, Director of Naval Air Warfare, Ministry of Defence
Capitán Jorge Benitez, FAA, Pucará pilot, Grupo 3
Lieutenant Commander Mike Blissett, RN, Sea Harrier pilot, No. 800 Sqn
Staff Sergeant Chris Bowman, army photographic interpreter, HMS *Hermes*
Teniente José Carlos, FAA, Skyhawk pilot, Grupo 5
Mr Tony Chater, Port Stanley resident
Air-Vice Marshal George Chesworth, RAF, Chief of Staff No. 18 Group, Northwood
Lieutenant Commander Hugh Clark, RN, Sea King pilot, Commander No. 825 Sqn
Capitán de fragata Jorge Colombo, AA, Super Étendard pilot, Commander 2nd Naval Fighter and Attack Escuadrilla

13

Comodoro Carlos Corino, FAA, Mirage pilot, Commander Grupo 8

Flight Sergeant Ray Cowburn, RAF, Harrier ground crewman, No. 1 Sqn

Lieutenant Commander Al Craig, RN, Sea Harrier pilot, No. 801 Sqn

Capitán de corbeta Roberto Curilovic, AA, Super Étendard pilot, 2nd Naval Fighter and Attack Escuadrilla

Air Marshal Sir John Curtiss, RAF, Air Officer Commanding No. 18 Group

Flight Lieutenant Dave Davenal, RAF, Victor operations officer, Ascension Island

Sub Lieutenant Phil Dibb, RN, Sea King pilot, No. 826 Sqn

Captain Sam Drennan, AAC, Scout pilot, No. 656 Sqn

Vicecomodoro Ernesto Duburg, FAA, Skyhawk pilot, Grupo 5

Squadron Leader John Elliott, RAF, Victor tanker pilot, No.55 Sqn

Wing Commander David Emmerson, RAF, Nimrod Detachment Commander, Ascension Island

Wing Commander Richard Fitzgerald-Lombard, RAF, Commander Engineering Wing, Wittering

Lieutenant Commander 'Fred' Frederiksen, Sea Harrier pilot, No. 800 Sqn

Corporal John Gammon, AAC, Scout crewman, No. 656 Sqn

Major Bob Gardner, Commander No. 47 Air Dispatch Sqn. RCT, Ascension Island

Flight Lieutenant Nick Gilchrist, RAF, Harrier pilot, No. 1 Sqn

Flight Lieutenant Jeff Glover, RAF, Harrier pilot, No. 1 Sqn

Capitán Horacio Gonzalez, FAA, Dagger pilot, Grupo 6

Flight Lieutenant Gordon Graham, Vulcan navigator, No. 101 Sqn

Captain John Greenhalgh, AAC, Scout pilot, No. 656 Sqn

Capitán Ricardo Grünert, FAA, Pucará pilot, Grupo 3

Lieutenant Martin Hale, RN, Sea Harrier pilot, No. 800 Sqn

Mr Graeme Hammond, Admiral's press liaison officer, HMS *Hermes*

Chief Technician 'Hank' Hankinson, RAF, bomb disposal team

Flight Lieutenant Mark Hare, RAF, Harrier pilot, No. 1 Sqn

Squadron Leader Peter Harris, RAF, Harrier pilot, No. 1 Sqn

Air Vice-Marshal Kenneth Hayr, RAF, Assistant Chief of Air Staff (Operations), Ministry of Defence

Sergeant Steve Hitchman, RAF, Chinook ground crewman, No. 18 Sqn, *Atlantic Conveyor*

Squadron Leader Bob Iveson, RAF, Harrier pilot, No. 1 Sqn

Flight Lieutenant Tom Jones, RAF, Chinook crewman, No. 18 Sqn

Capitán Narciso Juri, FAA, Learjet pilot, Grupo 2

Major Chris Keeble, 2nd Battalion the Parachute Regiment

Chief Technician Tom Kinsella, RAF, Chinook ground crewman, No. 18 Sqn

Squadron Leader Dick Langworthy, RAF, Chinook pilot, No. 18 Sqn

Comodoro Juan Laskowsky, FAA, Skyhawk pilot, Commander Grupo 5

Flight Lieutenant John Leeming, RAF, Sea Harrier pilot No. 800 Sqn

1er Teniente Hector Luna, FAA, Dagger pilot, Grupo 6

Flight Lieutenant Murdo Macleod, RAF, Harrier pilot, No. 1 Sqn

Mayor Carlos Martinez, FAA, Dagger pilot, Grupo 6

Squadron Leader Peter Martin-Smith, RAF, Ministry of Defence, Whitehall

Sergeant Ted Mawson, RAF, Harrier ground crewman No. 1 Sqn

Squadron Leader Neil McDougall, RAF, Vulcan pilot, No. 50 Sqn

1er Teniente Juan Micheloud, FAA, Pucará pilot, Grupo 3

Flying Officer Colin Miller, RAF, Chinook co-pilot, No. 18 Sqn

Lieutenant Clive Morell, RN, Sea Harrier pilot, No. 800 Sqn

Flight Lieutenant Dave Morgan, RAF, Sea Harrier pilot, No. 800 Sqn

Alférez Marcelo Moroni, FAA, Skyhawk pilot, Grupo 5

Flight Lieutenant Ian Mortimer, RAF, Sea Harrier pilot, No. 801 Sqn

Lieutenant Commander Rupert Nichol, RN, captain's staff HMS *Hermes*

Alférez Jorge Nuevo, FAA, Skyhawk pilot, Grupo 5

Capitán Carlos Pena, FAA, Learjet pilot, Grupo 2

Capitán Roberto Pastran, FAA, Canberra pilot, Grupo 2

Captain David Pentreath, RN, Captain HMS *Plymouth*

ler Teniente Carlos Perona, FAA, Mirage pilot, Grupo 8

Capitán de fragata Basilio Pertiné, AA, Electra pilot, 1st Naval Logistics Escuadrilla

Capitán de corbeta Alberto Philippi, AA, Skyhawk pilot, 3rd Naval Fighter and Attack Escuadrilla

Squadron Leader Jerry Pook, RAF, Harrier pilot, No. 1 Sqn

Group Captain Jeremy Price, RAF, Detachment Commander Wideawake airfield, Ascension Island

Lance Corporal Mark Price, AAC, ground signaller, No. 656 Sqn

Flight Lieutenant Hugh Prior, RAF, Vulcan air electronics officer, No. 101 Sqn

Squadron Leader Chris Pye, RAF, Vulcan engineer officer, Waddington

Sub Lieutenant Clive Rawson, RN, Sea King observer, No. 826 Sqn

Squadron Leader John Reeve, RAF, Vulcan pilot, No. 50 Sqn

Lance Corporal 'J' Rig, AAC, Scout crewman, No. 656 Sqn

ler Teniente Cesar Roman, FAA, Dagger pilot, Grupo 6

Teniente de navío Benito Rotolo, AA, Skyhawk pilot, 3rd Naval Fighter and Attack Escuadrilla

ler Teniente Hector Sanchez, FAA, Skyhawk pilot, Grupo 5

Mayor Juan Sapolski, FAA, Dagger pilot, Grupo 6

Lieutenant Commander Doug Squier, RN, Sea King pilot commander, No. 826 Sqn

Wing Commander Peter Squire, RAF, Harrier pilot, Commander No. 1 Sqn

Flight Lieutenant Alan Swan, RAF, commander bomb disposal team

Flying Officer Peter Taylor, RAF, Vulcan co-pilot, No. 50 Sqn

Lieutenant Commander Neil Thomas, RN, Sea Harrier pilot, No. 800 Sqn

Lieutenant Steve Thomas, RN, Sea Harrier pilot, No. 801 Sqn

Lieutenant Commander Simon Thornewill, RN, Sea King pilot commander, No. 846 Sqn

Squadron Leader Martin Todd, RAF, Victor tanker pilot, No. 57 Sqn

Mayor Juan Tomba, FAA, Pucará pilot, Grupo 3

Flight Lieutenant Rod Trevaskus, RAF, Vulcan air electronics officer, No. 50 Sqn

Wing Commander Fred Trowern, RAF, senior air liaison officer
  on General Moore's staff
Squadron Leader Bob Tuxford, RAF, Victor tanker pilot, No. 55
  Sqn
ler Teniente Ernesto Ureta, FAA, Skyhawk pilot, Grupo 4
Vicecomodoro Alberto Vianna, FAA, C-130 Hercules pilot,
  Grupo 1
Capitán Roberto Vila, FAA, Pucará pilot, Grupo 3
Lieutenant Commander 'Sharkey' Ward, RN, Sea Harrier pilot,
  Commander No. 801 Sqn
Chief Technician Fred Welsh, RAF, Harrier ground crewman,
  No. 1 Sqn
Commander Alan West, RN, Captain HMS *Ardent*
Flight Lieutenant Martin Withers, RAF, Vulcan pilot, No. 101
  Sqn
Flight Lieutenant Bob Wright, RAF, Vulcan navigator, No. 101
  Sqn
Vicecomodoro Ruben Zini, FAA, Skyhawk pilot, Grupo 5

Authors' Note

In this book, unless otherwise stated, all times are those local to the area being described in the text. The ranks stated are those held by the participants at the time described, with the Argentine ranks anglicized so that they are easier to follow for the English-speaking reader (a full list of comparative ranks is given in Appendix 1). Unless otherwise stated, all distances are given in statute miles and speeds in miles per hour; where units have been converted, the figures have been rounded out where appropriate.

1: Preparing to Meet the Unforeseen

3 – 19 APRIL

'The best scale for an experiment is 12 inches to the foot.'
Admiral of the Fleet Lord Fisher

The speed and comparative ease with which the Argentine forces had been able to overwhelm the small British garrison on the Falklands, and on the following day that on South Georgia, came as a shock to the British people. Initially there was a feeling of helplessness throughout the nation, which gave way to muted anger as film appeared on television showing the Royal Marines taken prisoner and flag-waving demonstrators celebrating the event in the streets of Buenos Aires.

At an emergency debate on 3 April, the first Saturday sitting of the House of Commons since the Suez Crisis in 1956, Prime Minister Margaret Thatcher announced that a strong naval force was to sail for the South Atlantic on the following Monday to repossess the islands, by force if need be. The move received the codename Operation CORPORATE.

Over that weekend there was frenzied activity at the Royal Navy bases, as ships were stocked and prepared for possible war. From the Naval Air Station at Yeovilton in Somerset, the Sea Harriers of Nos. 800 and 801 Squadrons hastily prepared to embark on their respective aircraft carriers, HMSS *Hermes* and *Invincible*. Normally these units were established at only five aircraft each; for CORPORATE the aircraft, pilots and ground crewmen of the Sea Harrier training unit, No. 899 Squadron, were shared between the two operational squadrons to bring No. 800 up to twelve aircraft and 801 up to eight. *Hermes* and *Invincible* also took on their resident anti-submarine helicopter squadrons, respectively Nos. 826 and 820, each with nine Sea Kings; and

19

Hermes took on a further nine Sea King transport helicopters of No. 846 Squadron for use by her contingent of marine commandos.

As the two aircraft carriers set sail from Portsmouth on 5 April they received a tumultuous send-off from large crowds of well-wishers. Lieutenant David Smith, one of the Sea Harrier pilots on *Hermes*, afterwards wrote to his parents: 'We sailed on 5 April to the most amazing sight I think I have ever seen. . . As far as the eye could see, the shores of both Portsmouth and Gosport were black with people cheering us away. It was the most heartening send-off which still lingers with us. I think it would be fair to say that few of the ship's company did not have a tear or two to shed.'

The noisy farewell contrasted sharply with the pensive silence on the warships when they left the land behind them, as their crews pondered on what the future might bring. Lieutenant Commander Andy Auld, the commander of No. 800 Squadron, heard one of the ship's Sea King pilots comment: 'I suppose the Spanish Armada enjoyed a send-off like this!'

By 6 April the Task Force on its way to Ascension Island comprised the two aircraft carriers, the assault ship *Fearless*, ten destroyers and frigates, and four replenishment ships. At this stage the ships carried, between them, twenty Sea Harriers and some fifty-four helicopters of various types – Sea Kings, Lynxes, Wessex, Wasps and Scouts.

One problem facing the British air commanders at this time was lack of reliable information on the size of the Argentine air threat likely to face the Task Force: over the years the intelligence community had concentrated its efforts looking east towards the Warsaw Pact rather than south towards Latin America. According to the best information then available, Argentina possessed some 16 Mirages, 26 Daggers, 76 Skyhawks, 9 Canberras, and 5 Super Étendards, plus a further 115 Pucará, Paris, Turbo-Mentor and Macchi light attack aircraft which could be a threat if the warships came within their range. That made a grand total of 247 enemy fighter and attack aircraft, sufficient to outnumber the Sea Harriers by more than twelve to one. Everybody agreed that was a 'worst case' figure, but intelligence officers prefer to deal in 'worst cases' and then worry themselves sick about the implications.

If it was to come to a fight, much would depend on the ability of the few Sea Harriers to overcome or at least contain the far larger enemy air forces. It was a tall order. The Mirages and Daggers, which alone appeared to outnumber the Sea Harriers by more than two to one, can fly at twice the speed of sound and would be able, literally, to run rings round their potential opponents. Then there were the postulated seventy-six or so Skyhawks, attack aircraft which, handled properly after they have dropped their bombs, can become mean little fighters.

Although it cannot fly faster than sound in level flight, the Sea Harrier did possess two advantages over its opponents in air-to-air combat, though neither had yet been proven in actual combat. The first of these was the ability to use VIFF – thrust Vectored In Forward Flight – and thereby outmanoeuvre enemy fighters. Some fanciful diagrams have been published showing how a Sea Harrier pilot could let an enemy get behind him, then use VIFF to jump out of the way, let his assailant go screaming past, then descend behind and loose off missiles to shoot it down. Such a theory ignores the realities of air combat: for one thing, no Sea Harrier pilot would ever willingly allow an enemy to get into such a missile-firing position behind him – and if the enemy did succeed in doing this, the relatively slow VIFF climb would not be fast enough to get the Sea Harrier out of trouble.

In fact, in combat VIFF would be used only in a very few specific situations. Its great disadvantage is that it rapidly slows the aircraft, and in combat that is usually the last thing a fighter pilot wants. 'Everybody has his own ideas on VIFF,' explained Flight Lieutenant David Morgan, a Royal Air Force pilot attached to No. 800 Squadron who was to end the conflict the top scorer among the Sea Harrier pilots. 'When on the offensive I personally would not use it unless by doing so I could finish the combat within a few seconds. That is to say, I would use it to point the nose of my aircraft higher than would otherwise be possible in order to get off a shot.' In other circumstances, Morgan felt the use of VIFF would probably help the enemy to escape. Thrust vectoring is considered a useful aid if the Sea Harrier is itself being attacked. If the pilot flies a violent manoeuvre and applies reverse thrust the aircraft decelerates very quickly indeed, far quicker than any conventional aircraft. Then the combination of rapid deceleration and violent evasive manoeuvre would give the attacking aircraft a very difficult shot even with a missile.

The other apparent advantage unique to the Sea Harrier in this conflict was that it carried the new AIM-9L version of the Sidewinder heat-seeking missile. Compared with previous types of infra-red air-to-air missile, which could home on subsonic targets only from the rear aspect, the AIM-9L could home on target aircraft from almost any aspect and even had a limited head-on capability. At least, the maker's brochure said it had. Since the advent of the missile age hardly a single one of these weapons had performed as well in action as the maker's brochure had said it would. Would the AIM-9L prove any different?

Quite apart from its dependence for fighter cover on a thinly spread force operating unproven equipment, the British Task Force was deficient in other aspects in the air. It had no airborne early warning aircraft to alert it of the approach of low flying raiders. Nor, initially, would there be any long range reconnaissance cover once the ships had passed beyond the operational radius of the Royal Air Force Nimrod patrol aircraft based on Ascension. The Sea Harrier squadrons were not fully trained for ground-attack missions, and they had only 'iron' bombs and unguided rockets with which to attack enemy warships. Initially none of these aircraft carried the chaff or infra-red decoy dispensers considered necessary for operations in the face of modern gun and missile systems. The transport helicopter force had sufficient lifting capacity to support landings on the islands only by relatively small raiding parties.

Some of these shortcomings would be corrected or partially corrected during the weeks that followed. By dint of much hard work and overtime at the British Aerospace factory at Kingston, which made the aircraft, and the Ferranti works at Edinburgh, which made the Blue Fox radar and other items of equipment, the final eight Sea Harriers on order for the Royal Navy were hastily completed and brought to operational standard. To provide them with the capability to drop chaff and infra-red decoys, several cartridge-dispensing systems were bought 'off the shelf' from the American Tracor company; these would later be flown south and fitted to many of the aircraft on board the carriers. The problem of providing airborne early warning radar for the warships would prove more intractable in the short term, however; it would lead to a crash programme to modify a Sea King for this purpose, but even though the work went ahead at the highest priority many weeks would pass before the prototype installation was ready to fly. To increase the size of the transport helicopter force three new squadrons were formed and prepared to move south: No. 825 with Sea Kings, and Nos. 847 and 848 with Wessex.

To meet other requirements the Royal Navy had to go beyond its own immediate resources. The Royal Air Force began a crash programme to fit Nimrods with in-flight refuelling equipment and began training crews in this unfamiliar type of operation.

Of the aircraft being sent south the most critical single type was the Sea Harrier. Only twenty-eight were available in total, and every one lost in action or by accident depleted the meagre air cover available to the Task Force by that amount. The only high-performance aircraft that could possibly be used to replace lost Sea Harriers was the Royal Air Force's GR 3 version of the Harrier; but this was a ground-attack aircraft and was not equipped, nor were its pilots trained, for air-to-air combat or carrier operations. So it came as a considerable surprise when No. 1 Squadron, based at Wittering near Stamford, received orders to prepare its pilots and Harrier GR 3s for the unaccustomed new roles.

The modifications required to the Harrier GR 3 fell into two main categories: those necessary for the aircraft to operate from carriers, and those to fit it for the newly acquired air-to-air fighting role. In the first category most of the changes were relatively minor: the fitting of lashing rings to the outrigger wheel legs, the drilling of holes in the airframe in strategic places to allow salt water to run out, minor changes to the nosewheel steering mechanism and the nozzle control system. Far more involved were the fitting of a radar transponder which would produce a distinctive blip on the shipborne radars used to control the aircraft on their return to the carrier, and the changes to the Harrier's inertial navigation system to enable it to provide flight instrument indications when aligned on the moving deck of a ship (the system fitted to the Sea Harrier had been designed for this purpose and was a quite different piece of equipment).

Of the modifications to improve the Harrier's operational capability, the most far-reaching centred on altering the aircraft to enable it to carry and launch Sidewinder air-to-air missiles (the

RAF operational requirements branch had been crying out for such modifications for years, but the necessary funds had never been available). The work involved the fitting of an electronic control and firing unit in the rear fuselage, and alterations to the aircraft wiring and weapons pylons. The task of incorporating the changes fell to No. 1 Squadron's engineers, backed up by Wing Commander Richard Fitzgerald-Lombard and the 625-strong Engineering Wing at Wittering. 'We were told we had to complete the work on the first batch of ten aircraft "as soon as possible",' he recalled. 'But putting two and two together we reckoned we had about three weeks before the aircraft would need to fly south to join the Task Force.' It would be a close-run thing: the installations of the radar transponder and the Sidewinder missiles had to be designed from scratch, then prototypes made and tested on the ground and in the air. The changes to the inertial navigation system, though previously considered by Ferranti (the makers), had never been tested under anything like operational conditions – and even when the inertial platform had been modified, the aircraft's moving map display could not be made to work if alignment took place on a ship.

By the end of the first week in April the No. 1 Squadron hangar at Wittering had become a hive of activity, as one by one the aircraft were wheeled in and modification work began. The British Aerospace factory at Kingston sent representatives from the Harrier design team and the drawing office to assist with the work; so did the government test establishments at Farnborough and Boscombe Down.

While this was happening Wing Commander Peter Squire, the commander of No. 1 Squadron, had the task of retraining his pilots for the unfamiliar new roles. There began an immediate series of lectures to acquaint them with the types of aircraft used by the Argentinians, and tactics to employ in air-to-air combat.

From mid-April No. 1 Squadron's pilots flew to Yeovilton to practise take-offs from the 'ski-jump' installed there, a replica of those fitted to the Royal Navy aircraft carriers. After a couple of tries each at the new technique, the pilots found it far easier to use than the semi-prepared field strips they normally flew from on exercises. Also at this time Peter Squire sent two of his officers, Squadron Leaders Bruce Sobey and Bob Iveson, to inspect a container ship moored at Liverpool; with Fleet Air Arm officers they looked over her closely and agreed that, with a few relatively minor alterations, her foredeck would be suitable for Harriers to land on and take off from. The ship's name was *Atlantic Conveyor*.

While all this work was taking place at Wittering, other Royal Air Force bases prepared equipment and personnel to support Operation CORPORATE. At Waddington near Lincoln selected Vulcan bombers of Nos. 44, 50 and 101 Squadrons were made ready to go to war. After many years of disuse, the flight refuelling receiver systems were brought back into service and crews began training to take fuel from Victor tankers. At the same time the conventional bombing equipment was refitted into the aircraft, to enable them to carry up to twenty-one 1,000-pound bombs in place of the nuclear weapons which constituted the bomber's normal armament. The Vulcans were also fitted with Carousel inertial navigation systems, to enable them to navigate accurately while flying at great distances from land. At Marham near King's Lynn Victor tankers of Nos. 55 and 57 Squadrons were fitted with improvised camera installations to enable them to operate in the ultra-long-range reconnaissance role; and most of the tankers were fitted with either Carousel or Omega long-range radio navigational systems. At Odiham in Hampshire No. 18 Squadron prepared seven Chinook helicopters to go south, with the installation of Omega, radar warning receivers, and numerous other changes.

At the *Condor* building on the north-eastern edge of Buenos Aires, where there was also now a flurry of activity, the relative strengths of the gathering British threat and the potential Argentinian response looked rather different. The huge modern steel and plate glass structure houses the high command of the Argentine Air Force (Fuerza Aérea Argentina); poised ironically on a concrete plinth in front of the building is a Gloster Meteor fighter, a reminder of times when relations between Britain and Argentina were happier. It was from *Condor* that General Lami Dozo, the Air Force commander, and his staff would direct operations during any forthcoming conflict.

If the Argentine landings on the Falklands came as a major surprise for the British forces, until the very last hours they were scarcely less so for the bulk of the Argentine armed forces that were not directly involved. And as the realization began to sink in that the warlike British moves represented more than mere bluster following a hurt to national pride, it became clear that the Argentine air forces were quite unprepared for the type of armed conflict now in the offing.

In fact, for various reasons, the Argentine Air Force and Naval Air Arm possessed fewer *usable* combat aircraft than was believed in London. The British figures had been based on reported deliveries of military aircraft to Argentina; but in many cases these had taken place more than a decade earlier, and information was scanty on those lost in accidents or pensioned off. Thus, instead of sixteen Mirage single-seat fighters thought to be available for action the Air Force had only eleven; instead of sixty-five Skyhawks they had forty-six, and instead of nine Canberras they had six. Instead of twenty-six Daggers they had thirty-four, however (the Dagger is an unlicensed Israeli-built copy of the attack version of the Mirage, with only a limited air-to-air capability, and more had been delivered than announced). So, instead of the 116 Air Force medium-range fighter and attack aircraft thought to have been available for action, the maximum number was ninety-seven. Lami Dozo has stated that the Air Force units committed to the conflict on the mainland never had more than eighty-two aircraft, and the authors have no reason to doubt this figure. To this can be added the Naval Air Arm with eleven Skyhawks and five Super Étendards, though because of the French arms embargo one of the latter would have to be cannibalized to provide spares for the other four. On the limited number of airfields on the Falklands there was room for only thirty-four Pucará, Turbo-Mentor and Macchi light attack aircraft. Instead of the total of 247 fighter and attack aircraft feared by British intelligence, therefore, the actual number available for action around the Falklands was nearer 130. The Sea Harriers were still outnumbered by more than six to one, but there were other factors which would further limit the Argentine air threat.

Of the aircraft able to reach the Falklands, only a small proportion were crewed by men fully trained to attack ships: the Air Force fighter-bomber and bomber units were trained mainly to support a land battle against one or other of Argentina's immediate neighbours. Only the pilots of the small Naval Air

Arm had training in the specialized art of attacking warships in open water. And, apart from the Super Étendards and their five Exocet missiles, the fighter-bombers and bombers had only old-fashioned 'iron' bombs and unguided rockets with which to attack enemy ships.

A further problem was that Port Stanley is 440 miles from the nearest usable airfield on the mainland at Rio Grande, a distance close to the maximum operational radius of action of the single-engined fighter and attack aircraft. For operations against targets at greater distances the naval Skyhawks could operate from the aircraft carrier *25 de Mayo*, and all Skyhawks and Super Étendards were equipped for in-flight refuelling, though the Air Force possessed only two KC-130 Hercules aircraft modified as tankers (the Argentine Navy possessed 'buddy' equipment to enable its Skyhawks to act as aerial tankers, but this would scarcely be used during the forthcoming conflict).

In any action against a British Task Force, the Super Étendard with its missile would represent by far the most powerful weapon in the Argentine arsenal. But the novelty of the aircraft gave rise to several problems for the 2nd Naval Fighter and Attack Escuadrilla operating them, as Commander Jorge Colombo explained: 'The 2nd Escuadrilla came into being only in November 1981, when our Super Étendards were delivered and the pilots returned after training in France. At that time the flying experience on the type was about forty-five hours per pilot. While in France we received only a basic training in flying the aircraft. We did no night flying training and we flew no tactical training missions.' Colombo's pilots had done relatively little more flying with the new aircraft before 31 March when, as the Argentine marines were about to land on the Falklands, he suddenly received orders to get his unit ready for operations with Exocet as rapidly as possible. It was no simple task, for the business of mating the aircraft's radar and attack computer with the missile had yet to be done on the Argentine aircraft.

During and since the conflict there has been press speculation that French technicians completed the necessary final work on mating the Exocet missile to Colombo's aircraft. This was not the case. President Mitterand had declared his support for Britain early on and imposed a rigid embargo on the delivery of military supplies or expertise to Argentina. Jorge Colombo was understandably bitter at this turn of events: 'At the beginning of April we still expected the French technical assistance team from Aerospatiale by mid-April which, under the terms of our contract, was due to come to Argentina to ensure the correct functioning of the aircraft and missile system. Shortly afterwards we were pained to learn that the French would not be coming. That meant valuable information on setting up the system would not be received, nor could we count on the experience and knowledge of those who had designed and built it. The other French technicians at Bahía Blanca at the beginning of the war [a small team from Dassault which manufactured the aircraft] were of no help in getting the Exocet ready.'

At Naval Air Base Espora near Bahía Blanca, where the 2nd Escuadrilla was based, Argentine technicians and engineers strove alone to master the intricacies of Exocet and the associated computer system; even the instructional manuals existed only in French. Working around the clock, the men managed it in two weeks. At the same time Colombo and his pilots had to train to operate the unfamiliar system. 'The missile launching technique, though complex, was more or less known,' he explained. 'It required the use of radar, flying at 500 knots [575 m.p.h.] a few metres above the sea, and working in pairs under strict radio silence. We trained in the Puerto Belgrano area against all types of vessels, warships and merchant ships, and the launch techniques were repeated over and over again until the pilots had the minimum skills to achieve their task.' Colombo also needed to discover whether it would be possible for his aircraft to fly missions from the short 4,100-foot runway at Port Stanley; if they could, it would greatly enhance the effectiveness of the Super Étendard against British naval forces approaching the Falklands. Accordingly a 4,100-foot length of runway was marked out at Espora and the pilots tried flying into and out of it. 'The take-off and braking distances were tested with the aircraft in the missile attack configuration. On a dry runway, brake curve values were attained which meant we could have landed at Puerto Argentino [Port Stanley], though with a very small safety margin; on a wet runway, landings were not possible. We could take off from a wet or dry runway, though there was no margin for error.' With the airfield at Port Stanley at best only marginally usable for the Super Étendard, Colombo considered it suitable only to receive aircraft critically short of fuel or with battle damage which prevented them regaining the mainland. To increase their operational radius of action to that necessary to attack warships east of the Falklands, 2nd Escuadrilla pilots began training in air-to-air refuelling from Air Force KC-130 Hercules tankers. By mid-April all the component parts of the mission had been practised and the time came to simulate the entire attack profile by a pair of aircraft: take off from Espora, refuel from a Hercules more than 300 miles out to sea, let down below the radar horizon of the 'enemy' ships taking directions from a Neptune reconnaissance aircraft shadowing them on radar, simulate Exocet attacks, break away, and return to base. The trial revealed no serious tactical shortcomings, so Colombo judged his unit ready for combat. On 19 April the first two Super Étendards took off from Espora for Rio Grande in Tierra del Fuego, on the southern tip of Argentina, their operational base if it came to an armed conflict with Britain over the Falklands.

While the 2nd Escuadrilla was preparing for action, other naval pilots were giving instruction to the Air Force fighter-bomber units on oversea operations. 'We had two weeks to give them a crash course in how to attack ships, and after the fighting started we gave them tactical advice after they made errors. In particular we tried hard to correct their habit of climbing after they delivered attacks on ships, which made them vulnerable to anti-aircraft and missile fire,' explained Lieutenant Benito Rotolo, a Skyhawk pilot with the 3rd Naval Fighter and Attack Escuadrilla. 'But it is not easy to change people's methods in just one or two weeks. When the Air Force pilots said they were flying low over the water, that was not my idea of low because I had been doing it for ten years. When I was training, the first time I went out I said, "Oh yes, I am low!", but I was at 100–150 feet. That was the "low" the Air Force pilots were flying and because of that several were later shot down.'

While the Argentine Navy and Air Force flying units prepared for action against the approaching Task Force, a massive transfer of men and equipment to the Falklands was in progress. The heavier items of equipment went by sea until 12 April, when the British government imposed a 200-nautical mile (230-statute mile) maritime exclusion zone centred on Port Stanley patrolled by nuclear submarines; thereafter very few ships reached the islands. The imposition of the maritime exclusion zone did nothing to hinder the airlift, however, and this continued unabated. During April C-130 Hercules transports of the Air Force, Electras and Fokker Fellowships of the Navy, Fokker Friendship and Fellowship airliners of the semi-military airline LADE, and Skyvan light transports of the Coast Guard, flew in more than 9,000 service and civilian personnel and 5,000 tons of equipment and supplies. By far the greater part of this influx came in through the airfield at Port Stanley (renamed Air Force Base *Malvinas*), the only one on the islands with a hard all-weather runway. To permit day and night operations a full system of lighting around the runway and taxiways was quickly installed. And to permit the airfield to be used by high-speed jet aircraft, army engineers began laying steel plating to extend the western end of the runway by some 200 feet; work also began to install a chain arrester gear, which would enable hook-equipped aircraft such as the Skyhawk and Super Étendard to pull up within the length of the runway even on wet days. On 25 April the first of five Macchi 339 light jet attack aircraft of the 1st Naval Attack Escuadrilla arrived to operate from Port Stanley.

Since Port Stanley town and airfield represented by far the most important single position to both sides, around it were concentrated the bulk of the ground anti-aircraft defence weapons sent to the Islands. Like so much of the Argentinian equipment, these had been purchased over many years and from many different suppliers. Potentially the most lethal of the anti-aircraft systems was the Franco-German Roland missile, fitted with full radar control for day and night operations. Only one such firing van was sent to the Falklands, however; it was set up midway between the town and the airfield. Considerably less dangerous to high-speed attack aircraft were the elderly British-made Tigercat missiles, of which three firing units were deployed in the area; and the Blowpipe shoulder-launched missiles, also of British manufacture, issued to infantry units. Supplementing the missiles – and somewhat more dangerous to low-flying aircraft as it turned out, because there were so many of them around – were the Oerlikon 35 mm fast-firing twin-barrelled guns, in many cases linked with Skyguard or Super Fledermaus fire-control radars (all of Swiss manufacture), and numerous German-made Rheinmetall 20 mm guns. To provide early warning of any attack on Port Stanley, and to direct defending fighters sent from the mainland, three US-built air defence radars were brought in. One was set up on Canopus Hill immediately to the west of the airfield, but soon afterwards it was blown over in a gale and played no further part in the conflict. The other two radars, a TPS-43 and a TPS-44, were positioned close to houses on the outskirts of Port Stanley itself; this made for poor radar siting but, as we shall later observe, it contributed greatly to the sets' survival.

Next in importance after the airfield at Port Stanley was the grass strip at Goose Green (renamed Air Force Base *Condor*). This became the main operating base of Reconnaissance and Attack Grupo 3, which deployed to the islands with twenty-five Pucará twin-turboprop aircraft. From Goose Green the unit sent detachments to operate from Port Stanley and the numerous small grass landing grounds dotted around the islands. To defend the airfield and garrison at Goose Green against air attack, three 35 mm Oerlikon guns were deployed with radar control, plus some 20 mm Rheinmetall weapons and Blowpipes.

The third of the main airfields used by the Argentine forces on the Falklands was at Pebble Island (Naval Air Base *Calderon*). As well as a staging post for Skyvan light transports from the mainland, the airstrip was the base for four Beech Turbo-Mentor turboprop light attack aircraft of the 4th Naval Attack Escuadrilla and accommodated a detachment of Pucarás. Near the airfield a lightweight Eltar search radar was installed; this set, and a similar one on Byron Heights 20 miles to the west, would play an important role in tracking Sea Harrier patrols when fighting started.

With surface movement on the islands severely restricted by the shortage of metalled roads, the only means of moving troops and supplies rapidly was by helicopter. To support its garrison, the Argentine Army brought over twenty-two Chinook, Puma, Bell UH-1 and Augusta 109 troop-carrying helicopters. On these would depend the defenders' ability to launch counter-attacks, when or if British ground troops returned to the Falklands.

As the Argentine forces strove to strengthen their hold on the Falklands, for the British forces Ascension Island nearly 3,900 miles to the north-east developed into a similar hive of activity. A

British-governed pimple of land midway between Africa and
South America and some 550 miles south of the equator,
Ascension is less than nine miles across at its widest point. The
airfield on the island, named Wideawake after a species of sea
bird which frequents the area, boasts a single 10,000-foot runway
able to take the largest transport aircraft. Built and paid for by the
US Air Force, Wideawake's *raison d'être* is as a means of supply for
the important satellite tracking station on the island. In return for
providing the use of the island Britain retains user rights on the
airfield, however; during the forthcoming conflict these rights
would be used to the full.

Initially only Royal Air Force Hercules and VC 10s, and
chartered civilian transports, flew into Ascension to unload and
refuel before returning north. Then more warlike machines began
to arrive. On 5 April a small detachment of Nimrod 1 patrol
aircraft of No. 42 Squadron arrived with ground crews, to operate
from Wideawake. These aircraft began flying patrols in support
of the approaching British ships, as well as covering patrols
around Ascension itself. The chances of an Argentine retaliatory
strike against the island were regarded as slight, but it was a
possibility that had always to be borne in mind. As one senior
Royal Air Force officer later commented: 'We would have looked
bloody stupid if a ship or submarine loaded with heavily armed
Argentinian marines had suddenly appeared off the coast in the
middle of the night, and the men had been able to land and blow
up our aircraft and installations!' On 12 April the far more
modern and effective Nimrod 2s, belonging to Nos. 120, 201 and
206 Squadrons, arrived on Ascension to take over the patrol task.

On 18 April there was a further strengthening of the Royal Air
Force contingent on the island, with the arrival of a detachment of
six Victor tankers of Nos. 55 and 57 Squadrons, including one
fitted with aerial cameras. These aircraft were capable both of
dispensing fuel and of receiving it, thereby providing a means of
flying ultra-long-range reconnaissance missions to the disputed
islands in the South Atlantic.

As 19 April drew to a close, the two sides' hastily prepared forces
were set on a collision course. Considerable distance still
separated the main bodies, though this was decreasing markedly

with each day that passed. Unless a political solution was found soon to the Falklands problem, an armed clash would be inevitable.

2: Initial Contacts

20 – 30 APRIL

'. . . contact, a word which perhaps better than any other indicates the dividing line between tactics and strategy.'

Rear Admiral Alfred Mahan

Starting at 2.50 a.m. local time on the morning of 20 April, four Victor tankers of Nos. 55 and 57 Squadrons, each laden with 48 tons of fuel, roared off the runway at Wideawake airfield at one-minute intervals. Flashing anti-collision and navigation lights, one after another the aircraft curved on to a southerly heading and were swallowed up in the darkness. If their mission went according to plan, just over six and a half hours later one of the aircraft would arrive in the vicinity of South Georgia some 2,850 miles away to search a huge area of sea off the north of the island for possible Argentine warships. For the first time since the withdrawal of the Antarctic patrol ship HMS *Endurance* on 4 April, British forces were to return to the area. Unknown to the Victor crews, and hopefully the Argentinians as well, *Endurance* was at the time a day's sailing to the north of the island in company with the destroyer *Antrim*, the frigate *Plymouth*, and the replenishment ship *Tidespring*. The nuclear submarine *Conqueror* was also in the area. Upon the results of the Victor's reconnaissance would depend whether or not British forces landed to retake the island.

Early in the reconnaissance mission there were equipment failures, which meant the Victor originally intended to fly to South Georgia had to abandon the attempt. Another of those in the force, captained by Squadron Leader John Elliott, was deputed to take its place. 'Once we knew that we were the crew to do the full mission, it was straightforward,' Elliott later commented. Straightforward, that is, for crews skilled in the art of

34

swapping fuel between large aircraft flying six miles high at night. Two hours after take-off and about 1,000 miles south of Ascension, two of the Victors gave all their spare fuel to the other two and then pulled round to return to their base. Two hours later and a further 1,000 miles from Ascension, Elliott took on more fuel from the Victor in company with him then it turned back; from now on he and his crew were on their own as they probed south into the unknown. For all anyone knew there was a chance that the Argentine Navy was in the area in strength, perhaps even with one or two guided missile destroyers. If that was the case, the Victor crew's only hope was that their radar warning receiver would provide sufficient warning of the enemy presence to the air electronics officer, Flight Lieutenant Ray Chapple, to enable them to move out of range before the missiles reached their altitude.

Dawn had broken when the Victor arrived off the north-eastern tip of South Georgia. Elliott descended the aircraft from 43,000 feet to 18,000 feet, its optimum height for a radar search, then the crew began to scour the area methodically, as briefed. Directed by its navigator, Squadron Leader Mike Buxey, the aircraft flew a 'creeping line ahead search'. After a southerly leg into the search area, the Victor wheeled west for 90 miles, which took it close to the island. It then headed north for 120 miles, west for a further 90 miles, south for 120 miles, west for 90 miles, then north for 280 miles before it climbed away to begin its return flight to Ascension. The search took just under an hour and a half, and during it the crew swept an area of more than 150,000 square miles of ocean for possible ships; a similar area, superimposed on the British Isles, would take in almost the whole of England, Scotland, Wales, Northern Ireland and the Irish Sea.

Elliott and his crew landed on Ascension late on the afternoon of the 20th, having been airborne for 14 hours and 45 minutes. There could be no fanfares at the time but the Victor had covered a distance of more than 7,000 miles and, in passing, had captured the record for the longest-range operational reconnaissance mission ever undertaken.

Once on the ground Squadron Leader Tony Cowling, the maritime reconnaissance expert attached to the crew, was able to analyse the radar photographs he had taken in the search area. From these he could say with reasonable certainty that there were

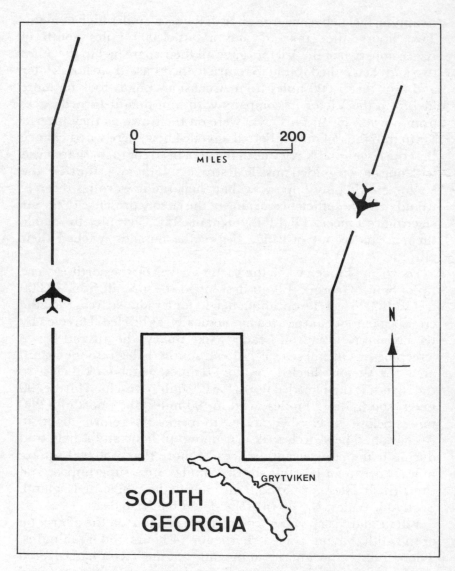

Search pattern flown by Squadron Leader John Elliott and his crew in a
Victor of No. 55 Squadron, during the radar reconnaissance off South
Georgia on 20 April. The flight covered more than 7,000 miles and took
14 hours 45 minutes; at the time it was the longest-range operational
reconnaissance mission ever flown.

no warships of any size off the coast in the area he had searched. Almost as important, he could also say that while there were ice floes off the south-eastern tip, there were none to the north of the island. It was negative intelligence, but it meant that no impediment had been discovered to the initial reconnaissance landings on South Georgia planned for the following day.

At first light on the 21st HMS *Antrim* launched her Wessex helicopter to fly a reconnaissance of the area around Fortune Glacier, where it was intended later in the day to land a small SAS party to observe the Argentine forces at Leith and Stromness some ten miles to the east. The pilot, Lieutenant Commander Ian Stanley of No. 737 Squadron, reported that although there was driving rain and strong winds, weather conditions in the area of the glacier were suitable for helicopters to fly in troops. Accordingly he returned to *Antrim* to pick up his party then, leading two transport Wessex from *Tidespring* similarly loaded, headed back to the glacier. Such is the speed at which the weather can change in this area, however, that the three helicopters now found their way blocked by thick low cloud and snow showers; they had no option but to turn round and go back to their parent ships, resolved to return later when the weather improved. Around noon visibility did improve, and the trio set out to make a second attempt. Again they ran into low cloud, with frequent driving snow squalls and sudden and violent changes in wind speed and direction. In spite of this the helicopters were able to continue to their objective, land the troops, and return to the ships.

For the helicopter crews it seemed that their problems had ended, but for the SAS men on the ground they had just begun. That night the weather on the glacier was at its Antarctic worst, with bitterly cold gale force 10 winds gusting to hurricane force – 80 m.p.h. – at times. Under such conditions it proved impossible to pitch the tents: one was torn from the men's hands and vanished downwind. By morning the SAS men were suffering badly from exposure and their condition was deteriorating; they radioed back that their position was untenable and asked to return to the ships.

When the three helicopters arrived in the area to pick up the men, they found weather even worse than the previous morning. The mountains to the south of the glacier were causing severe turbulence, with violent gusts of up to 80 m.p.h. interspersed with equally sudden lulls when the wind speed dropped to 10 m.p.h. In his anti-submarine Wessex – the only one of the three fitted with radar – Stanley made three unsuccessful attempts to get to the glacier while the other two waited to the north. Fuel shortage then forced all three to return to their ships. After refuelling the three went back again, and this time the weather relented for long enough for them to reach the ground party. No sooner were they down, however, when the weather closed in yet again, with strong winds which whipped up snow around the aircraft. A transport Wessex took off, but almost immediately the pilot entered 'white out' conditions with no horizon or reference points against which he could gauge the attitude of the aircraft. The wind took control and pushed the machine over sufficiently for one of the rotor blades to touch the ground; with the rend of tearing metal the helicopter then skidded some 50 yards and came to rest on its side. The men on board emerged, none with anything worse than a shaking, and boarded the other two Wessex. The pair took off to return to the ship, but soon afterwards the second transport Wessex ran into a 'white out', descended slightly, struck the top of a ridge, tilted to one side, and, as a rotor blade touched the ground, it too smashed on to its side. Ian Stanley, his own Wessex already overloaded, had no alternative but to leave the scene and continue with his load back to *Antrim*, waiting some 30 miles off the coast.

Having dropped his passengers, refuelled, and taken on blankets and medical supplies, the redoubtable Stanley lifted off *Antrim* again to try to rescue the men stranded on the glacier. On the way in he made radio contact with the men at the wrecked helicopter and learned that, almost miraculously, none had suffered serious injury (some of the men had been in both crashes). The ever-present danger of death from exposure remained, however, but Stanley's next two attempts to reach the scene of the crash were defeated by the strong winds and poor visibility. Reluctantly he returned to his ship to await a break in the weather. An hour later this came, and the Wessex lifted off, returned to the glacier, located the survivors, picked them up, and returned to *Antrim*.

As it turned out, Argentine troops appeared not to have detected the operation, but their presence in the area was throughout a complicating factor. For a demonstration of flying skill, determination and bravery that can have few equals in the history of aviation, Ian Stanley would later receive the Distinguished Service Cross.

On the night of the 22nd further parties of special forces landed on South Georgia, by helicopter and Gemini-powered rubber dinghy. Two of the Geminis suffered engine failures, however. Those on board one were rescued almost immediately, but the other boat drifted rapidly downwind and was soon lost to sight. Stanley took off to search for it, and, after an hour's fruitless search during the early morning darkness, located the men and rescued them at first light.

Thus far the British moves around South Georgia had proceeded without interference from the enemy, but on the afternoon of the 23rd intelligence was received to suggest that the Argentine submarine *Santa Fe* might be in the area. Immediately Captain Brian Young in *Antrim*, the Task Group commander, ordered all ships except *Endurance* (which was engaged in separate operations to the east of Grytviken) to retire some 200 miles to the north-east to reassess the situation.

On the 24th the Task Group received a powerful reinforcement in the shape of the guided-missile frigate HMS *Brilliant*, which carried two much-needed Lynx helicopters. At about the same time further intelligence came in which indicated that *Santa Fe* might attempt to enter Grytviken harbour on the morning of the 25th. Thus informed, the Task Group commander ordered the replenishment ship *Tidespring* to remain in the north-east while *Antrim*, *Brilliant* and *Plymouth* moved south to rejoin *Endurance* closer off the coast of South Georgia. The Task Group's helicopter force now comprised the Wessex on *Antrim* (Stanley's), two Lynx on *Brilliant*, two small Wasps on *Endurance* and one on *Plymouth*.

At first light the search for the *Santa Fe* began. While a Lynx from *Brilliant* swept westwards along the north coast of the island, Stanley took his Wessex stealthily towards Grytviken itself, with the radar switched off to avoid alerting the prey. At the time visibility was down to half a mile in places and the base of the cloud overcast was at 400 feet, so there were plenty of places for the Wessex to hide. Once in position off the coast the helicopter's observer, Lieutenant Chris Parry, made one sweep of the area using his radar and located a contact 5 miles off the coast. Stanley immediately headed towards it, and at a range of three-quarters of a mile caught sight of a submarine on the surface: the *Santa Fe*. The Wessex trembling at its maximum speed of just over 100 m.p.h., Stanley charged in to attack with two 250-pound depth charges and saw them explode in the water close off the boat's port side.

No longer able to dive, *Santa Fe* performed some tight turns then ran in towards Grytviken with oil and smoke issuing from her hull. Meanwhile Stanley had summoned to the scene the Lynx from *Brilliant*, and Wasps from *Plymouth* and *Endurance* carrying AS 12 wire-guided missiles. While the Wessex and the Lynx harassed the submarine with machine-gun fire, one of *Endurance's* Wasps scored a hit on the conning tower with an AS 12 which punched clean through and exploded as it was coming out on the other side. The battered submarine continued on its way and ran aground beside the jetty at Grytviken, and those on board scrambled ashore.

Now the attacking force had revealed itself, all pretence of stealth was abandoned and *Antrim* and *Plymouth* opened up a powerful bombardment just clear of the Argentine positions around the harbour to serve as a demonstration of force, the fire directed by a gunnery officer flown ashore by a Wasp. Meanwhile the Wessex and two Lynx began ferrying ashore the small available force of soldiers and marines. By the late afternoon British troops were closing on the enemy positions when, suddenly, white flags began to appear. The action at Grytviken had ended with no loss of life and just one man, a sailor on the *Santa Fe*, seriously wounded. On the following day the small Argentine garrison at Leith, 15 miles to the west, also surrendered. South Georgia was again in British hands.

While the manoeuvres to retake South Georgia were in progress, the main body of the carrier Task Group was closing rapidly on the Falklands. On 21 April it made its first contact with an Argentine aircraft. That morning Lieutenant Simon Hargreaves of No. 800 Squadron was ordered up in his Sea Harrier to investigate a radar pick-up 150 miles to the south of the warships. Initially the contact was thought to be a commercial airliner, several of which had come past during the previous days. But as

Hargreaves closed on the aircraft, a Boeing 707, he observed the blue and white Argentine flag painted on its nose: it was an aircraft of Transport Grupo 1, based at El Palomar near Buenos Aires, looking for the warships. With strict orders not to commit any warlike act, Hargreaves could only formate on the intruder and photograph it with his fixed starboard-facing camera. While he was doing this one of the crewmen on the Boeing photographed the Sea Harrier. It was an unexpected and strange encounter, with each side anxious to do nothing to aggravate the crisis. Afterwards the Boeing crew reported: 'British fleet at 19 deg 29 min south and 21 deg west, 2,300 km [1,430 miles] ENE of Rio de Janeiro. Fleet split into three groups, with eight ships in each of the two forward groups and an unknown number in the third group.' In fact the report was something of an exaggeration: at the time the Task Group in that area comprised only eleven warships and five replenishment vessels.

During the days that followed there would be more meetings with the reconnaissance Boeings, before the word was passed from London to Buenos Aires that further aircraft making such approaches would be intercepted and shot down.

On 23 April the Task Force suffered its first loss, when a transport Sea King from No. 846 Squadron off *Hermes* was forced to ditch and one crewman was killed.

Towards the end of April the Argentine Air Force units earmarked to support the defence of the Falklands from the mainland began moving to operational bases in the south of the country. The Canberra bombers and Learjet reconnaissance aircraft of Grupo 2 moved to Trelew in Chubut province; half the Daggers of Grupo 6 went to San Julian in Santa Cruz province; its remaining Daggers, the Skyhawks of Grupos 4 and 5 and the Mirages of Grupo 8, all moved to Rio Gallegos at the extreme south of the province.

The Naval Air Arm units prepared for action also. The four available Super Étendards of the 2nd Naval Fighter and Attack Escuadrilla established themselves at Rio Grande on Tierra del Fuego. Eight Skyhawks of the 3rd Escuadrilla were embarked on the aircraft carrier *25 de Mayo*, with a further three in reserve at their main base at Espora.

Since 17 April almost the entire warship strength of the Argentine Navy had been at sea in readiness to ward off the threatened British incursion into the area. On 29 April the fleet, designated Task Force 79, split into two groups and moved into position to cover the Falklands. The larger group, comprising *25 de Mayo*, the guided missile destroyers *Hercules* and *Santisima Trinidad*, and four smaller destroyers and frigates, moved into position just outside the British maritime exclusion zone and to the north-west of the islands. The smaller group, comprising the cruiser *General Belgrano* and two destroyers, moved into a similar position to the south-west of the Falklands.

On 30 April General Haig finally abandoned his shuttle diplomacy between London and Buenos Aires to find a peaceful solution to the crisis; he had done his best, but given the powerful feelings aroused in the two countries there would probably have been no solution acceptable to both. With that President Reagan rescinded his previous policy of attempting to deal even-handedly between the two sides, and came down firmly on the side of Great Britain. Also on that day, with the arrival of the British aircraft carriers in the area of the disputed islands, the previous maritime exclusion zone was re-designated a total exclusion zone: from now on any Argentine aircraft intercepted within the area was liable to be attacked without warning. Meanwhile, the Argentine government declared an exclusion zone of its own where British ships and aircraft would be attacked on sight. Barring some last-minute miracle, an armed conflict between the two nations was now inevitable.

3: 'Looks Like We've Got a Job of Work, Fellers . . .'

1 MAY

'It was clearly expedient to provide an early demonstration of force, to support the declared political resolve.'

Rear Admiral John Woodward

With the main body of his warships now inside the total exclusion zone, and political clearance to begin military action against Argentine forces on the Falklands, Rear Admiral Woodward's next step was to provide a demonstration of force to convince doubters on both sides that he was in earnest; it would also, hopefully, force the Argentinians to commit forces and reveal their capabilities and weaknesses.

The demonstration was to be staged on 1 May and would involve virtually the entire force of fixed-winged British aircraft that could reach the Falklands. Spearheading the action would be a single Vulcan bomber operating from Ascension and refuelled in flight, which would deliver an attack to cut the runway at Port Stanley during the early morning darkness. Immediately after dawn Sea Harriers would make low-level attacks on the airfields at Port Stanley and Goose Green. For the rest of the day the Sea Harriers would revert to the air defence role, ready to ward off the expected Argentine retaliatory attacks on the Task Force. To goad the enemy still further, during the late afternoon a small force of warships was to close on Port Stanley and deliver a bombardment of the airfield, as though in preparation for seaborne landings.

On the Argentine side an attack along these general lines was not unexpected. To meet it, jet fighter and attack units were standing by at the airfields at Rio Gallegos and Rio Grande nearest to the Falklands, as were the light attack units based on the Islands themselves. But politically the Argentine leaders felt it

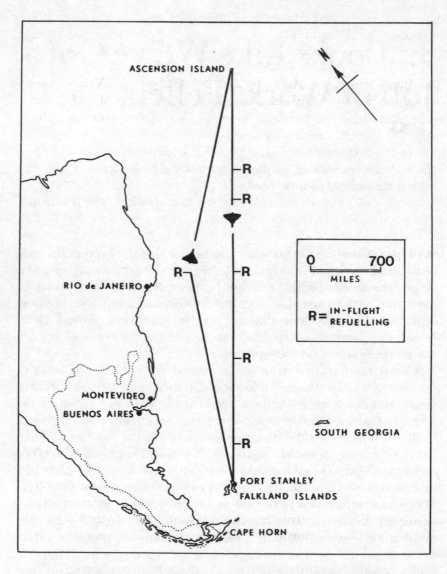

Route flown by Flight Lieutenant Martin Withers and his crew in a
Vulcan of No. 101 Squadron, during the attack on Port Stanley airfield
on 1 May. The round trip covered a distance of 7,860 miles and involved
six in-flight refuellings; at the time it was the longest-range operational
bombing mission ever flown.

expedient that the British should mount the initial blow in this next phase of the conflict.

The flight time from Ascension to Port Stanley by Vulcan was over eight hours, so any attack early on the morning of 1 May had to be launched the previous evening. By the shortest possible route the distance each way was 3,886 miles, roughly equivalent to that from London to Karachi; it was to be the longest-range attack ever mounted in the history of aerial warfare.

As the Royal Air Force planners had soon discovered, to get a Vulcan loaded with twenty-one 1,000-pound bombs from Ascension to Port Stanley would involve more than twice as much effort as was needed to get John Elliott's Victor to South Georgia for its reconnaissance mission.

Starting at 10.50 p.m. Ascension time (7.50 p.m. Port Stanley time), at one-minute intervals the eleven supporting Victor tankers of Nos. 55 and 57 Squadrons, then two Vulcans, roared off the ground from Wideawake airfield. 'Black Buck', as the operation was codenamed, was on its way. One Victor and one Vulcan were reserves, but it immediately became clear that both would be needed. As they climbed away to the south one Victor crew found they could not wind out their hose to transfer fuel; the reserve aircraft took their place and they turned back. The cabin of the primary Vulcan could not be pressurized and it too had to go back. The news reached Flight Lieutenant Martin Withers of No. 101 Squadron, at the controls of the reserve Vulcan, shortly after he had taken off. Those on board the aircraft remember that there was a long and pensive silence, then Withers commented, 'Looks like we've got a job of work, fellers. . .' There was no need for further discussion: the reserve crew had been briefed fully and prepared for the mission as assiduously as had those now forced to abandon it.

The first transfer of fuel took place about one and three-quarter hours after take-off, at a point some 840 miles south of Ascension. Four Victors topped off the tanks of four others, then turned back. The remaining Victor topped off the Vulcan's tanks but continued with the formation. Even during the first refuelling, a problem manifested itself which was to become cumulatively greater with each hour that passed and would finally jeopardize the success of the entire mission: for various reasons – in particular the need to fly the combined formation at speeds and altitudes which were not the optimum for either the Vulcan or the Victor – the force was burning fuel at a rate greater than had been planned. Thus when the four tankers turned back, they had all had to bite deeply into their fuel reserves in order to send the remaining aircraft south with full tanks.

Two and a half hours, and some 1,150 miles, south of Ascension, one of the Victors topped off the Vulcan's tanks yet again then turned back. Soon afterwards two Victors passed fuel to the remaining three aircraft and they too turned back.

The third transfer of fuel to the Vulcan took place four hours, and 1,900 miles, south of Ascension. At about the same time there were tense scenes on the island as the initial wave of four Victors came in to land. The single runway at Wideawake airfield runs between rocky outcrops and can be entered or left only at its western end; as usual, the wind was blowing from the east, which meant the Victors had to end their landing runs at the end of the runway opposite from the exit taxiway. And because all four aircraft arrived back extremely short of fuel, there was no time for the previous aircraft to turn round and taxi off the runway before the next one had to land. As the first Victor touched down it ran to the end of the runway and braked to a halt. The second did likewise and pulled up just clear of the first. The third repeated the process and stopped behind the second. Thus when the fourth Victor approached to land, with Squadron Leader Martin Todd at the controls, the stage was set for the spectacular aeronautical equivalent of a motorway pile-up. There was little margin for error: if he misjudged his approach or if there was a relatively minor failure to his aircraft, the Royal Air Force stood to lose one-third of the Victor tankers committed to the mission, and the very machines that would soon be needed to take fuel out to the aircraft returning from the distant south. Todd put his Victor down firmly on the western end of the runway, lowered the nose wheel to the ground, streamed the huge braking parachute, and felt himself pushed into his seat straps as the aircraft began to decelerate. Ahead of him sat his comrades' Victors, their anti-collision lights blinking in the darkness. 'There were the other three at the end of the runway, waiting for us to stop. If our brakes had failed or anything, Christ, I hate to think of it. . .' Martin

Todd later commented. But there was no failure of judgement or equipment. The Victor pulled up well clear of the other aircraft. Todd released the brake parachute then, with a burst of power, swung his machine through a semi-circle and headed towards the runway exit. In relieved procession the other three Victors followed.

Meanwhile, back at the attack formation, there was yet another problem. Flight Lieutenant Alan Skelton passed fuel to the remaining two Victors, then turned north. As he pulled clear, however, his Victor developed a fuel leak. The leak itself was not large, and in normal circumstances it would not have mattered much, but he was a long way from home and had cut his reserves to a minimum to assist the other aircraft. With some urgency, the crew radioed Ascension and requested that a tanker be scrambled to meet them south of the island.

After five and a half hours' flying, 2,750 miles south of Ascension, the Vulcan's tanks were topped up once again. Squadron Leader Bob Tuxford, at the controls of the Victor which had passed the fuel, then prepared to refill the tanks of the remaining tanker also. But a further unforeseen problem arose, as he later explained: 'There is an unwritten rule in air-to-air refuelling, a variation of Sod's Law, which says: "If you're going to find any really bumpy weather it will be right at the point where you have to do your tanking."' The small formation now found itself over a violent storm, with the tops of the turbulent clouds extending to the 31,000-foot flight altitude of the aircraft, at exactly the point where the final transfer of fuel between Victors was due to take place.

From his vantage point in the Vulcan, in formation a couple of hundred yards to the right of the Victors, Martin Withers watched Flight Lieutenant Steve Biglands close in behind Tuxford's aircraft to take on fuel: 'It was dreadfully turbulent, we were in and out of the cloud tops, there was a lot of electrical activity with St Elmo's fire dancing around my cockpit. The Victor was trying to refuel in that, he was having enormous problems. We could see the two aircraft bucking around, with the refuelling hose and basket going up and down about 20 feet.'

Eventually, after some superb flying, Biglands managed to get his probe into the refuelling basket and the transfer of fuel began. But the triumph was short-lived. 'Suddenly Steve called on the radio and said, "I've broken my probe!" That left us in a rather awkward position,' Tuxford recalled. With his probe broken, Biglands could take on no more fuel. The sole alternative now open, if the mission was to continue, was for Tuxford and Biglands to exchange roles, and for Tuxford to go in behind Biglands and take back the fuel he had just given plus sufficient to take the Vulcan on to Port Stanley.

Now it was Bob Tuxford's task to try to take fuel from the aircraft bobbing up and down in front of him: 'I went in behind Steve's hose and had just as much difficulty as he did, trying to get in. I finally managed to make contact on a very unstable hose, and took on about half of the fuel. Then the hose started to whip about and I lost contact. It took three or four minutes to make contact a second time, and just at that point we broke into clear skies with the stars shining above and no turbulence.' From then on the fuel transfer was straightforward, except that at its end Tuxford was well down on the amount of fuel he needed. The turbulence and the need for the two aircraft to change places had taken the second-to-last Victor well to the south of where it should have turned back, so it needed more fuel to complete its flight; this, coupled with the broken probe which prevented him taking on any more fuel, meant that it was essential for Biglands to retain a reasonable reserve to get him back to Ascension.

As Biglands pulled his Victor round and headed north, there remained a possible legacy of the broken probe which threatened the continuation of the mission: if the end of the broken refuelling probe was now jammed in Tuxford's hose, the Vulcan would be unable to take on any more fuel either. To find out, Withers formated on the refuelling basket to have a look at it. The Vulcan closed until the end of the hose was just six feet in front of its windscreen and Flight Lieutenant Dick Russell in the co-pilot's seat flashed a hand torch to look it over; in the half light the basket seemed all right. The only way to be absolutely certain was for Withers to push in his probe and take on a little fuel to prove the system. He did, and it was functioning perfectly.

Now the final pair of aircraft were more than 3,000 miles south of Ascension, with the Vulcan within just over an hour's flying of its target. Inside the Victor an earnest discussion was taking place. 'We were considerably lower on fuel than we should have been,' Tuxford explained. 'Now we had a decision to make: either to go on, give the Vulcan the fuel it needed to make its attack, and prejudice our own position because if we didn't pick up some more fuel on the way back we would have to ditch; or turn back at that stage while we both had sufficient fuel to get back to Ascension. I was the captain of the aircraft and I had to make the decision, but I asked my crew what they thought. One by one they came back and said, "We have to go on with the mission." '

The Victor's problems were unknown to Martin Withers and the crew of the Vulcan. Throughout the flight radio traffic had been held to an absolute minimum so as to betray as little as possible to any unfriendly listeners. So it came as a profound shock when, about half an hour later, as the Vulcan was in the middle of its final transfer of fuel before the target, suddenly and unexpectedly the red lights on the Victor flashed on to indicate that the refuelling was over. The Vulcan was still some 6,000 pounds of fuel short of what it should have had at this point in the mission. Withers broke radio silence with a brief request for more fuel, but Tuxford told him curtly that there could be no more: 'Not being familiar with the tanking game, not knowing how far I had stretched myself to put him where he was, all he knew was that he wanted a certain amount of fuel. If only he had realized how much discussion had already taken place in my aeroplane, about how far we could afford to stretch ourselves to get him there. . .' The Victor peeled away and headed north; unless it could take on more fuel on the way back, it would inevitably crash into the sea some 400 miles south of Ascension.

Although the Vulcan was short of fuel also, Martin Withers had the great advantage of knowing that one Victor tanker plus a reserve were planned to meet him on his return journey to top up his tanks. With his crew he now put the problems of the previous hours behind him and made final preparations for the attack. Dick Russell, attached to the crew as a flight refuelling expert, climbed out of the co-pilot's seat and Flying Officer Peter Taylor, who normally flew with Withers, climbed in. At a point 290 miles to the north of the target Withers pulled back his throttles; the bomber dropped its nose to maintain speed and began a long descent to low altitude, to remain below the cover of any early warning radars the Argentinians might have set up on the island. Falling at about 2,000 feet per minute, the Vulcan continued towards its target, covering a further 57 miles before it levelled out

2,000 feet above the sea. From there it made a more gentle descent to 300 feet. Since leaving Ascension nearly eight hours earlier the navigator of the aircraft, Flight Lieutenant Gordon Graham, had not had a chance to get ground fixes to confirm his position; and now, with the Vulcan maintaining strict radar and radio silence so as not to betray its approach, he had to place complete trust in the accuracy of his dead-reckoning navigation. Graham could only hope that the Carousel inertial navigator, hastily installed into the aircraft before it left England, was functioning as accurately as the maker's brochures said it would.

As the estimated range of the target came down below 60 miles the Vulcan's radar operator, Flight Lieutenant Bob Wright, finally turned on his H2S bombing radar; at first it failed to come on properly and there were anxious moments as he reset his controls. Without a serviceable bombing radar an accurate attack would be impossible: the risk of inflicting casualties on the Falklanders themselves was too great, and even at this late stage the attack might have to be abandoned. In the end Wright succeeded in getting a good picture on his screen, but there was no sign of the expected returns from the 2,300-foot-high summit of Mount Usborne in the middle of East Falkland. Suspecting the mountain was still below the Vulcan's radar horizon Withers eased the aircraft up to 500 feet and then, suddenly, the feature appeared on Wright's screen almost exactly where Graham had said it would be: the dead-reckoning navigation backed up by the intertial system had functioned perfectly and the bomber was correctly positioned and properly aligned to begin its bombing run. At the same time, more ominously, the aircraft's radar warning receiver started to give out a short high-pitched buzz at ten-second intervals: the receiver was picking up signals from the American-built TPS-43 early warning radar at Port Stanley, its scanner rotating at six revolutions per minute.

Now within 46 miles of his target, Withers pushed forward his throttles to get full power and eased back on the stick to pull the Vulcan into a rapid climb to its attack altitude of 10,000 feet. The climb took two minutes then Withers reduced power, levelled out once more, and concentrated his entire attention on holding the aircraft on its attack heading of 235 degrees (almost due southwest).

Because there would later be some controversy about the

attack it needs to be pointed out here that Withers was carrying out a textbook runway-cutting operation, exactly as taught at the Department of Air Warfare at Cranwell. Certainly the operation could have been carried out far more effectively using the Royal Air Force's new Tornado strike aircraft, fitted with its ultra-modern radar and attack system and dropping the specially developed JP 233 runway-cratering weapon. But neither the Tornado nor the JP 233 was yet ready for action. Martin Withers was having to make his attack using the methods of a different era. Essentially the radar and the general-purpose bombs carried by the Vulcan represented the technology of the 1940s; the attack system linked to the radar belonged to the 1950s. Taking into account the known inaccuracies of the Vulcan system, the *best* chance of hitting the runway was to fly across it at an angle of 30 degrees and release the twenty-one bombs in a line at quarter-second (50-yard) intervals. That was why Withers was now holding a heading of 235 degrees, 30 degrees off that of the single runway at Port Stanley which was aligned almost east to west. It was a tactic which would give a reasonable chance of scoring one and with luck two hits on the runway. The 10,000-foot attack altitude was chosen to give the bombs sufficient vertical momentum to punch their way through the runway; they were fused to detonate underneath it to cause maximum possible disruption of the surface. That attack altitude would also give the Vulcan a useful measure of immunity from the anti-aircraft guns and missiles the Argentinians had positioned in the area.

As he ran in at 400 m.p.h. Withers had the sun visors in front of him pulled down. 'I was worried about the loss of night vision from the flak I expected to come up. I really thought it would be like 5 November when the Argies opened up,' he later commented. In the rear cabin Bob Wright concentrated on keeping the markers on his radar screen over the green-painted echoes from offset points in the target area. The airfield at Port Stanley could not be relied upon to give a good echo, so he was using ground features nearby which did give good echoes; fed with an accurate distance and bearing from the target of each of the offset points, the Vulcan's bombing computer continually worked out the correct steering signals to take the aircraft to its bomb-release point, and presented these on a left-right needle indicator in front of Withers.

'It was a smooth night, everything was steady, the steering signals were steady, and the range was coming down nicely. All of the switching had been made and 10 miles from the target we opened the bomb doors,' Withers recalled. 'I was expecting flak and perhaps missiles to come up but nothing happened. The AEO didn't say anything about the defences and I didn't ask – I left that side of things entirely to him. I was concentrating entirely on flying the aircraft.' In fact the air electronics officer, Flight Lieutenant Hugh Prior, had plenty to occupy his thoughts, though he decided not to worry the rest of the crew by mentioning them at this critical time. As the bomb doors opened he heard in his earphones a distinctive high-pitched scratching note from his radar warning receiver, as a Skyguard fire-control radar tried to lock on to the bomber; Skyguard was linked to 35 mm Oerlikon anti-aircraft guns whose shells might, at a pinch, reach the Vulcan's altitude. Prior pushed the button on his control panel to set in operation the ALQ-101 jamming pod fitted under the starboard wing of the bomber, and almost at once the enemy radar signals ceased.

Finally, about two miles short of the target to allow for the forward throw of the bombs, the bombing computor set in motion the release mechanism and over a period of five seconds the Vulcan disgorged its twenty-one bombs. From the time Withers had levelled out at 10,000 feet until the last bomb left the aircraft had taken about six minutes. Now the bombs were away the bomb doors were closed; Withers pushed open his throttles to apply full power once again and thrust his control column to the left to wind the huge bomber into a 45-degree bank before pulling it into a tight turn: there was no point in staying within range of the defences any longer than absolutely necessary.

It took the bombs about twenty seconds to reach the ground, during which time the Vulcan had turned through about 60 degrees. Sitting in the co-pilot's seat to the right of Withers, Pete Taylor glanced over to his left; about 7 miles away to the west he made out the street lights of Port Stanley through a gap in the blanket of low cloud. Suddenly, much nearer, the clouds over the airfield were lit up from below; it was as if someone had switched on a bright but flickering light behind a window of translucent glass. Then the darkness returned and the crew felt rather than heard the distant crump of the explosions merged together.

Nobody in Port Stanley who heard the explosions, at 4.46 a.m. local time on that Saturday morning, will ever forget it. Artist Tony Chater was in bed with his wife Ann at their home in the centre of the town when the bombs detonated: 'I was half awake at the time and the whole house shook. It was as though there had been an earthquake, then we heard the "boomboomboomboom" of the bombs going off, very muffled. Shortly afterwards I just made out the sound of an aircraft in the distance.' To the Chaters, as to many of the Falklanders within earshot, the sound of the explosions gave a tremendous moral fillip; 'There was terrific jubilation in Stanley. From then on we really felt very confident that the British forces were going to come to our rescue.'

A couple of minutes after the Vulcan completed its turn, by which time it was well out of range some 14 miles away from the target and climbing rapidly, the Port Stanley gun defences finally opened fire. The noisy display of defiance continued for some minutes before one by one the guns fell silent.

On board the Vulcan there were no feelings of jubilation to match those of the residents of Port Stanley. The exertions of the previous eight hours had drained the crew of emotion. And there was another consideration: 'After the attack the crew were very quiet, rather sad. We had just started a shooting war. It had all been rather cold-blooded, creeping in there at 4.30 in the morning to drop bombs on the place,' Martin Withers later commented. 'But we had a job to do and we thought that job worth doing.'

The crew had no way of knowing it yet, but Bob Wright's stick of bombs had cut a swath of destruction running south-west from the centre of the airfield. His first bomb landed almost in the centre of the runway, penetrated as planned, and then detonated to cause a large hole with considerable 'heave' around the lip. The second bomb caused similar damage to the southern edge of the runway. One of his later bombs landed between the airfield's only repair hangar and a Pucará attack aircraft parked nearby, causing severe damage to both. Considering the age and limitations of the Vulcan's bomb-aiming system, the attack had been as successful as could reasonably have been hoped.

As the bomber clawed its way back to high altitude, where each pound of fuel would take the machine twice as far as it could low down, Hugh Prior prepared the post-attack signal. He had been briefed to send one of two codewords: if the attack appeared to have been successful, 'Superfuse'; if it appeared not to have been successful and the Argentinians had been alerted, 'Rhomboid'. If the attack had been abandoned for any reason without alerting the enemy, he was to remain silent. Everyone in the crew agreed that the attack appeared to have been successful so Prior sent the briefest of messages with 'Superfuse', on his high-frequency radio, and received an immediate acknowledgement from Ascension. There were no further radio transmissions from the Vulcan while it was in the target area. 'We did not wish a good morning to the ships of the Task Force as some people have said,' Hugh Prior insists.

To those concerned with the 'Black Buck' operation, the receipt of the 'Superfuse' codeword gave an immediate boost to morale, coupled in some cases with immense relief. In Bob Tuxford's Victor, about 1,000 miles north of the Vulcan and heading towards Ascension desperately short of fuel, it meant there was no further need to hold radio silence for fear of jeopardizing the mission. Tuxford's air electronics officer, Flight Lieutenant Mike Beer, began passing to Ascension details of the crew's predicament and where and when they needed to rendezvous with a tanker to take on more fuel. At the Ministry of Defence building in Whitehall there was a cheer in the Royal Air Force operations room as the news was received. Air Vice Marshal Kenneth Hayr, Assistant Chief of the Air Staff (Operations), dashed upstairs to carry the good news personally to the Chief of the Air Staff, Air Chief Marshal Sir Michael Beetham.

The feelings of self-congratulation soon subsided, however, with the realization that the operation was still only half complete. The second, and in many ways more difficult, part of the mission was that of getting all the aircraft safely back to Ascension. Both the Vulcan and Tuxford's Victor were short on fuel, though if the worst came to the worst Withers might have diverted to Brazil. Bob Tuxford did not even have that option: 'It was a long, dry journey back. We discussed a lot of things, including the practical aspects of bailing out of a Victor into the sea – you would not try to ditch it, the aircraft is the wrong shape. We had our radar on to see if there were any ships in the area, but in fact there was none in the right place.'

In the event Tuxford was able to rendezvous with the tanker

sent to meet him, and he took on the vital fuel without incident. So did Flight Lieutenant Alan Skelton who, it will be remembered, had suffered a fuel leak in his Victor four hours out from Ascension. That left only the Vulcan requiring succour.

The receipt of the 'Superfuse' codeword also gave a boost to morale on HMS *Hermes*, now moving into position 100 miles east-north-east of the Falklands in readiness to launch the planned strikes against the airstrips at Port Stanley and Goose Green.

Of the two targets, that at Port Stanley was considered by far the more important, and nine of the twelve available Sea Harriers were to be sent against it. Although the Vulcan attack had denied the Sea Harriers any possibility of enjoying strategic surprise, a degree of tactical surprise was still possible if the attack was carefully planned. To confuse the defences, the Port Stanley attacking force was split into two main elements. First to attack would be four Sea Harriers each loaded with three 1,000-pound bombs, mostly fitted with radar air-burst fuses. These aircraft, the toss bombers, were to approach the airfield at low altitude from the north-east; at a point three miles from their targets they were to pull up into 30-degree climbs, release their bombs, then turn away to the south-east. Thus released, the salvo of half-ton bombs would fly for nearly half a minute before bursting over the Argentine anti-aircraft gun positions on Mary Hill and Canopus Hill, respectively to the north-west and south-west of the airfield. While the defenders were thus distracted and concentrating on the east, the remaining five Sea Harriers, the lay-down bombers, were to run in low from the north and north-west to attack the airfield buildings and parked aircraft with 600-pound cluster bombs, and the runway with 1,000-pound parachute-retarded bombs. After bombing, the aircraft were to remain at low altitude and withdraw to the east behind the toss bombers.

The attack on Goose Green, some 50 miles to the west of Port Stanley, was to be a far less complex affair with a straight run-through at low altitude by three Sea Harriers dropping parachute-retarded and cluster bombs.

Only the Sea Harriers of No. 800 Squadron on *Hermes* were to take part in these attacks. As the raiders went in to bomb, No. 801 Squadron on *Invincible* was to launch six Sea Harriers, loaded with

Sidewinder missiles, to mount combat air patrols off the east coast of the Falklands; these aircraft would thus be in position to pounce on any Argentine fighters in pursuit of the bombers.

It was still dark as the pilots on *Hermes* boarded their Sea Harriers, the ship's entire complement drawn up on her flight deck laden with bombs. 'It was a peculiar feeling, the adrenalin pumping around like mad,' Flight Lieutenant Dave Morgan recalled. 'Everyone was very quiet, people were not saying a great deal. There were some half-hearted jokes and a few nervous titters about the place, but everyone was fairly withdrawn.' The pilots completed their checks, then started the engines.

At 7.50 a.m. Port Stanley time it was beginning to get light as Lieutenant Commander Andy Auld, commander of No. 800 Squadron, pushed forward his throttle. His Sea Harrier accelerated towards the bow of the ship, thrust into the air by the 'ski-jump', then headed out over the sea slowly gathering speed. At measured intervals the rest of his squadron followed. In the half light the aircraft orbited over their ship and formed up, then headed west-south-west towards the Islands, flying just 50 feet above the waves. At about 8 a.m. the Goose Green raiders broke away and headed west.

Shortly after 8.05 a.m. the Port Stanley attack force reached the coast of East Falkland, as briefed, at Macbride Head some 20 miles due north of the target. There the force split into two: Lieutenant Commander Tony Ogilvy led four toss bombers off to the south-east, before turning south-west into his bombing run; Andy Auld led the five lay-down bombers in an orbit to give the necessary separation at the target from the first wave. His force then swept south towards the target.

At his home in Port Stanley Tony Chater, his wife and two young sons were listening to the news and Radio Newsreel on the BBC World Service; they had just learned that the aircraft whose attack had woken them during the early hours was a Vulcan from Ascension.

Right on time the toss bombers pulled up and let go their bombs, then each aircraft turned sharply away from the defended area. Their twelve bombs continued on in formation for a further twenty-seven seconds, then the radar fuses detonated them in mid-air to rain down thousands of jagged splinters on the defending gun positions.

At the Chaters' home the sound of more exploding bombs brought everyone in the family to their feet and out into the garden to see what was going on. Suddenly the father caught sight of a couple of small aircraft to his north, hugging the ground as they ran in. 'They came in round Mount Low, dipped through the narrows, turned, and went in to attack the airfield,' he recalled later. In fact these were two of the three lay-down aircraft led by Lieutenant Commander Mike Blissett, heading towards the target from the north-west.

Blissett rounded Mount Low seconds after the air-burst bombs exploded over their targets. 'I did not see them go off,' he recalled, 'but I saw the columns of smoke and dust still in the sky.' Leading the lay-down bombers he saw a great deal of firing ahead, with tracer rounds criss-crossing the airfield. As he swept low over the water with two miles to go he saw the gunners start to concentrate on his aircraft. 'There was a lot of fire from just off the western end of the runway, and more from the hills to the south-west, all coming towards me,' he continued. 'I did a very hard 6 to 7 G jink to the left, held it for a few seconds, did an equally hard jink to the right then levelled out and ran in to bomb. Going flat out I pulled up to 170 feet, released my cluster bombs at the airfield buildings, then bunted back to low altitude to get clear as quickly as possible.'

From their positions around the town to the west of the airfield, the Argentine gunners loosed off long bursts of automatic fire at the fleeting targets hugging the ground in the distance. Even the battery of obsolete Tigercat missiles to the south of the town tried to join in the fight. Tony Chater recalled: 'The Harriers were more or less over the airstrip by the time the rockets were fired from the football field. My wife Ann saw one roar off down the harbour, pull up into the clouds and explode. Lots of people saw another of the rockets, fired at a flat angle, strike the surface of the football field then ricochet off and career into the sky.'

When Dave Morgan arrived over the middle of the airfield in the last Sea Harrier to attack, everything seemed to be happening. He saw bombs exploding, smoke rising from fires and aircraft, shells and missiles going in all directions; a Tigercat missile scorched past his nose, aimed at one of the aircraft in front. Morgan was in the act of releasing his cluster bombs when: 'Suddenly there was a bloody great explosion behind me and the rudder started vibrating like mad. At the time I was hit I was going pretty fast, 550–600 knots [630–690 m.p.h.], with the throttle hard forward. The aircraft was still responding to the controls; I took a quick look inside the cockpit to see if the engine instruments looked all right. They did.' As he eased forwards on the stick to get the aircraft back to relative safety close to the ground, he heard a rattle on his radar warning receiver as a gun control radar locked on to the Sea Harrier. Morgan blipped open his airbrake for an instant to release the packet of chaff radar reflective strips held there, at the same time pulling into a hard turn to the left and going even closer to the ground. Whether it was the chaff or the manoeuvre or the low flying or the opening range that broke the radar lock-on, he never knew. Probably it was a combination of all of them. So far as he was concerned the important thing was that the warning note had ceased, and with it the risk of his being engaged with accurate radar-laid fire.

While the attack on Port Stanley airfield was in progress, Lieutenant Commander 'Fred' Frederiksen led his three Harriers southwards down Falkland Sound before running in to attack Goose Green airfield from the north-west. Approaching fast and very low, the raiders achieved almost complete surprise at their target. As the aircraft pulled up to begin their bombing runs one of the pilots saw the muzzle flashes of small-arms fire aimed at them, but that was the sole reaction from the ground. The Sea Harriers released their bombs and were clear before the defenders could bring heavier weapons to bear. As the raiders swept in one of the Pucarás had been preparing to take off, and the exploding cluster bombs wrecked the aircraft, killing the pilot and six ground crew.

During the two attacks only Dave Morgan's Sea Harrier had suffered any battle damage. Once clear of the defences he throttled back to cruising speed and the vibration decreased markedly. On the way to the carrier one of his comrades formated on him and made a careful inspection; Morgan was told there was a hole in the middle of his fin, but it appeared that nothing vital had been hit.

On their way back from their targets in ones and twos, No. 800 Squadron's Sea Harriers passed beneath the screen of six aircraft from *Invincible* above cloud at 15,000 feet providing top cover. The bombers came past with no enemy aircraft in pursuit but the

covering force remained in position: for most of the next hour
Hermes would be vulnerable, her flight deck covered in aircraft
being refuelled and fitted with Sidewinder launchers and missiles.

Dave Morgan landed on *Hermes* without difficulty, climbed out
of his Sea Harrier, and strode round to the tail to join the knot of
people surveying the damage. A shell, probably a 20 mm, had
made a hole about the size of a ten-pence piece on the port side of
the fin, then detonated and blown out a hole the size of a man's fist
on the starboard side. The twisted metal could be cut away and
patched over without difficulty, however, and before the end of
the afternoon the aircraft would be ready for action again.

Martin Withers was elated. Soon after the last of the raiding Sea
Harriers arrived back on HMS *Hermes* his Vulcan, by now more
than 2,100 miles to the north and critically short of fuel, arrived at
the final tanking rendezvous off the coast of Brazil. In front of
him, exactly according to plan, he caught sight of the white belly
of a Victor swinging into position. It was, he later commented,
'the most beautiful sight in the world!'

Withers moved into close formation and pushed his probe into
the refuelling basket, and initially the precious fuel flowed
smoothly into the Vulcan's tanks. Then, as pressure in the hose
built up, suddenly a curtain of translucent fuel spilled over the
aircraft's windscreen. Even with his windscreen wipers going
Withers could see only the blurred outline of the tanker in front,
on which he had now to maintain close formation: 'It was just like
driving through a car wash,' he later remarked. Under normal
conditions Withers would have broken contact and made another
attempt to get his probe properly in the basket, but he did not
know whether either component had suffered damage and could
not be sure, if he broke contact, whether he would ever be able to
regain it. Even if one-tenth of the fuel was being spilled, nine-
tenths was going into the Vulcan's tanks, and each minute he
could hold the precarious contact a further ton of fuel was passed,
to increase greatly the chances of the bomber getting back to
Ascension. Bob Wright had been watching the operation,
standing on the ladder between the two pilots' seats. Now he
noticed that almost level with his eyes, across the bottom of the
centre windscreen, there was a narrow strip clear of fuel. Through

this he gave Withers and Russell a running commentary on the position of the tanker, which enabled the pilot to hold his position. It took ten minutes to fill the Vulcan's tanks with sufficient fuel to get to Ascension with a reasonable reserve, then Russell eased back on the throttles to break contact. Immediately the Victor ceased passing fuel, the airflow cleared the spillage off the windscreen.

Suddenly all was sunshine and blue skies in the Vulcan cockpit; it was as if a great burden had been lifted off the crew's shoulders. 'After that fuel was on board, the other four hours back to Ascension were a bit of a bore,' Withers later remarked. 'Only then was the tension off and we knew we were going to make it. Those last four hours seemed to last for ever.'

With Martin Withers and his crew safely on their way, the scene of the action returns to the south, for now, as expected, the Argentine Air Force arrived to contest the airspace around the Falklands. Flight Lieutenant Paul Barton of No. 801 Squadron from *Invincible* was flying on combat air patrol with another Sea Harrier to the west of the Task Force, when their directing ship made radar contact with the incoming enemy. 'I remember the controller saying, "I've got trade for you, two bandits closing from the west range 120 miles", and he gave us a vector towards them. Then he said, "Er, 15 miles astern of them are two more, another raid strength two. Er . . . er . . . there's two more behind them. . ." He was a very inexperienced young sub-lieutenant, and with each call his voice was getting higher and higher.'

Reinforcements were on their way but initially it would be six enemy fighters, probably Mirages, against just a pair of Sea Harriers; the latter had only four Sidewinders between them. In a turning fight it was generally conceded that the Sea Harrier was better than the Mirage, but it was not three times better. If the enemy supersonic fighters were handled properly they would probably launch a series of co-ordinated high-speed slashing attacks from different directions, which would make mincemeat of their far slower opponents. If they did really well the Sea Harriers might knock down one or two of their adversaries before they were destroyed — and two-for-two would be an excellent exchange rate for the far larger Argentine Air Force. It was, as

Barton later recounted, 'an arse-gripping situation to be in'.

The two Sea Harriers stayed at 15,000 feet and accelerated to fighting speed, keeping their noses pointed towards the reported incoming enemy aircraft. From their controlling ship they could get no altitude measurements on the enemy aircraft, but from the rapidly unwinding range between the two forces it was clear they were getting very close. As the range came down to single figures, still with no visual contact with the enemy aircraft, the tension in the Sea Harriers became almost unbearable. 'There were John [Lieutenant Commander Eyton-Jones] and I wheeling around, and the controller saying, "There are four contacts within two miles of you. . ."' Barton continued. 'It was very worrying, my mouth was tab dry. If they are two miles away and you can't see them, you have to think they are behind you.' Flying in battle formation, line abreast about 2,000 yards apart, the two Sea Harrier pilots anxiously searched the sky around them, in particular the blind zone behind the companion aircraft. Still there was nothing to be seen. Finally Barton realized what was happening. He eased down his nose to gain speed, then stood his aircraft on its tail to make a radar search of the sky on top of the layer of high cloud above – and there were the enemy aircraft, up around 35,000 feet. That explained the odd-sounding reports they had received from the ship!

'If we had the choice we would have fought the Sea Harriers at high altitude. But we could not draw them up,' explained Colonel Carlos Corino, the Grupo 8 commander whose Mirages were involved. For the mission the Mirages each carried two 1,700-litre (375-gallon) drop tanks, which allowed them about twelve minutes in the operational area at high altitude or five minutes lower down. But with the tanks and either a pair of Matra Magic infra-red homing missiles or a single Matra 530 radar semi-active missile, the Mirage had a very poor turning circle at high speed and low altitude. 'The important thing was not to try to follow the Sea Harrier for very long at low altitude, because the Mirage III can very quickly end up in front,' Corino commented. 'Also, the Sea Harrier's missiles' large angle-off kill capability made one not want to get tempted into trying to follow it.'

Even had the numbers been more equal, the Sea Harrier pilots had no intention of allowing themselves to be lured to high altitude where the Mirage could exploit its superior performance.

The sparring lasted for several minutes before fuel shortage, the ultimate arbiter in so many air actions, brought an end to the proceedings. The Mirages turned west for their bases, the Sea Harriers returned to their carrier.

At midday the destroyer *Glamorgan* and the frigates *Arrow* and *Alacrity* moved in close to Port Stanley preparatory to bombarding the airfield. As they came into view from the island, three Turbo-Mentors of the 4th Naval Attack Escuadrilla took off to attack the warships. At the time Lieutenant Commander 'Sharkey' Ward and Lieutenant Mike Watson of No. 801 Squadron were on combat air patrol in the area, and were called in to intercept. The two Sea Harriers curved round to the south, then descended through the cloud layer. 'As we came out of the bottom of the cloud we saw them, about a mile away. They saw us at about the same time,' Ward recalled. He recognized the machines as enemy and opened fire with cannon as he swept past at high speed, though without seeing any hits. 'They went straight up into cloud, I went after them. In the cloud I very nearly hit one. I just missed his right wing as I came past him, very close.' The pair of Sea Harriers turned round and nosed back underneath the cloud layer again, in time to see the Turbo-Mentors jettison their bombs and flee for the safety of the Port Stanley gun defences.

Ward and Watson then returned to their patrol line off the coast, where soon afterwards they were confronted by a pair of Mirages which behaved in a manner similar to those Barton and Eyton-Jones had met earlier. 'We turned towards them, they turned away. So I decided to spoof them. We headed north at 360 knots [415 m.p.h.] at medium level. And immediately we did that they started to close on us from behind, obviously under ground radar control and going *very* fast. Our ship controller called out the ranges: 40 miles . . . 35 . . . 30 . . . 25 . . . 20. They were obviously going for us. When they got to about 15 miles I said "Let's go!" and we turned hard through 180 degrees and started looking for them on our radar. From our ship's reports, we knew they were very high.' Ward looked up and saw what he thought at first were three condensation trails; it looked as if the enemy aircraft were coming down to engage him. But he was mistaken: 'I tried to lock one of my missiles on one of them, but the "contrails" turned out to be smoke trails from missiles they had fired at us!

They must have fired from well out of range, because the nearest missile went past me by a long way and fell into the sea. I watched as the other two missiles followed.' Still reluctant to close with the Sea Harriers, and with little confidence in aged missiles they knew to be inferior, the Mirage pilots saw little alternative to firing at extreme range and hoping for a lucky hit.

Following these skirmishes there was a lull in the air-to-air activity, but the intensive helicopter operations continued around the British warships. Three Sea Kings maintained an almost continuous defensive anti-submarine screen some 7–12 miles in front of the main body of the Task Force, and an additional helicopter conducted a search for enemy surface ships out to a distance of 200 miles. During the late morning a more aggressive anti-submarine hunt was launched when Lieutenant Commander Tony Hogg of No. 826 Squadron led a force of three Sea Kings, each carrying a spare four-man crew, off *Hermes*. They moved to a position 180 miles away, off the north coast of the Falklands, and joined the frigates *Brilliant* and *Yarmouth* where it was thought the modern Argentine submarine *San Luis* might be operating. When they arrived in the area each Sea King lowered its spare crew to the deck of one of the frigates, then the search began. For the first time in action the Royal Navy was to employ the technique it had developed for refuelling helicopters in flight from warships (the Sea King is too large to land on a normal frigate). Hovering over the ship's stern, the helicopter lowered a hook to pick up the fuel line, which was then winched up and plugged into a pressure coupling. The fuel was then pumped up to replenish the helicopter's tanks. Each such refuelling took about fifteen minutes, during which the ship performed its normal anti-submarine manoeuvres and the Sea King followed, as one Royal Navy officer put it, 'like a dog on the end of a bit of string'.

During the latter part of the afternoon the Argentine Air Force returned to the fray, this time with a concerted attack on the British warships. Some forty sorties were launched: Canberras of Grupo 2, Skyhawks of Grupos 4 and 5, and Daggers of Grupo 6, with the Mirages of Grupo 8 flying top cover.

The Mirages formed the vanguard of the attacking force, and once again Paul Barton chanced to be airborne and on the combat air patrol station nearest their line of approach; with him as wing man was Lieutenant Steve Thomas. This time Lieutenant

Commander Paul Raine, an experienced and very competent controller, was directing them from HMS *Glamorgan*, which had a full radar height-finding capability. At first the Argentine fighters repeated their initial sparring game, then headed straight for the Sea Harriers at medium altitude as though bent on a fight. Thomas picked up the enemy aircraft on his radar: they were flying in echelon about 1,200 yards apart, slightly higher than he was. He thought it a rather odd type of formation for fighters to use in combat. 'I locked my radar on to the leader, then began looking for the others – I couldn't believe that a pair of fighters would come in alone like that,' he recalled. Tactically it was a poor formation, because if the rear man came under attack from behind there was no way the leader could go quickly to his aid. Barton, too, was taken aback: 'This is the sort of thing one learns not to do on Day 1 at the Tactical Weapons Unit. We would never dream of flying that sort of formation, so it was mildly surprising that they did.'

Having made first radar contact on the enemy, Thomas took over the lead of the pair and headed straight at the incoming raid. Meanwhile Barton accelerated to maximum speed and pulled away to the right, bent on hooking round to the side of the enemy fighters and disrupting their attack.

Thomas caught sight of the enemy aircraft at 8 miles and recognized them immediately: they were Mirages, and a few seconds later they launched their attack from head-on at far too great a range and in any case beyond the homing capability of their infra-red missiles. 'At 5 miles their leader launched a missile at me, but I saw it diverge and go down to my left. At the same time something came off the second aircraft; it was tumbling, obviously a missile which had misfired. I did not feel threatened by either missile.' As the enemy pair hurtled towards him Thomas tried to lock-on one of his Sidewinders but without success. Then he eased back on his stick and dropped his right wing: 'I began turning hard to the right, and passed about 100 feet above the top of their leader. I could make out every detail of the aircraft, its camouflage pattern, and see the pilot in his cockpit.'

Meanwhile Barton was swinging round on to the tails of the Mirages. As they swept past his nose he loosed off a brief burst at the rear aircraft with his cannon, but did not see any hits.

The two Mirage pilots, Captain Garcia Cuerva in the lead aircraft with Lieutenant Carlos Perona as his wing man, knew the Sea Harriers were in their general area but had lost sight of them. Cuerva led the pair in a curve to the left, but as he did so Barton, unseen by either of them, swung behind Perona into a missile-firing position. 'If he had seen me, any red-blooded fighter pilot would have broken hard towards me as I turned in. But he did nothing,' Barton commented. The Sea Harrier pilot heard a growl in his earphones as the homing head of his starboard Sidewinder picked up the infra-red emissions from the enemy aircraft, then he pressed the button to lock-on the missile and heard the insistent 'nee-nee-nee' sound to confirm it was ready to fire. He eased his fighter down a little, to about 12,000 feet, to silhouette the Mirage against the cold background of the powder-blue sky, then squeezed the firing button. With a muffled roar the Sidewinder sped off its launcher leaving a trail of grey smoke. 'At first I thought it had failed. It came off the rail and ducked down. It took about half a mile for it to get its trajectory sorted out, then it picked itself up and for the last half mile it just homed straight in.' During all of this Barton saw the rear Mirage continue unconcernedly behind its leader, now in a slowly tightening turn to its left. 'The missile hit him on the port side of the fuselage, then the whole rear half of the aircraft disappeared in a great ball of flame. The front half went down burning fiercely, arcing towards the sea.'

The first thing Perona knew of the attack was when his Mirage broke up into a flaming mass around him. He immediately jettisoned the canopy and pulled the handle to fire his ejection seat, but even before he could do so the nose section had pitched down violently so that when the seat went off he was blasted forwards and downwards, at about 45 degrees to the horizontal. At the time Barton was convinced that nobody could have survived from the fireball in front of him; from his vantage point Perona on his seat looked like just another piece of wreckage falling clear. Several seconds later, when he reached 10,000 feet in his fall, Perona was released from his seat and his parachute opened automatically. He came down just off the coast of West Falkland in shallow water, and walked ashore.

Steve Thomas saw Barton's missile strike, as he was curving vengefully on the tail of the leading Mirage. He locked on one of

Main Argentine Air Bases
Used in the Falklands Conflict

ARGENTINA

BUENOS AIRES

ESPORA

PUERTO BELGRANO

N

CHILE

TRELEW

COMODORO RIVADAVIA

PUERTO DESEADO

0   200
STATUTE
MILES

SAN JULIAN

TOTAL
EXCLUSION
ZONE

SANTA CRUZ

FALKLAND
ISLANDS

RIO GALLEGOS

PORT
STANLEY

PUNTA
ARENAS

RIO GRANDE

TIERRA
DEL
FUEGO

ISLA DE LOS ESTADOS

CAPE HORN

his Sidewinders and launched it, but as he did so the Argentine pilot realized what was happening and started a high-speed dive towards a patch of cloud below. When last seen the missile was close to and closing rapidly on the tail of the Mirage, then both plunged into the cloud.

At the time Thomas could claim only one Mirage 'possibly destroyed'. In fact, the Sidewinder went off on its proximity fuse close to the enemy fighter and caused considerable damage. Streaming fuel from his punctured tanks, Cuerva knew he could not regain the mainland so headed for Port Stanley to try to bring his crippled aircraft down on the runway there.

With a dozen or so of his neighbours Tony Chater was in his garden in Port Stanley watching the comings and goings above. 'We saw a couple of aircraft go past over to the north-east, very low and too far away to identify,' he recalled. Then another aircraft came straight towards the town from the west. 'Suddenly the Argentinian guns opened up at it, everything they had in and around the town joined in the firing. They hit it once, twice, and down she came. She smashed into the ground and the Argentinians cheered like a football crowd. We Falklanders were very dejected, it was a bad moment for us.' Later, however, the residents' spirits were lifted considerably when they learned that the aircraft they had watched being shot down was not a Sea Harrier. It was Garcia Cuerva's Mirage, finished off by his own side. The pilot did not survive.

While all this was happening, elements of the main attack force were approaching the British warships at low altitude. Lieutenant Cesar Roman was flying with a flight of three Daggers of Grupo 6, cruising over West Falkland at 480 m.p.h. about 300 feet above the ground. Each fighter-bomber carried two 1,000-pound bombs and two large drop tanks. 'On the way in we saw a Sea Harrier making a tight climbing turn, then it flew into cloud and that was the last we saw of it. We also sighted a Sea King apparently on a radar search, but it was quite a long way from our line of approach so we continued on the planned route,' Roman explained. 'When we arrived at the point where we should have found the ships there was no sign of them. But we had enough fuel so we continued on the same heading. As we were about to turn for home we glanced to one side towards Puerto Argentino [Port Stanley] and saw three warships in the distance going towards

Puerto Argentino itself. We also saw the splashes of artillery fire from the coast, aimed at the warships.'

The warships Roman had seen were *Glamorgan, Arrow* and *Alacrity*, which had just completed the initial bombardment of Port Stanley airfield. 'The flight leader immediately assigned us our targets. I was to go for the ship nearest the coast, the leader would go for the middle ship, and the No. 2 man, on the left, was to take on the warship furthest away. The leader drew ahead slightly, but we all attacked within a space of a few seconds and dropped our bombs almost together. We had caught them by surprise and there seemed to be little or no anti-aircraft fire,' Roman continued. 'All three of us continued past the warships, put on full power and picked up speed, then pulled up into cloud and set course due west.' The three Daggers returned to San Julian without incident.

During the snap attack all three warships suffered minor damage. The worst was to *Arrow*, which picked up eight hits from 30 mm cannon across her funnel and engine air intake; in each case the damage was spectacular rather than serious, however, for the high-explosive rounds detonated on impact and blew out a line of holes each about a foot across, in the outer plating of her superstructure. One man suffered splinter wounds. *Glamorgan* suffered minor splinter damage. *Alacrity* was shaken by a bomb exploding nearby, and took on a little water before her damage-control team was able to seal off the leak.

The ease with which the Daggers had been able to surprise the British warships highlighted the shortcomings of the latters' air defence and fire-control radars during operations close to the shore. In almost every case the radars carried on the three ships had been designed some two decades earlier, and none had the modern circuitry which would effectively filter off ground returns and enable a set to track incoming aircraft over land. It was a problem that was to dog the Royal Navy throughout the conflict, whenever its warships moved close inshore and were liable to attack from the air. Only the modern Type 22 frigates carried radars that were able effectively to filter out the land clutter; there were only two of these, *Broadsword* and *Brilliant*, and although they were also fitted with the Sea Wolf self-defence missile system they did not have 4·5-inch guns with which to bombard enemy positions. It was decided that during future bombardments of

Port Stanley airstrip by day, a Type 22 would accompany the gun-carrying ship.

As the Daggers pulled away from their targets, a further skirmish was developing higher up. Flight Lieutenant Tony Penfold and Lieutenant Martin Hale of No. 800 Squadron were on patrol in their Sea Harriers when they came under attack from Daggers of Grupo 6 at high altitude, operating in the fighter role and carrying Shafrir infra-red homing air-to-air missiles. Penfold's radar had gone unserviceable so Hale was leading the section. 'We were in standard defensive battle formation [in line abreast, about a mile apart] and we ran in towards them. Tony got a visual pick-up on them at about 8 miles. He called "Targets at 12 o'clock [in front], high". I looked up from my radar screen and the first and only thing I saw of them was a very obvious missile trail in front of me, coming from whatever type of aircraft was up there. He was at between 30,000 and 35,000 feet, we were at 20,000 feet,' Hale later recalled. 'The trail probably went horizontal for two or three hundred yards, then it curved quite definitely down in my direction. I took what we considered to be the appropriate evasive action: I broke to port rapidly and entered a nearly vertical dive. At the same time I blipped open my airbrake to dump chaff. For what seemed far too long, the missile continued to gain on me quite dramatically.'

It was a thoroughly unnerving experience for the Sea Harrier pilot: 'People talk about your life flashing before your eyes when you are near to death. I had never experienced it before, but there were a couple of seconds when a portion of my life passed before my eyes.' Just before he entered cloud at 5,000 feet Hale looked back and saw the missile trail begin to waver: it had broken lock, almost certainly because it was fired at too great a range.

A very relieved Sea Harrier pilot eased his aircraft out of the dive. 'I turned back towards the fight, poked my head out of the cloud, and was climbing back up to where I thought they would be. I kept my eyes pretty much glued to my 6 o'clock [the rear] to see if there were any of their guys trying to get in behind me. As I was in the climb I heard Tony call that he had fired a missile and it looked like a long shot. I looked up and saw a missile trail very high, then an explosion.' Penfold had knocked down the Dagger which had given Hale such a fright; its pilot was Lieutenant José Ardiles, cousin of the famous football star.

By now it was dusk but still the attackers came in, this time six Canberras of Grupo 2 approaching in two flights of three. They came in at very low altitude from the north-west, on almost the direct line from their base at Trelew. As the bombers were descending to low altitude they were observed on one of the ship's radars, however, and Lieutenant Commander Mike Broadwater and Lieutenant Al Curtiss of No. 801 Squadron were vectored out to intercept. Searching with radar at an altitude of 5,000 feet, the Sea Harriers made contact with one of the flights and curved round to engage. Curtiss got into a firing position first and loosed off a Sidewinder at one of the Canberras about 50 feet above the waves.

At the controls of the leading bomber was Captain Alberto Baigorri. 'We were intercepted about 150 miles before reaching Puerto Argentino,' he later recalled. 'The No. 3 in my flight called that there was a missile heading my way. I looked to my right and saw it hit the No. 2 aircraft, piloted by Lieutenant de Ibañez and with Lieutenant Gonzales as navigator. The bomber continued flying with an engine on fire then, as it started to go down, I saw de Ibañez and Gonzales eject before it hit the water.' From behind, Curtiss had also seen his Sidewinder explode close to the Canberra and pieces fall clear; but when the bomber continued on he launched a second missile, which was still in flight when the Canberra crashed into the sea.

Meanwhile, Broadwater was lining up his aircraft for a missile shot on one of the bombers. Baigorri caught a glimpse of the hunter closing in. 'Above me I saw a Sea Harrier looking to see whose turn it would be next! I broke to the right and called to my No. 3 man to break to the left.' Broadwater loosed off both of his missiles at one of the evading Canberras, then shortage of fuel forced the two Sea Harriers to break off the action and return to *Invincible*.

After he had shaken off the attacker Baigorri returned to the scene of the crash to look for his comrades, but found no sign of them. While he was circling close to the water his Canberra was seen by the crew of a Royal Navy Lynx helicopter on patrol and reported as being 'apparently in difficulty'. Later this would give rise to the notion that one of Broadwater's missiles might have inflicted serious damage on a Canberra too, though this was not the case.

The hunt for the Argentine submarine *San Luis* continued through the night of the 1st, though after dark the three Sea Kings of No. 826 Squadron were forced to break off and return to HMS *Hermes*. Supporting the operation the helicopters each spent over ten hours airborne, with a crew change in the hover halfway through; they refuelled from the frigates a total of ten times. In the course of the hunt Sea King VX 577 spent 10 hours and 20 minutes in the air, to establish a new world record for the longest time airborne by a helicopter on an operational mission.

That night *Hermes* moved in closer to the Falklands and the Sea King transport helicopters of No. 846 Squadron started to fly off intelligence-gathering patrols from G Squadron of the Special Air Service, taking them to positions from which they could keep watch on Argentine movements. In the weeks that followed the SAS reports would have an important bearing on the unfolding battle.

Throughout the day the Argentine cruiser *General Belgrano* and her consorts had patrolled between Isla de los Estados and Burdwood Bank to the south-west of the Falklands, their tasks being to prevent British warships joining the Task Force from the Pacific and to provide warning of any movement towards the mainland from that direction. Meanwhile the main body of the surface fleet, including the carrier *25 de Mayo*, was at sea to the east of Comodoro Rivadavia, and after dark set course towards the main British Task Group at 20 knots. Tracker reconnaissance aircraft were launched, and shortly before midnight one of these located the quarry on radar: one large and six medium-sized ships, 150 miles due north of Port Stanley and some 300 miles south-east of the force now bent on attacking them. Preparations immediately began for an air strike on the British ships using all eight Skyhawks on the carrier, to be launched from a position just outside the total exclusion zone shortly before dawn the following morning (although *25 de Mayo* could launch jet aircraft at night, the Argentine Navy considered her too small for landings in the dark).

During the evening of 1 May there was a great deal to think about for both sides. The Sea Harrier had emerged from its baptism of fire without a single loss and had shown it could certainly hold its own against the Mirage, the best fighter the Argentinians had. On the British side there was considerable surprise at the poor combat handling displayed by the enemy aircraft; their pilots seemed to have little idea of correct tactics when it came to a fight. 'We were ahead, we were confident we would stay ahead, but we couldn't believe they would continue to use the same pathetic tactics,' said Flight Lieutenant Ian Mortimer of No. 801 Squadron. 'That night we looked at each other and said that if the fighting continued at that intensity hardly any of us would get home. That day we on 801 had had seven missiles fired at us. Most had been fired out of range, or the parameters were all wrong; they had even fired Matra Magics at us from head-on, and it doesn't have a head-on homing capability. But we figured that if they continued throwing missiles at us at that rate, sooner or later some were going to hit.'

In Argentina the position looked rather different. During the day a total of ten Mirage, twelve Dagger, six Canberra and twenty-eight Skyhawk sorties had been dispatched from the mainland to engage the enemy forces east of the Falklands. Of this total thirty-five, or about two-thirds, had reached their assigned combat areas. Two Mirages, a Dagger and a Canberra had been shot down by the enemy, in one case assisted by the defenders at Port Stanley. It was clear that in air-to-air combat the Mirages and Daggers were no match for the Sea Harrier with late-model Sidewinders, especially when the Argentine pilots were being forced to engage on the enemy's terms at medium altitude. On the other hand, there had been several reports of Sea Harriers having been destroyed by the gun and missile batteries on the Islands, and if these were even partially true the Task Force's air cover was now seriously depleted.

The Vulcan's stick of twenty-one 1,000-pounders across the airfield at Port Stanley sent out a shudder which extended far beyond Tony Chater's bedroom three miles away. In fact the reverberations were felt more than 1,200 miles away, in the *Condor* building in Buenos Aires. The single hole in the middle of the runway put an end to any hope that fast jet aircraft would be able to use the airfield as a refuelling stop after attacking enemy warships. Even more important, Martin Withers's attack had demonstrated that the Royal Air Force had the ability to bomb airfields in Argentina if it chose to do so. In sending the Task

Force into action at all the British government had reacted in a way quite different from that predicted; who could now say with any confidence where they would stop? Accordingly the decision was taken to withdraw from the south the remaining Mirages of Grupo 8, the Air Force's only specialized interceptor unit, and redeploy them to cover airfields on the mainland. The decision was to have far-reaching consequences. It meant that at a stroke the Argentinians had abandoned any chance of securing air superiority over the Falklands and the surrounding waters. The Daggers with their simple avionics were less capable in the air fighting role than the Mirage, and would in future be used only as bombers.

To deliver the twenty-one bombs on to the airfield at Port Stanley the Royal Air Force, and in particular the Victor tanker force, had taken considerable risks and encountered difficulties which tested men and machines to their limits. The effort expended had been out of all proportion to the amount of damage actually caused to Port Stanley airfield. But the effect of the attack on Argentine Air Force thinking and its combat capability was out of all proportion to the damage also.

The bloody war of attrition in the air, feared by Ian Mortimer and his comrades flying Sea Harriers after the first day's fighting, would never take place. During the weeks to follow British air crews would face danger in many forms, but never again from Argentine fighters sent determinedly to destroy them.

4: Time of Attrition

2 – 20 MAY

'It may well be a hundred to one against a hit with a heavy torpedo on a ship, but the chance is always there and the disproportion is grievous. Like a hero being stung by a malarious mosquito.'

Winston Churchill

2 MAY

During the night following the action on 1 May, there was naval activity on both sides. The patrol boat *Alférez Sobral* put out from Port Stanley to conduct a vain search for the Canberra crew which had parachuted into the sea. And off the north coast of the Falklands the Royal Navy hunt for the submarine *San Luis* continued into the darkness of the following morning. According to Argentine Navy reports *San Luis* was able to close to within 1,400 yards of one of the frigates and launch a torpedo attack, but without scoring any hits. Royal Navy officers are sceptical about this claim, however, and neither warship detected the distinctive sound of an incoming torpedo on its sensitive sonar listening equipment. Several homing torpedoes, depth charges and anti-submarine mortar rounds were expended by the frigates and helicopters during the hunt, against suspected submarine contacts on or near the sea bottom. In the event *San Luis* was able to escape, though not before her crew had been given a taste of what it was like to be on the receiving end of an all-out submarine hunt by the Royal Navy. The boat played little further part in the conflict.

Also during the night the opposing groups of warships launched aircraft to try to locate each other. Shortly after midnight Flight Lieutenant Ian Mortimer took off from *Invincible* in a Sea Harrier to investigate radar signals coming from a source to the north-west of the British warships. He flew the probing mission with his radar on 'standby', ready for use but not transmitting, and used his radar warning receiver to search for emissions from the enemy. Finally he found what he was looking for: the familiar sound of a British Type 909 missile control radar sweeping its beam across his aircraft, then beginning to lock on. The Type 909 is the control radar for the Sea Dart missiles fitted to several Royal Navy warships, but the same radar and missiles were carried by the Argentine destroyers *Hercules* and *Santisima Trinidad*, and he did not intend to allow one of these to engage him. 'Realizing what it had to be, I turned and fled,' Mortimer later recalled. 'When I got to a safe distance I turned back, put on my radar, and pointed it in the direction where the threat signals had come from and saw six ships on my screen.' Bearing this important information, Mortimer sped back to his carrier.

Just before dawn *25 de Mayo* arrived in position to launch her air strike, about 200 miles to the north-west of the British warships. But now fate intervened. The wind, usually strong in these latitudes at this time of the year, was calm, and this meant that the ship's Skyhawks could not be catapulted carrying bomb-loads and sufficient fuel to reach their target and return. As it was getting light the Argentine commander, Rear Admiral Juan Lombardo, ordered the carrier and her escorts to turn back to safer waters nearer the mainland until the weather improved.

It should be pointed out that these same calm conditions imposed no hindrance on jet operations from the British carriers: Sea Harriers could be launched even when their ship was moving downwind. They could land, by day or night, regardless of whether the ship was moving into wind, downwind or across wind. If visibility was poor, the jump-jets could make slow approaches; and if the deck was pitching severely they could still land, using the old helicopter trick of setting down amidships near the point about which the carrier's motion pivots and where the vertical movement is at a minimum. The British carriers were thus able to operate Sea Harriers over a vastly greater range of sea and weather conditions than was possible for *25 de Mayo* with her Skyhawks. In combat the concept of the short take-off and vertical landing fighter-bomber was making very good sense indeed.

Later in the day a further attempt by the Argentine Navy to strike at the British Task Force also came to nothing. Commander Jorgo Colombo led a pair of Super Étendards of the 2nd Escuadrilla from Rio Grande, with the intention of carrying out the first attack with Exocet. The initial in-flight refuelling off the coast failed, however, and the aircraft returned with the precious missiles still on their launchers.

Meanwhile the cruiser *General Belgrano* and the two destroyers continued their patrol between Isla de los Estados and Burdwood Bank, now heading back towards the former. Trailing the ships was the British nuclear submarine *Conquerer*. Following an exchange of signals via satellite with the Royal Navy fleet headquarters at Northwood on the outskirts of London, the boat's commander received orders to attack the cruiser even though she was 30 miles outside the total exclusion zone. *Conquerer* launched a salvo of torpedoes at the *General Belgrano*, two of which scored hits and inflicted severe damage. Two hours later the warship sank, and in spite of protracted rescue operations by the Argentine Navy 321 of her crew were lost.

Both during and since the conflict there has been a great deal of controversy about the attack on the *General Belgrano*, at a time when she was outside the total exclusion zone and when both the northerly and the southerly groups of Argentine warships were heading back to the mainland. Argentine official sources make no mention of the ships having been recalled to port, however, and in each case the withdrawal was temporary: *25 de Mayo* and the ships with her were to head east again when the weather became suitable for her to launch the air strike; and *General Belgrano* was simply on the westerly leg of her east-west patrol line. There is no doubt that, had the weather allowed, *25 de Mayo* would have launched her air strike at the British warships from outside the total exclusion zone; and had the Skyhawk and Super Étendard strikes been successful and hit one or both of the British aircraft carriers, *General Belgrano* was in position to join in any surface action against the remainder of the Task Force.

Following the loss of *General Belgrano* the Argentine surface fleet returned to the waters immediately off the mainland, where it would remain for the rest of the conflict. British nuclear submarines would maintain a blockade of the naval bases, though the possibility of a sudden high-speed sortie getting out to sea was to exercise the minds of British planners during the weeks to follow.

3 MAY

During the evening of 2 May the patrol craft *Comodoro Somellera* and *Alférez Sobral* put out from Port Stanley to resume the search for the two Canberra crewmen who had come down in the sea to the north of the Falklands. Shortly after midnight Lieutenant Commander John Chandler, flying a Sea King of No. 826 Squadron, closed on a small surface contact detected on radar. Initially the vessel had been showing lights, but as the helicopter closed in they were extinguished. Then, as the Sea King moved in closer still, the vessel opened fire on it with automatic weapons. Chandler pulled away to a safe distance, his aircraft undamaged, and called in supporting helicopters. The destroyers *Coventry* and *Glasgow* launched their Lynx helicopters, each carrying a pair of the new and untried Sea Skua missiles which had been hastily issued to front-line units as the Task Force moved south. *Coventry*'s Lynx was first on the scene and, guided in by Chandler's Sea King, picked up the enemy ship on radar, achieved a lock-on, and closed to 8 miles where it fired two Sea Skuas in succession. Both missiles homed on the ship's radar echoes, scored direct hits, and detonated. There followed a secondary explosion of ammunition then the vessel, the *Comodoro Somellera*, sank. *Glasgow*'s Lynx began searching for survivors, but shortly afterwards it came under fire from another Argentine patrol craft in the area. The latter was picked up on radar, a second attack with a pair of Sea Skuas carried out, and a further two detonations seen. Two days later *Alférez Sobral*, with most of her bridge blown away and her captain and seven crewmen dead, would limp into the mainland port of Puerto Deseado. Neither crewmen from the shot-down Canberra was rescued.

4 MAY

Late on the evening of 3 May eleven Victor tankers and two Vulcans had taken off from Ascension, to launch the second 'Black Buck' attack on Port Stanley airfield. The lessons of the first attack had been well learned, and major changes made in the refuelling procedures. 'In Black Buck 1 there had been one huge formation going south, slowly getting smaller and smaller. In our mission there were two smaller formations,' explained Squadron

Leader John Reeve of No. 50 Squadron, the captain of the Vulcan.
'The first comprised our Vulcan and the refuellers who were to
get us two-thirds of the way to Port Stanley before the last one
turned back. The second wave of tankers took off about five
minutes after us, and flew at a slightly greater height and speed so
they caught us up well down the route. Their job was to get a
single Victor full of fuel to refuel us immediately before we began
our descent for the target. It worked extremely well.' Indeed, the
entire mission went smoothly except at the target, where the luck
which had sustained Martin Withers's first mission deserted the
second at the critical moment. The stick of twenty-one 1,000-
pounders from Reeve's Vulcan narrowly missed the western edge
of the runway, causing no significant additional damage to the
airfield. All aircraft involved in the operation returned safely to
Ascension.

Thus far during the conflict all the major losses had been on the
Argentine side. But now the run of luck enjoyed by the British
forces was suddenly to come to an end. That morning Lieutenant
Commander Gordon Batt led a second attack on Goose Green, by
three Sea Harriers of No. 800 Squadron. He and Lieutenant Nick
Taylor were to attack the parked Pucarás with cluster bombs,
running in from the south-east; once they were through the target
Flight Lieutenant Ted Ball was to run in from the south-west and
drop three 1,000-pound parachute-retarded bombs to crater the
airstrip. 'I turned in towards the target looking for Nick, because
he had to be clear before I dropped my bombs. I caught sight of
him running in, exactly where I expected him to be,' Ball later
recalled. Then Taylor's aircraft was hit by heavy-calibre ground
fire, almost certainly 35 mm Oerlikon. 'Suddenly his Sea Harrier
burst into flames; it continued flying for some way then it crashed
into the ground with a huge ball of fire. Probably he was killed
before he hit the ground, otherwise he would have had time to
eject. At first I was mesmerized by the scene, but then I had to get
on with the job of dropping my own bombs and getting out of the
area.'

The loss of the Sea Harrier pilot was mourned throughout the
British Task Force, but worse was to befall shortly afterwards.
Since early that morning a Neptune patrol aircraft of the 1st
Naval Reconnaissance Escuadrilla had been shadowing the
British warships, and reported the main concentration to be

about 100 miles south of Port Stanley. Again the Argentine Naval Air Command ordered a Super Étendard strike and at 9.45 a.m. Lieutenant Commander Augusto Bedacarratz and Lieutenant Armando Mayora took off from Rio Grande. Each aircraft carried external fuel tanks under the port wing and fuselage, and a single Exocet missile under the starboard wing. Fifteen minutes after take off the attack aircraft topped off their fuel tanks from a KC-130 Hercules tanker, then continued eastwards at medium altitude before their approach to the target area where they let down to 50 feet above the waves. Throughout this phase the two attack aircraft maintained visual contact on each other and kept strict radio and radar silence, their pilots relying on infrequent broadcasts from the Neptune to update their position on the target. When they arrived in the area where the warships had been reported the two aircraft pulled up to about 120 feet, briefly switched on their radars to locate the exact positions of the targets in front of them, launched their Exocets and withdrew at high speed. This was modern war at its most impersonal: neither pilot had any idea at which ship he had aimed his missile.

It was just after 11 a.m. when the destroyer HMS *Sheffield*, on radar picket duty about 20 miles west of the main body of the British Task Group, picked up radar contact on an aircraft closing at low altitude from the west; but the contact disappeared from the radar screen shortly afterwards.

The first positive sign of the approaching danger came about two minutes later when Lieutenants Peter Walpole and Brian Layshon, on the bridge of *Sheffield*, glanced over the starboard bow to see a trail of smoke close to the sea and the missile about a mile away and closing rapidly. Five seconds later the Exocet struck the destroyer amidships and smashed its way deep into her hull with what her commander Captain Sam Salt later described as a 'short, sharp, unimpressive bang'. Since the event there has been speculation on whether the missile's 364-pound warhead detonated fully, and from examination of the available evidence the authors consider it unlikely that it did so. A half-ton missile impacting at 680 m.p.h. and brought to a halt within about 30 feet by a ship's structure will cause considerable damage, and almost certainly there would have been sufficient unused rocket fuel to start an intensely hot fire in the area where the missile came to rest. At the time *Sheffield*'s crew were on normal defence watches

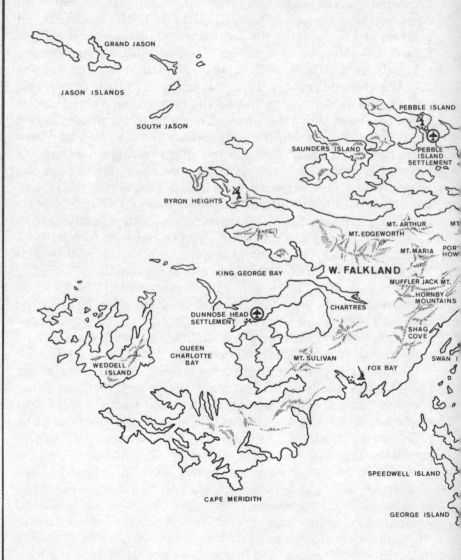

The Falkland Islands

GRAND JASON

JASON ISLANDS

SOUTH JASON

PEBBLE ISLAND

SAUNDERS ISLAND

PEBBLE ISLAND SETTLEMENT

BYRON HEIGHTS

MT. ARTHUR

MT. EDGEWORTH

MT. MARIA

PORT HOW

KING GEORGE BAY

W. FALKLAND

MUFFLER JACK MT.

HORNBY MOUNTAINS

DUNNOSE HEAD SETTLEMENT

CHARTRES

SHAG COVE

QUEEN CHARLOTTE BAY

MT. SULIVAN

FOX BAY

SWAN I

WEDDELL ISLAND

SPEEDWELL ISLAND

CAPE MERIDITH

GEORGE ISLAND

⊕ MAIN AIRFIELDS

✗ AIR SEARCH RADARS

⚓ MAIN CONCENTRATIONS ANTI-AIRCRAFT WEAPONS

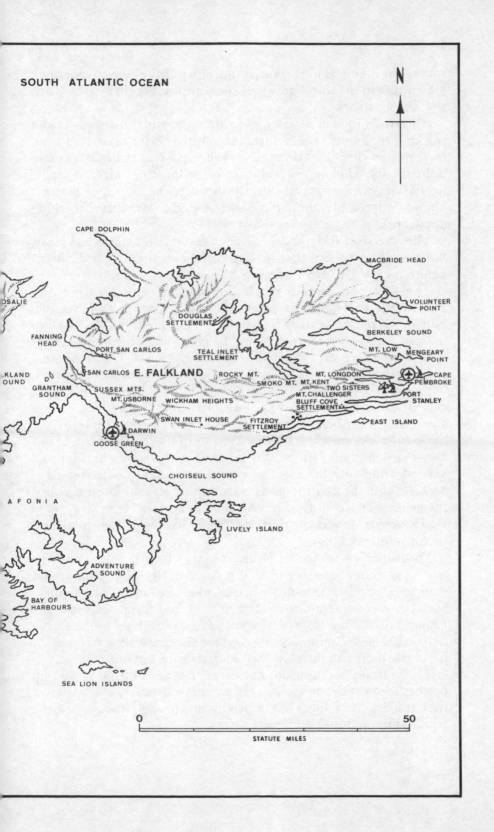

SOUTH ATLANTIC OCEAN

N

CAPE DOLPHIN

MACBRIDE HEAD

OSALIE

VOLUNTEER
POINT

FANNING
HEAD

DOUGLAS
SETTLEMENT

BERKELEY SOUND

PORT SAN CARLOS

TEAL INLET
SETTLEMENT

MT. LOW

MENGEARY
POINT

KLAND
OUND

SAN CARLOS   E. FALKLAND   ROCKY MT.

SMOKO MT. MT. KENT

MT. LONGDON

TWO SISTERS

CAPE
PEMBROKE

GRANTHAM
SOUND

SUSSEX MTS.
MT. USBORNE   WICKHAM HEIGHTS

MT. CHALLENGER

PORT
STANLEY

BLUFF COVE
SETTLEMENT

SWAN INLET HOUSE

FITZROY
SETTLEMENT

EAST ISLAND

DARWIN
GOOSE GREEN

CHOISEUL SOUND

AFONIA

LIVELY ISLAND

ADVENTURE
SOUND

BAY OF
HARBOURS

SEA LION ISLANDS

0

50

STATUTE MILES

rather than at action stations, and most of the twenty-one men killed were in the ship's galley or the computer room nearby when the Exocet struck.

Almost immediately *Sheffield*'s damage-control teams began working to contain the fire, but the ship's water main had been fractured in the initial impact, and the task was made even more difficult by choking, acrid smoke from the burning cable insulation, which spread rapidly through the ship and made it almost impossible to survive below-decks without breathing apparatus.

The course of the second Exocet missile launched is less clear, but there is evidence that it passed close to the frigate *Yarmouth* before it crashed harmlessly into the sea.

The first outsiders to reach the stricken warship were Sub Lieutenant Phil Dibb and his crew in a Sea King of No. 826 Squadron, on anti-submarine patrol in the area. Suddenly Dibb noticed a destroyer in front of him belching smoke from its hull: 'I said to my observer, "What ship is that in our 1 o'clock at about 7 miles, either *Sheffield* or *Coventry*, making a lot of smoke?" He said, "Oh, a Type 42, they all smoke." I said, "Not like this one!" We closed in and saw that she was drifting, with dark smoke streaming out of her amidships. We could get no reply to our radio calls, the missile had knocked out her sets. We winched our crewman on focsle, which was covered with shaken and injured sailors, some with burns.' The crewman returned with details of *Sheffield*'s plight and the assistance required, and Dibb climbed his helicopter a couple of hundred feet and reported the news to HMS *Hermes*. It was the first the flagship knew of the attack and its consequences.

From then on a stream of helicopters plyed between *Sheffield* and the other warships, flying in fire-fighting teams and equipment and returning with wounded crewmen. The fight to save the warship continued for the next four hours, but it was a losing battle. Finally, with the flames gaining hold and nearing her magazines, Captain Salt asked for the remainder of his crew to be taken off and the ship was left to burn itself out.

The volume and unusual nature of the radio traffic picked up by the Argentine monitoring station at Port Stanley made it clear that at least one Exocet had scored a hit, though it was not clear which ship or ships had been victims.

Had *Sheffield*'s crew detected the true nature of the attack in time, her defence would have been to fire chaff rockets in a carefully designed pattern. During their trajectories the rockets would have disgorged many millions of metalized glass-fibre needles, each thinner than a human hair, to produce several radar-attractive targets to decoy the missile safely clear. Theoretically the destroyer would have had about twenty-five seconds' warning of the approach of the Exocet itself, from the time the missile's radar homing head began transmitting during the final 5 miles of its flight. According to some accounts these all-important signals were missed because, at the time, *Sheffield* chanced to be transmitting with her powerful satellite communications equipment. When Walpole and Layshon first saw the missile from the bridge of the destroyer, just a few seconds before impact, it was too late to initiate any counter-measure. The hard-won lessons from the loss of *Sheffield* would be applied by the British Task Force during the weeks that followed.

Three hours after the last of *Sheffield*'s crewmen was taken off, at 6.15 p.m. Falklands time (9.15 p.m. London time), the British Broadcasting Corporation gave out the news of the loss:

> In the course of its duties within the total exclusion zone around the Falkland Islands, HMS *Sheffield*, a Type 42 destroyer, was attacked and hit late this afternoon by an Argentine missile. The ship caught fire, which spread out of control. When there was no longer any hope of saving the ship, the ship's company abandoned ship. All who abandoned her were picked up.

For Jorge Colombo's Super Étendard escuadrilla at Rio Grande, where the men had been waiting expectantly throughout the afternoon, the broadcast from London was the first indication that *Sheffield* had been their victim. It will never be known with certainty which pilot's missile struck the destroyer. In published accounts it has frequently been suggested that the attack on the destroyer was mounted in retaliation for the sinking of the *General Belgrano* two days earlier, with the implication that the two events were linked. We now know that the 2nd Escuadrilla had attempted an Exocet attack on British warships on 2 May, before *Belgrano* was hit, only to be foiled by a flight refuelling failure.

Provided only that the operational conditions were suitable, the Super Étendard attack on 4 May would almost certainly have gone ahead regardless of whether any major Argentine Navy ship had been hit.

Following the loss of *Sheffield* the British Task Group pulled away well to the east of the Falklands, to reassess its operations in the light of the new situation. Never again during the conflict would the aircraft carriers spend any length of time so close to the islands, and when supporting operations there the Sea Harriers would be forced to operate at distances close to the aircraft's maximum radius of action.

The loss of the Sea Harrier at Goose Green caused a further change to the Task Force's operations. Never again were these precious aircraft to be hazarded in low-level attack missions involving flights over well defended targets. From now on, when attacks on ground targets were required, the Sea Harriers would either bomb from a high level or use toss bombing methods, which were less risky but also far less accurate.

5 MAY

After the withdrawal of the surface ships of the Royal Navy Task Force to the east, the weather closed in around it and there was a period of little air activity apart from normal reconnaissance and air defence patrols.

Off the Argentine coast, however, a full-scale anti-submarine hunt developed after a Tracker aircraft of the 1st Naval Anti-Submarine Escuadrilla from *25 de Mayo* reported a possible contact on a submarine 180 miles north-east of Comodoro Rivadavia. A Sea King of the 2nd Naval Helicopter Escuadrilla, also from the carrier, joined the hunt and reported a sonar contact which was attacked with homing torpedoes. No results were observed.

Shortly after this incident *25 de Mayo* disembarked her aircraft and returned to Bahía Blanca. She would play no further part in the conflict.

At this time there was an odd sequel to the Sea Harrier attack on Goose Green on 1 May, when Lieutenant Antonio Jukic was killed when the Pucará in which he was about to take off was hit by cluster bomblets. Now the Argentine government decided to elevate the unfortunate pilot to the status of war hero. The story was concocted that he had lost his life in a lone attack on the British fleet and that immediately after his bombs had hit the aircraft carrier *Hermes* and started a serious fire, his aircraft had been destroyed by a guided missile; the imagined scene was the subject of a dramatic painting, copies of which were passed to journalists. News of the true facts behind the canard quickly spread around the Argentine Air Force, however, where it caused considerable resentment amongst pilots with operational units.

6 MAY

The bad weather around the British Task Force continued, and on this morning it led to the loss of two Sea Harriers from HMS *Invincible*. At about 9 a.m. the two fighters were flying separately on combat air patrols when a Sea King on reconnaissance reported a radar contact well to the south of the warships. Both Sea Harriers moved in to investigate, and nothing was seen again of the aircraft or pilots in spite of an intensive search of the area afterwards. Although the chances of it happening in that way are thousands to one against, the most likely explanation is that the two Sea Harriers collided. There is no evidence that Argentine forces were anywhere near the area, and they report no engagements that can be linked with the missing machines.

With the loss of the Sea Harrier two days earlier, this brought the number of aircraft available to protect the Task Force down to seventeen; reinforcement aircraft were on their way from England, but it would be almost two weeks before they arrived in the operational area to fill the gaps in the carrier air groups.

7 MAY

The bad weather continued through 7 May, during which Grupo 1 sent one of its C-130 Hercules freighters from Comodoro Rivadavia to Port Stanley. The aircraft landed on the undamaged part of the runway, off-loaded supplies and key personnel, then picked up men wounded during the previous actions and returned to the mainland. For the remainder of the conflict the Hercules force, soon joined by Naval Electra and Fokker Fellowship transports, would fly an average of two missions per day into the Falklands, which would do much to boost the morale of Argentine troops. During these operations the radars on the Falklands played an important role in providing warning of the Sea Harrier patrols, thus enabling crews to pick their way past the enemy fighters and avoid interception.

8 MAY

The bad weather and poor visibility continued, bringing a virtual halt to Sea Harrier operations. On this day and the previous three, No. 800 Squadron on *Hermes* flew a total of only four Sea Harrier sorties.

9 MAY

During the day the destroyer *Coventry* and the frigate *Broadsword* were operating off Port Stanley. Lieutenant Commander Gordon Batt and Flight Lieutenant Dave Morgan of No. 800 Squadron took off from *Hermes* to make a high-level bombing attack on Port Stanley airfield, only to find their target shrouded in cloud, which forced them to abandon the mission. As the pair swung away Morgan turned on his radar and observed a contact about 60 miles away out to sea. He called *Coventry*, the control ship in the area, and asked if the contact was friendly; they were told there was no British ship in that area and they were to investigate. As the pair approached the contact Batt let down through cloud and identified it as a large stern trawler, flying the Argentine flag and bearing the name *Narwal*. Morgan relayed the report to *Coventry* and soon afterwards received orders to engage the vessel. Although each aircraft carried two 1,000-pound bombs, these had been rigged for dropping from high altitude, with a seven-second arming time after release before they became 'live'. As the Sea Harrier could not return to the carrier with the bombs, however, it was decided to aim them at the enemy ship. After releasing their bombs, one of which lodged in the *Narwal*'s hull without exploding, the Sea Harriers strafed the ship with cannon. Damaged about the engine room, the trawler wallowed to a stop and her crew began to abandon her. Later Sea King helicopters landed a boarding party to take possession of the ship and take her crew prisoner; one of those on board was found to be an

Argentine naval officer, and captured documents indicated that the ship had been involved in intelligence gathering. *Narwal* sank under tow the next day.

Also on the 9th the Argentine Air Force lost two pilots in a flying accident in bad weather, in a manner reminiscent of that which had claimed the lives of two Sea Harrier pilots three days earlier. A pair of Skyhawks of Grupo 4, approaching the Falklands to attack British ships at low altitude and in poor visibility, smashed into the steep side of South Jason island off the north-west of West Falkland. Both pilots died immediately.

Soon afterwards *Coventry* picked up on radar a slow moving aircraft contact near Port Stanley and engaged it with a Sea Dart missile. The weapon exploded close to a Puma helicopter of the Argentine Army, knocking it out of the sky and killing all on board.

10 MAY

Poor weather continued to limit air operations around the Falklands. At Port Stanley airfield the rain and the almost nightly naval bombardments combined to make life a misery for the Argentinians dug in there. The diary of Army Sergeant Juan Ochoa, serving there with B Battery of the 601st Anti-Aircraft Battalion operating 35 mm guns, gives an idea of the wretched conditions the men had to face. On the 10th he noted:

> At 0210 hours naval gunfire started with about ten shells falling a few metres away from our old position. We went to our allocated shelter trenches and ours started to fill with water, turning it into a pool. We went off to another larger hole where we stayed, sodden, until 0800 hours. Despite being soaked, we slept well. Everybody woke up thoroughly wet because the trench was pouring with water, down the walls as well as on the ground. It was cloudy with continual drizzle, and after a breakfast of coffee I took off all my clothes to dry them over the generator for the fire control radar.

11 MAY

At Ascension Island there were rarely problems with the weather, and a new capability developed for Operation CORPORATE was used for the first time: the Nimrod 2 with flight refuelling. Refuelling once on the way down, a crew from No. 206 Squadron flew 2,750 miles south-south-west of the island to provide anti-submarine cover for the major reinforcement convoy carrying troops to retake the Falklands.

The flight-refuelling modification bore all the hallmarks of a hasty improvisation, as Wing Commander David Emmerson, the Nimrod detachment commander, later explained: 'The Nimrod had an ex-Vulcan refuelling probe attached to what had been the pilot's escape hatch above the cockpit. Leading from the rear of the probe, down to the cabin floor and along the floor to the refuelling gallery two-thirds of the way down the fuselage, was a length of standard canvas-on-rubber flexible bowser hose which people treated with a great deal of respect and avoided when walking past.' For all that, the new system worked well, and would make it possible for the Nimrod 2 to provide comprehensive radar and electronic reconnaissance wherever required.

12 MAY

Shortly after midday Grupo 5 sent two flights of four Skyhawks from Rio Gallegos to attack British warships bombarding Port Stanley airfield. The leading flight ran in to bomb but found the warships – the destroyer *Glasgow* and the frigate *Brilliant* – ready for them. *Brilliant* engaged with Sea Wolf and shot down two of the Skyhawks, while a third crashed into the sea trying to avoid a missile. All three pilots, Lieutenants Bustos, Nivoli and Ibarlucea, were killed. As the survivor pulled clear the second flight, led by Captain Zelaya, arrived on the scene. Zelaya himself and two others made for *Glasgow*; the remaining Skyhawk went for *Brilliant*. Again the Sea Wolf operators prepared to engage, but at the critical moment the system suffered a technical hiccup and they were unable to do so. The sailors watched helplessly as the Skyhawk closed in rapidly and released its bombs: they struck the water, bounced right over *Brilliant* and fell back into the sea on the far side.

'The ships were heading south-south-east and from their wakes we could see they were going fast,' Zelaya recalled. 'A few kilometres before we reached the target they began firing at us. I didn't see any missiles, but I could hear the explosions of the anti-aircraft shells. As I neared the bomb-release point I concentrated my entire attention on the target. The sight of her huge radar scanner, continually rotating, remains etched on my memory.' After releasing their bombs the Skyhawk pilots returned to low altitude and sped clear of the warships. Zelaya heard his pilots call in: 'Lieutenant Fausto Gavazzi shouted "Viva la Patria! [Long live the Motherland!] I hit it! I'm sure I hit it!"'

In fact Gavazzi had scored a direct hit on *Glasgow* with a 1,000-pound bomb. It struck her amidships, smashed clean through her hull, emerged out the other side and exploded in the sea several seconds later when the ship was safely clear. On its way through the ship the bomb managed to miss all the structural frames; it knocked over a high-pressure air-bottle without fracturing it and smashed a fuel tank without starting a fire. The ship had enjoyed the narrowest of escapes, but even so there remained the bomb's entry and exit holes, each some 3 feet across, close to the waterline on either side. *Glasgow*'s damage-control parties made a good first-aid repair using timber, bedding and steel plates but if she rolled at all the destroyer took on a lot of water. *Glasgow* was forced to withdraw from the operational area for more extensive repairs.

Fausto Gavazzi would not be given long to savour his success. As the surviving Skyhawks came past Goose Green on their way home, trigger-happy Argentine anti-aircraft gunners opened up at the aircraft coming from the east. Gavazzi's aircraft was hit, rolled over on to its back and smashed into the ground with the pilot still on board.

Even as the fighter-bombers neared Rio Gallegos their problems were not over. Zelaya recalled: 'During the final descent we found that our windscreens were covered in salt particles [caused by salt spray picked up by the aircraft during their approach flights to the Islands at low altitude], which obstructed the view ahead. We tried to get rid of it by blowing hot air, but our efforts were useless. Over the radio we heard that Ensign Vazquez, a member of the flight that had attacked before us, was returning with the same problem. Because of this, when he landed he ran off the runway. We afterwards learned that he was the sole survivor of his flight.'

It had been a hard day for Grupo 5: four aircraft and pilots lost, one aircraft damaged running off the runway and another with battle damage.

The encounter demonstrated that Sea Dart, the sole anti-aircraft missile system fitted to *Glasgow* and her sister Type 42 destroyers, though effective enough against higher-flying targets, was far less effective against aircraft approaching an ultra low altitude; and it was clear that the Argentinian pilots, who had practised attacks against their Navy's Type 42 destroyers, knew of this weakness. Also, when used to engage low-flying aircraft, the Type 42's gun-control radar suffered considerably from surface clutter and the accuracy of fire from the 4·5 inch gun suffered accordingly.

Brilliant's Sea Wolf had shown that when it functioned properly it was extremely effective against low-flying aircraft; but, like many computer-controlled systems, it was liable to 'sulk' at the most inconvenient time.

These problems were bad enough, but at least they were now known to the Royal Navy. As yet the Argentine Air Force had no inkling of the factor which was to limit greatly the effectiveness of its anti-shipping attacks throughout the war: that, even when bombs did hit British ships, they usually failed to detonate. In most cases the bombs used by the Air Force fighter-bombers against shipping were standard British 1,000-pounders, well-proven weapons similar to those used by the British forces though with a considerably smaller range of fusing options. The Argentine dilemma could be summed up as follows: either the fighter-bombers could release their bombs from altitudes above 200–300 feet, and risk suffering swingeing losses from the ships' missiles; or they could avoid the missiles by attacking from very low altitude, below 100 feet, but in that case the bombs' arming systems would not have time to operate before the weapons struck their targets, and they would hit while still 'safe'. Technically it is a perfectly simple matter to design an arming system to make a bomb 'live' immediately after it leaves the aircraft. But that would have meant that when making such low-level attacks the aircraft would have been literally 'hoist by their own petards' – blown up by their own bombs.

There was a further problem. Even if the bomb did arm itself properly before it struck the warship, there remained the question of how long a delay should be set on the fuse between impact and detonation. If a short delay was used, of the order of a quarter of a second, then to avoid falling debris from bombs from aircraft in front, succeeding aircraft had to attack with at least twenty-five seconds' gap between each. If, on the other hand, the fighter-bombers attacked at shorter intervals to swamp the defences, the detonation of the bombs had to be delayed by between twelve and thirty seconds after impact, so that the last aircraft was clear before the first bomb exploded. Almost certainly that was the fuse setting of the bomb which struck HMS *Glasgow*, but during this delay the bomb had time to punch its way clean through the ship's hull and get well clear before it went off.

Because the bombs used were fitted with the longer-delay fuses, the attacking pilots expected to be well clear before they went off. When they looked back to observe the results, it was easy to imagine the smoke which often belched from the British warships (when they manoeuvred at full power on gas turbines) was caused by fires starting by exploding bombs. As a result a considerable period would elapse before the Argentine Air Force High Command realized the extent of the problem – and in the meantime there would be several claims of damage inflicted on enemy ships, erroneous but made in good faith, from attacking pilots.

In view of the narrow escapes of *Glasgow* and *Brilliant*, Admiral Woodward decided that there would be no further naval bombardments of Port Stanley airfield during the daylight hours.

13 AND 14 MAY

Again poor weather imposed a brake on air operations. On the evening of the 14th, however, this provided useful cover for the landing on Pebble Island of forty-five men of D Squadron of the Special Air Service, from two Sea Kings of No. 846 Squadron. Once down the men moved quietly on their objective, the airstrip manned by Argentine Navy personnel. While one troop blocked the approaches to the airfield to prevent possible counter-attack, the remainder moved rapidly between the parked aircraft placing demolition charges in the cockpit of each and at strategic points about the airfield. Then, covered by supporting fire from warships off the coast, the men withdrew. When the charges detonated they put out of action all the aircraft on the airstrip: six Pucarás of Grupo 3, four Turbo-Mentors of the 4th Naval Attack Escuadrilla, and a Skyvan transport belonging to the Coast Guard. The attack was a serious blow to Argentine air strength on the Islands. Not only did it knock out nearly a third of the light attack aircraft based on the Falklands, but it put the nearest airstrip to the mainland out of action for the remainder of the conflict. Of the attack Admiral Woodward later commented: 'In my view this single operation is easily the best example of a successful "All Arms" special operation we are likely to see in a very long while. A short-notice operation carried out with speed and dash – no dead, one injured [on the British side] and eleven aircraft written off in one hour.' The time, from the initial conception to the completion of the raid, had been just five days.

15 MAY

While the weather continued to restrict operations around the Task Force, the latter prepared to receive the massive injection of men and equipment about to arrive in the convoy from Ascension. With the main amphibious landings on the Falklands due to begin in only a few days, the British High Command needed to be sure that the Argentine Navy warships had indeed restricted their activities to the waters immediately off their coastline. The blockade of the mainland ports was being mounted by nuclear submarines, but in this context these craft could be likened to short-sighted boa constrictors: they were stealthy and immensely powerful, but able to detect their prey only over relatively short distances. Nobody could be absolutely certain that a task group of Argentine warships, having been able to sneak past the blockade, was not waiting quietly at sea for the opportunity to strike. The extensive cloud cover prevented the few reconnaissance satellites passing over the area from proving conclusively that no such task group was at sea.

To find the required answers, during the early morning darkness of the 15th Wing Commander David Emmerson and a crew from No. 201 Squadron took off from Ascension for a flight which was to test the new in-flight refuelling capability of the Nimrod to the utmost. Refuelling twice on the way, the aircraft flew to a point about 150 miles north of Port Stanley, headed due west until it was some 60 miles off the coast of Argentina, then turned north-east to take it parallel with the coast. Flying past each of the main enemy naval bases in turn, in an unarmed aircraft at altitudes between 7,000 and 12,000 feet in broad daylight and within easy range of the fighter bases, the crew felt extremely vulnerable. 'It was a gorgeous winter's day, with the sun shining and hardly any cloud to hide in,' Emmerson recalled. 'We felt just like goldfish in a bowl; anyone who looked in our direction could have seen us. Normally the visual look-out is one of the less popular duties in the Nimrod. But while we were off the Argentine coast almost every piece of perspex on our aircraft had a pair of very intent eyes staring out from behind it!'

Using their highly sophisticated Searchwater radar, the Nimrod's operators swept a great swath of sea more than 400 miles wide and 1,000 miles long, which took in almost the entire area of the east coast of Argentina. Within that zone they could say with near certainty that there was no vessel larger than a medium-sized launch whose position they had not recorded. As well as plotting the ships in the area they could determine the general type of each one: Searchwater is able to show an approximate profile of any ship within range and give its length. Simultaneously, the aircraft's sensitive radar receivers scoured the ether for the tell-tale emissions from possible enemy warships at sea.

When the Nimrod landed on Ascension that evening, having been airborne for 19 hours and 5 minutes and refuelled three times, its crew could say with a high degree of confidence that there was no Argentine Navy task group at sea in the area they had examined. As with John Elliott's long-range reconnaissance mission off South Georgia twenty-seven days earlier, the Nimrod returned bearing only negative information. But such an outcome had been half expected, and hoped for, by Admiral Sir John Fieldhouse and his staff at Northwood. Thus informed, the fleet commander could reposition his nuclear submarines for an even more effective blockade of the Argentine naval bases.

The Nimrod's remarkable flight covered a distance of more than 8,300 miles and exceeded by a handsome margin that by John Elliott's Victor, to advance further the world-distance record for an operational reconnaissance mission. And the Nimrods had not finished yet: on seven out of the ten nights following, they would fly similar missions to check that the enemy warships remained in port.

At about the same time as David Emmerson and his crew were landing at Ascension, the Argentine defences around Port Stanley received a powerful addition on board a C-130 Hercules transport which braved the blockade and landed on the battered runway that evening: a 155 mm artillery piece with the range to enable shore gunners, for the first time, to reply to the troublesome Royal Navy warships whose almost nightly bombardments had made the lives of soldiers in the area such a misery. During the days that followed more such weapons would be flown in.

16 MAY

During a reconnaissance sweep by a Sea Harrier that morning, the Argentine supply ship *Bahía Buen Suceso* was observed alongside the jetty at Fox Bay and another, the *Rio Carcaraña*, was seen in Falkland Sound. Two pairs of Sea Harriers from No. 800 Squadron carried out a strafing attack on the *Bahía Buen Suceso* and bombed and strafed the *Rio Carcaraña*; after the attack both ships were abandoned. The aircraft encountered some return fire, and one collected a bullet hole in the tail.

That night there was to have been a further attempt by a Vulcan to knock out the runway at Port Stanley, but strong headwinds were forecast and the operation was cancelled.

17 MAY

Since the end of the first week in May the most powerful weapon in the Argentine anti-shipping armoury, the Super Étendards of the 2nd Escuadrilla, had remained on the ground at Rio Grande awaiting the location of suitable targets. The Neptune reconnaissance aircraft, one of which had directed the attack on *Sheffield*, were old and unreliable and their electronic equipment was proving almost impossible to keep serviceable. 'This forced us to look for alternatives,' explained Commander Jorge Colombo. 'Naval senior officers, and officers from the Operations Centre at Puerto Argentino [Port Stanley], met to devise another means of locating the enemy. The admiral in charge of naval operations on the Malvinas gave radar crews at Puerto Argentino the task of analysing the tracks of Harriers and Sea Harriers seen on their screens. The positions where Harriers first appeared on the screens, and where they disappeared on their return flights, were plotted continually. The premise was that the aircraft could not be very far from their carriers when they appeared and disappeared.'

This method of locating the aircraft carriers was, admittedly, only an approximate one. While within 50 miles of the carriers Sea Harrier pilots had orders to descend below the radar horizon from Port Stanley, to prevent the Argentinians locating the main Task Group in exactly that way. On the first occasion Super Étendards attempted to use such methods to find their target, the precaution paid off. On the 17th a pair of aircraft carrying Exocets arrived in the area east of the Falklands where the ships were suspected of being, but when they popped up to locate their target and launch the attack, they found nothing. Rather than conduct a longer search on radar, which would inevitably have betrayed their presence and resulted in almost certain interception by Sea Harriers, the pair abandoned the mission and returned to base. For the 2nd Escuadrilla, there would be another time.

During the previous weeks, other British forces had assembled and moved south in readiness for the planned landings to retake the islands. By the final week in April engineers at Royal Air Force Station Wittering had completed work to prepare ten Harrier GR 3s of No. 1 Squadron for fighter operations from aircraft carriers. Simultaneously, at the Royal Naval Air Station at Yeovilton, the eight Sea Harriers from the final production batch had been hastily completed and impressed into the newly formed No. 809 Squadron. Between 30 April and 5 May these aircraft made their way south, some flying the 4,000-odd miles to Ascension Island in a single hop refuelled by Victor tankers. The nine-hour flights were the longest ever made in the jump-jets, but in their cramped cockpits the pilots coped remarkably well. 'I drank only half a cup of coffee that morning, and I didn't drink anything else until I was halfway through the flight. We had pee-bags with us, but in the Harrier they are totally impractical because to use them we would have had to unstrap completely,' commented Squadron Leader Peter Harris of No. 1 Squadron. 'I had no problems, when I got out at Ascension I wasn't standing cross-legged or anything like that. The only thing was that I had a sore bum which lasted for several hours – in the bar that evening I had to do my drinking standing up!'

The pilots of the last Harriers to arrive on Ascension had little time to relax, because on 6 May all the Sea Harriers and six of the GR 3s took off from the island and landed vertically on the foredeck of the container ship *Atlantic Conveyor*, at anchor just off the coast. Already stowed on the ship's deck were several helicopters: six Wessex of No. 848 Squadron and a replacement Lynx, of the Royal Navy; and four Chinooks of No. 18 Squadron, Royal Air Force. As the jump-jets sat on the open deck of the ship, where they were to remain for the voyage south, all except one was covered with a special bag of heavy-duty plastic to keep off the salt spray. The remaining aircraft, a Sea Harrier, remained fully fuelled and armed near to the bow, ready to get airborne at short notice in case the ship and her valuable cargo came under air attack.

The four Harrier GR 3s of No. 1 Squadron remaining on the island would be available if the Task Force required further aircraft. In the meantime, fitted with Sidewinder missiles, these provided the sole fighter defence for Ascension and its vitally important airfield. By day the Harrier was adequate to counter any Argentine aircraft with the range to reach the island. By night it was a different matter, however, for as a ground-attack aircraft the GR 3 carried no search radar. To overcome this deficiency pilots were issued with night-vision binoculars which clipped on their flying helmets. Thus equipped, the Harriers became makeshift night fighters and were held at readiness to intercept, identify, and, if necessary, engage approaching aircraft. In the clear tropical skies the system was very effective. 'The night-vision glasses worked very well,' recalled Flight Lieutenant Murdo Macleod. 'On a cloudless night one could see the lights from Ascension from 80 to 100 miles, and the cockpit lights and jet pipes of aircraft at considerable distances.' From time to time Harriers were scrambled to investigate unidentified aircraft picked up by the island's radar, but on each occasion they proved to be airliners going about their lawful business or sometimes incoming aircraft with unserviceable identification equipment.

18 MAY

That morning, with the arrival in the operational area of *Atlantic Conveyor*, the troop transports, several supply ships and further escorts, a massive transfer of men and equipment took place between ships well to the east of the Falklands. No. 809 Squadron split into two and gave four Sea Harriers to No. 800 on *Hermes* and the other four to No. 801 on *Invincible*; all of No. 1 Squadron's Harrier GR 3s were allocated to *Hermes*. Thus far the Task Force had lost three Sea Harriers, less than had originally been feared, but this now gave rise to a problem on the aircraft carriers: because the two new squadrons were intended to make good losses, in which case they could use the servicing teams already on the ships, neither had its full complement of engineers. No. 809 Squadron had brought none at all, while No. 1 Squadron had only eighteen specialists to deal with the points of difference between the GR 3 and the Sea Harrier. For the remainder of the conflict the servicing teams on both carriers would be undermanned and under considerable pressure.

19 MAY

Throughout the day the transfers between ships continued. One useful addition for the defence of the aircraft carriers, brought south on the supply ship *Fort Austin*, was four Lynx helicopters fitted with special electronic equipment developed by the Royal Air Force to serve as Exocet decoys (the task was not as dangerous to the crew as it might sound, because the Exocet has no ability to home on airborne targets and will pass harmlessly beneath a helicopter flying at 100 feet). Two Lynx decoys went to each carrier, and for the remainder of the conflict one would be held on deck at immediate readiness at all times.

That evening, during an operation to transfer SAS teams between ships, a Sea King of No. 846 Squadron had its tail rotor strike a large sea bird, possibly an albatross, and crashed into the sea. HMS *Brilliant* was swiftly on the scene to pick up survivors, but twenty-two of those on board were killed.

Meanwhile *Hermes* was making a high-speed dash well to the west of the Falklands, where she flew off a single Sea King of No. 846 Squadron. Exactly what happened after that, and what the true purpose of the helicopter's mission was, has been a matter of considerable press speculation since. According to some accounts the helicopter landed SAS teams near one or more of the air bases on the mainland, to report to the Task Force by radio when aircraft were taking off and assembling to launch attacks. What is clear is that the Sea King finally put down near Punta Arenas in southern Chile, where she was destroyed by her crew who went into hiding before handing themselves over to the Chilean authorities three days later.

20 MAY

Long before the story of the Sea King in Chile was revealed, *Hermes* was speeding back to her more accustomed position with the main body of the Task Force east of the Falklands. Throughout most of the day the weather in the area was poor, which served as a useful shield for the carrier. It also provided cover for the ships carrying troops and supplies towards the Islands for the landings planned to take place the following day, the 21st.

With the newly arrived Sea Harriers the Task Force now had a total of twenty-five of these aircraft, sufficient to provide a bare minimum of air cover over the landing area. Since the troops would require air support when they were ashore, it was decided to remove the Sidewinders and launchers from the No. 1 Squadron Harrier GR 3s and use these machines in the ground-attack role, for which the aircraft were equipped and the pilots trained.

Late that afternoon the weather cleared sufficiently for No. 1 Squadron to mount its first attack, against a fuel dump Argentine troops had established at Fox Bay on the eastern side of West Falkland. Wing Commander Peter Squire led the mission accompanied by his two flight commanders, Squadron Leaders Bob Iveson and Jerry Pook. Each Harrier was loaded with two cluster bombs. Because the target was close to the limit of their radius of action, the small force approached the islands cruising at 30,000 feet to make the most of the available fuel. Then, after passing Cape Dolphin on the north of East Falkland, the Harriers descended to low altitude and picked their way to the western side of West Falkland to approach their target from the north-west to achieve maximum surprise. 'We flew in battle formation, a wide V with about a mile between aircraft, with the two rear machines covering their own tails and that of the Boss in the lead. At that time we were still concerned about possible Argentinian fighter attacks,' recalled Iveson. 'We swept in low over the hills, then suddenly in front of us was our target: rows of jerrycans and 40-gallon drums laid out carefully on the ground, so that supposedly a single bomb would not set off the lot. But in fact they had laid them out in almost a perfect shape for a cluster bomb pattern! I saw the Boss go in first; his cluster bombs hit, and the fuel dump started to go up with a lot of secondary explosions,' he continued. 'Then I went in, attacking from 30 degrees to the right of the Boss's line. Finally Jerry Pook came in on a similar line to the Boss and put down his bombs. So far as I could see not a shot was fired at us. We ran out past East Head, turned north-east up Falkland Sound and then started our climb back to high altitude to return to the carrier.'

As darkness fell there was an expectant air throughout the British Task Force, as men and equipment were prepared for the amphibious assault to take place the next day. The conflict had entered its most critical phase. If the landings were successful the remaining period of Argentine military presence on the Falklands could be measured in weeks. But if the landings failed, or if the defenders were able to impose such heavy losses on troops coming ashore that there was a stalemate, the conflict might drag on almost indefinitely.

Everything would depend on the amphibious forces being able to land a sizeable number of troops before the Argentine land, sea and air forces could counter-attack. Then it would be for the screening British warships and aircraft to do all they could to deter, slow and weaken the enemy blows. As in previous wars, the outcome would depend to a large extent on the skill, bravery and determination of individual men under fire.

5: D-day at San Carlos

20–21 MAY

'May 21st was a heavy day.'

Flight Lieutenant Dave Morgan

During the evening of the 20th the British amphibious landing force and its escorts ran in towards Falkland Sound from the north, giving the Argentine positions on East Falkland a wide berth. The troops and their equipment were embarked on the luxury liner *Canberra*, the assault ships *Fearless* and *Intrepid*, the landing supply ships *Sir Percival, Sir Tristram, Sir Geraint, Sir Galahad* and *Sir Lancelot*, and the motor vessels *Europic Ferry* and *Norland*, with the ammunition ship *Fort Austin* and the supply ship *Stromness* in support. Escorting these ships and their valuable cargoes were the destroyer *Antrim* and the frigates *Ardent, Argonaut, Brilliant, Broadsword, Yarmouth* and *Plymouth*.

The force approached in anti-aircraft formation, with the transports and supply ships bunched together and the escorts disposed evenly along the front, sides and rear. It was a necessary precaution although, in the darkness and the poor weather, the chances of air attack were slight. 'There was a strong north-westerly wind, sea state 4 or 5, it was overcast and misty – perfect weather conditions for our approach,' commented Commander Alan West in *Ardent*.

The ships ran in under the watchful eye of a Nimrod of No. 206 Squadron down from Ascension, again with David Emmerson on board. The concentrated force of ships showed up clearly on the aircraft's Searchwater radar, as the prying beam swept the area for other warships at sea. Again the Nimrod flew a track which took it parallel to the Argentine coast and some 60 miles to the east. If anything would induce the Argentine Navy to return to

100

sea, it would be the knowledge that a British amphibious force was approaching the Falklands. But during the night the waters around the Islands and the mainland coast remained devoid of Argentine warships. The nuclear submarines, awaiting the order to pounce, could only wait.

Just before midnight, as the landing ships and their escorts were approaching Falkland Sound, the destroyer *Antrim* and the frigate *Ardent* broke away and sped through the narrows to positions from which they were to carry out shore bombardments, off Fanning Head and in Grantham Sound respectively. While they were moving in a pair of Sea Kings of No. 826 Squadron positioned themselves at the north of the Sound and conducted a sonar search for possible enemy submarines.

San Carlos Water, along whose shores the landings were to take place, lies at the north-western tip of East Falkland. The main stretch of water runs almost north to south, is just over 1 mile wide and 4 miles long, and is deep enough to accommodate the largest ships. For ships wishing to avoid attack by aircraft, San Carlos Water has the attributes of a slit trench: it lies in a natural amphitheatre, surrounded by hills on all sides except the south-east and the entrance at the north-west. Because of this, aircraft attacking at low altitude could only fly along the main north-south axis of the waterway, with the south-easterly approach rather more difficult than that from the north-west. The lengthy coastline of the Falklands is pock-marked with numerous natural harbours of all sizes, but none came close to San Carlos Water in the degree of protection it gave against attack from the air. And, fortunately for the British troops now about to land, the area had been left virtually undefended by the Argentine Army.

While the main assault force was approaching its objective, some forty SAS men landed by helicopter in the Goose Green area and mounted a noisy diversionary attack. This lasted throughout the night and, according to Argentine sources, was taken as battalion-strength attack on their positions.

The first ship to enter San Carlos Water was the frigate *Plymouth*, ready to provide gunfire support should troops going ashore meet opposition. One by one the assault ships and transports followed, dropped anchor, and began offloading.

Dawn found the British commandos and paratroops well established ashore, with patrols moving to secure the high ground

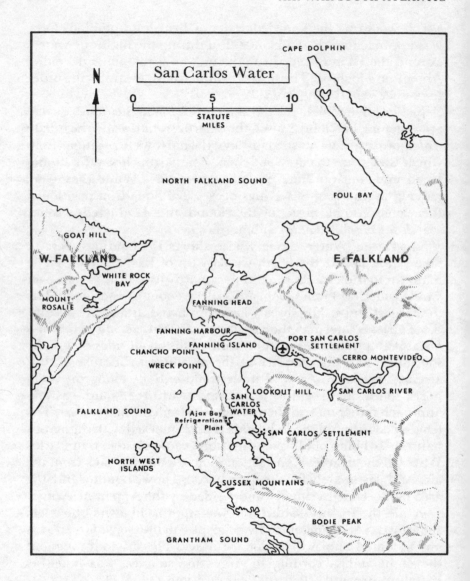

N

San Carlos Water

0   5   10

STATUTE
MILES

CAPE DOLPHIN

NORTH FALKLAND SOUND

FOUL BAY

GOAT HILL

W. FALKLAND

E. FALKLAND

WHITE ROCK
BAY

MOUNT
ROSALIE

FANNING HEAD

FANNING HARBOUR

FANNING ISLAND

CHANCHO POINT

WRECK POINT

PORT SAN CARLOS
SETTLEMENT

CERRO MONTEVIDEO

LOOKOUT HILL

SAN CARLOS RIVER

SAN
CARLOS
WATER

FALKLAND SOUND

Ajax Bay
Refrigeration
Plant

SAN CARLOS SETTLEMENT

NORTH WEST
ISLANDS

SUSSEX MOUNTAINS

BODIE PEAK

GRANTHAM SOUND

surrounding the inlet. There had been a brief skirmish with a small force of Argentine troops in the area; as the survivors withdrew they shot down two Gazelle helicopters of the Royal Marines. The escorting warships, apart from *Plymouth* which remained in San Carlos Water, were disposed outside the inlet to ward off counter-attacks coming from on land, below the sea, or in the air. *Broadsword* and *Argonaut* mounted an anti-submarine screen immediately to the north of Falkland Sound; *Yarmouth*, *Brilliant* and *Ardent* did the same across the Sound to the south of the landing area. *Antrim* was positioned off Fanning Head to block the entrance of San Carlos Water to attacking aircraft and provide gunfire support to the troops ashore if needed.

The dispositions placed HMS *Ardent* in Grantham Sound, in the most exposed position of all. As well as blocking the approach of possible enemy submarines from the south, she was to provide gunfire support to cover the withdrawal of the SAS from Goose Green, disrupt any attempt by the Argentine garrison there to advance on the landing area, and hinder operations from the airstrip. At dawn the commando spotter ashore reported the first target to *Ardent* and, at measured intervals, her 4·5-inch gun blasted shells at the enemy positions. From the start it was clear that the landing force would receive none of the cloud cover it had enjoyed the previous day. 'When dawn came it was crystal clear. Once I saw the weather it was obvious we were in for a very tough day,' recalled Alan West, *Ardent*'s captain. 'I remarked to someone that it was the anniversary of the opening of the Battle of Crete in 1941, except that on this occasion we were landing troops rather than pulling them out.' (The Royal Navy lost several ships to air attack off Crete.)

The first Argentine aircraft to arrive on the scene, a Pucará from Grupo 3 conducting a dawn reconnaissance, had the misfortune to pass over one of the withdrawing SAS patrols without realizing it. A soldier loosed off a Stinger shoulder-launched infra-red missile at the aircraft, which homed on one of the engine exhausts and detonated. The first thing the pilot, Captain Jorge Benitez, knew of the attack was when his Pucará bucked under the force of the explosion. 'I never saw the missile,' he later recalled. 'I was flying at very low altitude and it must have been fired from astern. The Pucará did not show immediate signs of damage so I continued flying, but after about a minute the controls began to fail and I was forced to eject.' (Although the Pucará is a two-seater, when used on operations the aircraft was almost invariably flown with only one pilot on board.) From the bridge of *Ardent*, a couple of miles away, Alan West saw the Pucará go down on fire and its pilot eject. Once safely on the ground just south of the Sussex Mountains, Benitez released his parachute and began the long walk to Goose Green; he would get there just after dark that evening.

Also at first light *Hermes* and *Invincible* began launching pairs of Sea Harriers, to fly combat air patrols to block the approach of Argentine attack aircraft coming from the mainland. As is so often the case in aerial warfare, these patrols had to be planned to take into account several widely diverging, even conflicting, requirements. The patrols needed to be as close as possible to the area of the amphibious landings they were to protect, but not so close that the fighters could not complete their interceptions before the incoming enemy aircraft reached the target area defended by surface-launched missiles. Almost invariably a low-level interception ends in a tail chase, and when the enemy aircraft reached the missile engagement zone the Sea Harriers had to break away to avoid being fired on by 'friendly' weapons. To conceal their approach flights and the patrol areas from the enemy radars at Port Stanley and Pebble Island, the Sea Harriers needed to be at low altitude; for best visual pick-up ranges on enemy aircraft coming in close to the ground they needed to be at about 8,000 feet; for optimum fuel consumption and therefore longest time on task they needed to be at 25,000 feet or above. In addition to these conflicting requirements, the aircraft carriers themselves remained under continual threat of attack from the Super Étendards and their Exocets and so needed to remain as far as possible to the east of the Islands.

The compromise arrived at was for the patrols to be flown near Pebble Island and halfway down Falkland Sound, respectively to the north-west and the south-west of the landing area and about 30 miles from it. While on their oblong patrols orbits the fighters were to fly at 8,000 feet or just below the cloud base, whichever was the lower. To allow the Sea Harriers ten minutes on patrol at a distance of more than 200 miles from their carriers, the fighters would have to approach and withdraw at altitudes around 25,000 feet and in full view of the Argentinian radars; to conceal the carriers' positions as far as possible, the Sea Harriers were to remain below the radar horizon from Port Stanley while they were within 50 miles of the ships. At thirty-minute intervals throughout the daylight hours, pairs of Sea Harriers would launch from alternate carriers to relieve those on patrol. As a means of providing air defence for the landing area the plan was far from watertight: both in time and space there would be gaps through which low-flying fighter-bombers could penetrate to their targets.

The plan provided for two Sea Harriers to be on one of the patrol lines at any one time, and that for only two periods of ten minutes each hour. Given that it would take attacking fighter-bombers ten minutes to pass the patrol line on their way in, bomb their target, and pass the line on their way out, there was a 25 per cent chance that the Sea Harriers would be in position to intercept once any given raiding force.

This defence could easily have been swamped by a massed attack at low altitude by thirty or forty Argentine fighter-bombers, perhaps with a few fighters with air-to-air missiles to keep busy or shoot down the patrolling Sea Harriers. Such an attack would have saturated the ships' missile defences, allowing the raiders to bomb with minimal losses. To meet this possibility each carrier was to keep two Sea Harriers at cockpit readiness throughout the day, ready to be scrambled. But the British planners' main hope was that such a co-ordinated attack would be beyond their enemy counterparts.

Closely following the pair of Sea Harriers from *Hermes* that mounted the first combat air patrol came a couple of Harrier GR 3s of No. 1 Squadron, the first to deliver an attack in support of troops ashore. The pilots, Squadron Leader Jerry Pook and Flight Lieutenant Mark Hare, were to attack helicopters reported by an SAS team in the Mount Kent area; since any counter-attack on San Carlos would depend on helicopters to airlift troops and their weapons, these were now priority targets for the British forces.

The pair arrived at their target just as it was getting light to find a Chinook, two Pumas and a Bell UH-1 sitting on the ground, well apart. Neither Harrier pilot was able to score hits on the initial attacking run, so the pair pulled hard left around Mount Kent and came in for a second pass. Hare lined up on the Chinook and opened fire with his 30 mm cannon: 'I saw my exploding rounds walking along the ground towards the helicopter; when I saw them exploding on it I held my sight there, then it blew up with a spurt of flame and I pulled away,' he later commented. The pair made further attack runs during which each set fire to a Puma, but in the half-light it proved almost impossible to line up on the Bell UH-1 for an accurate attack. 'Unfortunately that one got away scot-free,' Hare continued. 'All the time, the other three helicopters were burning away magnificently. On what turned out to be the last pass I heard a "thud". I told Jerry my aircraft had been hit, I pulled away to the north, and he joined me.' On his return to *Hermes* he found that his aircraft had three bullet hits: one through the engine intake and out the top, one which had caused damage to a gun mounting, and one which had passed through the wing fuel tank.

Shortly after Pook and Hare landed on *Hermes*, Wing Commander Peter Squire and Flight Lieutenant Jeff Glover took off, briefed to provide close air support for troops in the landing area. The mission went sour almost from the beginning. As he climbed away Squire was unable to retract his undercarriage and was forced to return to the carrier. Glover went on alone. When he arrived in the San Carlos area, he asked the army forward air controller if there was a target for his cluster bombs. Back came the reply that there appeared to be no Argentine troops in the area, so he was asked to fly to Port Howard, 20 miles to the south-west, and attack enemy positions there. Glover made a high-speed low-altitude run through the area from north to south, but saw nothing to indicate an Argentine presence. In fact a few shots were fired at the Harrier as it sped clear, though without scoring hits and without the pilot knowing. Glover reported that he had seen nothing, and received a request to photograph the area so the defensive positions could be picked out for later attack.

Any such return to a defended area is always fraught with danger, so the Harrier pilot headed over the centre of West Falkland to give time for things at Port Howard to quieten down. Then, about fifteen minutes after the first run, he returned, this time approaching from the south-west. As Glover passed over the small settlement, flying fast and low with his port-facing camera clicking, he again saw nothing of the enemy. The first he knew of their presence was when his aircraft shuddered under the impact of exploding enemy shells – first one, then two more in rapid succession; almost immediately it flicked into an uncontrollable roll to the right. One of the Port Howard residents, Kathy Patrick, watched the action and later wrote: 'This time they were ready for him. It seemed as though every gun in the garrison opened up and we watched, appalled, as directly over our heads the plane did a roll and part of the wing came off.'

With considerable presence of mind Glover waited until the Harrier had rotated through 320 degrees in its roll then pulled the handle of his ejector seat, so that when he left the aircraft he was going almost vertically upwards. As he was hurled into the 600 m.p.h. air blast he lost consciousness. On the ground, Kathy Patrick watched him fall clear: 'As the plane went down in a great smoking ball the pilot ejected, coming down in the creek between Port Howard and Packes. The Argies were all cheering, shouting and firing rifles into the air as we were hurried home. "*La casa, la casa*" was the order.'

When Glover came to he was under water. As he struggled to the surface he felt a stabbing pain from his left shoulder (his left arm, shoulder and collar bone were broken); his flying helmet and oxygen mask were gone, torn off by the wind blast or when he struck the water. Deep in shock, the injured pilot forgot to inflate his life-jacket, but fortunately for him there was sufficient air trapped in his rubberized immersion suit to keep him afloat. 'I came up and saw my parachute floating in the water in front of me. I had a good look around and saw the shore about 200 yards away. I started trying to swim towards it on my back but I got nowhere fast – I had not released my parachute harness,' he later recounted. Glover gave up the attempt, stopped to collect his thoughts, and concentrated on releasing himself from his parachute. While doing this he caught sight of a rowing boat with half a dozen Argentine soldiers pulling in his direction. 'In the front of the boat was an officer, and under his direction the soldiers came alongside me and hauled me on board; as they lifted me, my arm hurt like hell. The officer spoke to me in good English. He said he was a doctor, asked where it hurt, and said I would be all right, he would look after me,' the pilot continued. For Jeff Glover, the war was over. (Later, as has been widely reported, Glover would be introduced to the Argentine soldier credited with shooting down the Harrier with a shoulder-

launched Blowpipe missile. However, on reflection, and in view of
the three explosions he heard before his aircraft began to roll, he
now believes the most probable cause of the damage was three
hits from explosive 20 mm rounds.)

Much had happened, yet it was still only 9.45 a.m. In the
landing area, now in broad daylight but still unmolested by the
enemy, the massive task of unloading the transports continued,
with landing craft and helicopters scuttling between the ships and
the shore. Although the Argentine High Command on the Islands
had received a report more than an hour earlier that British
warships had entered the northern end of Falkland Sound and
were bombarding the coastline, this had been discounted as yet
another diversionary attack. Not until 10 a.m. did a Pucará on
reconnaissance penetrate to the landing area and report the
existence of twelve ships, some of which were unloading troops
and equipment.

The first air attack came five minutes later, delivered by a
single Macchi 339 of the 1st Naval Attack Escuadrilla based at
Port Stanley. Lieutenant Guillermo Owen Crippa swept low over
the hills surrounding San Carlos Water and suddenly found
himself confronting what looked like 'the entire British fleet'.
Nonplussed by his discovery, Crippa braved the return fire and
delivered an attack on HMS *Argonaut* with 30 mm cannon and
four 5-inch rockets, in which he inflicted some damage to the
ship's upper deck fittings and caused wounds to three of her crew.
His munitions exhausted, the pilot then pulled out of the area. For
the lone attack he would later receive the Argentine Medal for
Heroism and Bravery in Combat, the highest decoration awarded
in the Navy during the conflict.

Some thirty minutes after that, at 10.35 a.m. the first attacking
force from the mainland arrived; Major Carlos Martinez flew at
the head of six Daggers of Grupo 6 on an armed reconnaissance of
the reported landing area. The fighter-bombers came in over the
north of West Falkland, well clear of the Sea Harriers on patrol
over Falkland Sound, and as he passed over Mount Rosalie,
Martinez caught sight of ships in San Carlos Water and three
warships in position outside in the Sound (*Broadside, Argonaut* and
Antrim). Martinez himself went for *Broadsword*, Captain Rodhe
and Lieutenant Bean went for *Argonaut* and Captain Moreno led
the remaining three aircraft against *Antrim*. The Daggers attacked

with 1,000-pound bombs and strafed the ships with 30 mm cannon; the warships replied with everything they had – *Antrim* even loosed off one of her huge obsolete Seaslug missiles, more in an attempt to distract the attacking pilots than with any hope of hitting aircraft flying so low. A Sea Cat missile, fired either by *Argonaut* or *Plymouth*, hit Bean's aircraft and it crashed into the sea. Before the aircraft struck the water one of his comrades saw the pilot eject, but his body was never found.

After attacking, the Daggers ran out to the south and came past *Ardent* in Grantham Sound bombarding targets in the Goose Green area. The frigate engaged the aircraft with her 4·5-inch gun and Sea Cat missiles but there were no hits on either side.

Meanwhile HMS *Brilliant*, the ship assigned the task of fighter director that day, was attempting to guide the Sea Harriers on combat air patrol into position for an interception. But with their bombs gone the Daggers were able to accelerate almost to supersonic speed and even in the dive the Sea Harriers had little margin of speed to catch them. When the British pilots, Lieutenant Commander 'Fred' Frederiksen and Lieutenant Martin Hale of No. 800 Squadron, caught sight of their adversaries it was already too late. Hale recalled, 'We picked them up visually as they were coming down the Lafonia side of the Sound, just over land at low level and running out at high speed. I was the nearer to them. I dropped in behind the left-hand man in their formation and got a good missile lock. The range was a bit on the high side but I decided to give it a try and launched a Sidewinder.' His missile chased after the Dagger but the distance was too great and it exploded some way short of its intended victim. The Sea Harriers followed the attackers out to the west without being able to close the range, then shortage of fuel forced them to break off the chase.

The most serious damage from the attack was to *Antrim*, which was struck on the stern by a bomb which pierced her missile loading doors, narrowly missed a fully armed Seaslug missile, smashed through a fan compartment and a pyrotechnic locker, then demolished a calorifier before it came to rest in a lavatory area. Fortunately for the crew, the bomb failed to explode; the only casualties from the forty or so hits on the ship with 30 mm cannon shells were two men seriously wounded and others with minor cuts from flying splinters. *Broadsword* was also damaged during the strafing attack and suffered four casualties. All the other bombs missed their targets, and none of the other ships suffered damage.

After the initial bombing attack *Antrim* moved into the comparative safety of San Carlos Water so that a disposal team could begin work to remove the unexploded bomb lodged in her stern. At the same time *Argonaut, Broadsword* and *Brilliant* moved closer to the entrance of the inlet to give each other mutual support against attacking aircraft; by now it was almost certain that there was no Argentine submarine anywhere in the area.

While this was happening, shortly before noon, a pair of Harriers of No. 1 Squadron flew an armed reconnaissance along an arc centred on the landing area and running 10 to 15 miles inland from it. The pair were briefed to attack enemy troops advancing towards the beachhead to launch a counter-attack, but the area was devoid of movement.

The next air action opened just before noon when Major Juan Tomba and Lieutenant Juan Micheloud of Grupo 3 took off from Goose Green in their Pucarás, to attack targets in the beachhead area. As they approached Grantham Sound *Ardent* engaged them at extreme range with her 4·5-inch gun. 'They thought better of it and turned away, then they ran in towards us making a much more keen-looking attack. Our gun was firing at them and we launched a Sea Cat. When they were quite close, about 3,000 yards from us, they both turned away. Whether it was because of our fire or because there were Sea Harriers around, I don't know,' commented Alan West. 'The next thing we saw was two Sea Harriers come plummeting down from the heavens, go from about 500 knots [575 m.p.h.] to very slow with clouds of black smoke, and sit on the tail of one of them, at which the Pucarás started jinking like mad.'

The Sea Harriers were part of a three-aircraft patrol from No. 801 Squadron, led by Lieutenant Commander 'Sharkey' Ward; they were on the point of leaving the area to return to their ship. HMS *Brilliant* had reported slow-moving enemy aircraft to the south of the landing area and asked Ward to investigate. As the trio passed overhead at 15,000 feet Lieutenant Steve Thomas caught sight of one of the Pucarás: 'He popped out from under cloud in front of us, going south at low level. He was over land when I first saw him and in his light colouring he stuck out like a sore thumb. I told "Sharkey" I had seen him and went down to attack.' Lieutenant Commander Al Craig followed.

Thomas and Craig made their attack on Tomba's Pucará using guns, but they were overtaking far too rapidly and failed to score hits. In the meantime Michcloud was able to make good his escape. Then it was Ward's turn to attack Tomba's aircraft, also using cannon. 'On the first pass I hit his left aileron and shot it to pieces. Then I pulled up; I was going a lot faster than he was. I pulled off to the left, turned, and came in behind for another attack. This time I had my flaps lowered and I slowed right down behind him. I opened fire and hit his right engine, which caught fire and I saw bits falling off the aircraft,' Ward remembered. 'On my third pass I got in behind nicely and opened fire and saw his left engine start to burn, part of his canopy fly away, and pieces fall off the fuselage. As I pulled away to the left thinking, "This is incredible, he hasn't gone down yet!" I saw the pilot eject. The aircraft continued on, hit the peat, and slid to a halt. The pilot landed by parachute not far from the aircraft. I thought he was a very brave chap, staying with it for so long.' Tomba landed without injury, and began the walk back to Goose Green.

The next attacking force to set out from the mainland, four Skyhawks of Grupo 5 led by Captain Pablo Carballo, ran into difficulties almost from the outset. When the aircraft made their rendezvous with the KC-130 Hercules tanker off the coast, one of them was unable to take on fuel and had to turn back. Later another of the fighter-bombers was unable to transfer fuel from one of its drop tanks and it too had to abandon the mission. The remaining two Skyhawks crossed over the centre of West Falkland then entered Falkland Sound. In the channel the pair sighted a large ship in front of them; in fact it was the Argentine freighter *Rio Carcaraña*, lying abandoned after having been attacked by Sea Harriers five days earlier. Carballo headed towards it preparing to attack. 'When we got near I saw it was not a warship. It was large and white and, fearing that it might be one of ours, I decided not to attack.' In the heat of the moment he omitted to communicate the decision to his wing man, however; Carballo pulled away but Ensign Carmona, busy concentrating on his attack, continued on and released his bombs at the freighter. Carmona's aircraft was now disarmed and Carballo ordered him to return to base.

Carballo continued on up the eastern side of Falkland Sound alone: 'I was passing rapidly by the small bays and entrances to the sea when all of a sudden, on entering Bahía Ruiz Puente [Grantham Sound], in front of me there appeared a frigate. My first thought was, "It's not as big as I had imagined!" Then I ran in to attack. As I closed in, almost touching the water to avoid being picked up on their radar, the frigate grew larger and larger.'

Since the Pucará had been shot down, things had been quiet around HMS *Ardent* in her bombardment position in Grantham Sound. The air raid warning state had been relaxed from Red to Yellow and on her bridge Alan West had felt the tension ease. 'I let the crew have a slight break to have some food at their posts while ammunition was being passed from aft to forward. We were quite pleased with ourselves. By then we had fired nearly 190 rounds of 4·5-inch, five Sea Cat missiles and some 20 mm at the Pucarás. They seemed to have respect for our weapons, especially Sea Cat. I was surprised they hadn't pressed home their attacks on us more, we were all alone. Then suddenly somebody on the bridge shouted "Aircraft closing!" and pointed. We looked in that direction and coming straight towards us from the south-west, over land, was a single Skyhawk about 4,000 yards away and closing very fast. He was right on the bow. I put on full wheel and called for full speed. As he flashed over us we were just beginning to turn, the 4·5-inch had no time to get on to him and the only thing that could fire was the 20 mm. He dropped two bombs, one of which fell short and the other passed over us. He continued past us, banked round and flew down the sound.' For Alan West and his crew it was a salutary lesson on how rapidly things could change if fortune ever deserted them.

Lieutenant Commanders Neil Thomas and Mike Blissett of No. 800 Squadron were arriving at their patrol position over Falkland Sound when HMS *Brilliant* told them to go after the aircraft which had just attacked *Ardent*. The pair of Sea Harriers accelerated to fighting speed and descended below the puffs of cloud at 1,500 feet, as they headed out over West Falkland. The pilots never did see anything of Carballo's Skyhawk on its way home, but suddenly it no longer mattered.

'When we were about 3 miles east of Chartres Settlement I caught sight of four Skyhawks in front of me about 3½ miles away, flying across my nose from left to right; they had just crossed the coast on their way in,' remembered Blissett, who immediately called for Thomas to break hard to starboard. 'As we passed over the top of them they saw us, their nice arrow formation broke up, and they began to jettison underwing tanks and bombs.' The Skyhawks, belonging to Grupo 4, pulled hard to starboard to avoid the attack but the Sea Harriers followed in hot pursuit.

Blissett was the first to reach a firing position. 'I was in the lead with Neil to my left and about 400 yards astern, with all of us in a tight turn,' he remembered. 'The Skyhawks were in a long echelon, spread out over about a mile. I locked a Sidewinder on one of the guys in the middle and fired. My first impression was that the missile was going to strike the ground as it fell away – I was only about 200 feet above the ground. But suddenly it started to climb and rocketed towards the target. At that moment my attention was distracted somewhat as a Sidewinder came steaming past my left shoulder – Neil had fired past me, which I found *very* disconcerting at the time! I watched his 'winder chase after another of the Skyhawks, which started to climb for a patch of cloud above, then the aircraft disappeared into the cloud with the missile gaining fast.'

With that distraction passed, Blissett glanced back to watch the progress of his own Sidewinder. 'Suddenly, about 800 yards in front of me, there was a huge fireball as the aircraft blew up in the air; there was debris flying everywhere. As I started to lock on my second missile I caught sight of something flickering to my left, out of the corner of my eye: it was the Skyhawk Neil's Sidewinder had hit, tumbling out of the clouds with the back end well ablaze. It came down cartwheeling slowly past my aircraft about 100 yards away, looking like a slow-motion replay from a film.' Blissett loosed off his 30 mm ammunition in a series of bursts at one of the surviving Skyhawks then, by now getting very short on fuel, the Sea Harriers broke off the chase and began climbing away for the long flight back to *Hermes*.

It was approaching 2.30 p.m. the start of the most dangerous period for the British amphibious forces and their escorts. Until now the attacking aircraft had been probing the defences and learning the positions of important targets. But in the three and a half hours since the first mainland-based aircraft flew over the landing area there had been time for their pilots to return to base and tell what they had learned, for plans to be drawn up for more effective attacks, and for the next wave of attacking pilots to be briefed and fly out to the target area.

In recognition of the greater threat the Sea Harrier patrols had been stepped up, with three pairs of aircraft per hour instead of two. Lieutenant Commander 'Fred' Frederiksen and Lieutenant Andy George of No. 800 Squadron were on patrol when one of the first of the new raiding forces came in: four Daggers of Grupo 6 led by Captain Horacio Gonzalez. The raiders had been seen on radar before they descended to low altitude west of the Falklands, however, and directed by *Brilliant* Frederiksen and George headed west to intercept them. Meanwhile the low-flying raiders had headed south-east from Jason Island, and after making a landfall at King George Bay on West Falkland they swung on to a north-easterly heading to take them through a gap in the high ground towards their target.

As the Daggers crossed the coast Frederiksen, by then over Chartres Settlement at 2,500 feet, caught sight of them three miles away to the right; at the time he thought the aircraft to be Skyhawks. 'I put Andy George into one mile trail on me to keep an eye open for any escorts that might be behind them as we accelerated and I went in behind the left-hand element. Having checked there were no escorts, Andy went for the right-hand element. I went for the tail man in the left element; there was no sign that they had seen me. . .' The tail man in the left element was Lieutenant Hector Luna, who recalled: 'We were about four minutes from the target and flying very low; I could see the peaks of the mountains covered by cloud as we flew down the valley between them. And at that moment I saw a Sea Harrier turning above me. I tried to advise my leader but my radio malfunctioned. Then I looked in my mirror and saw a second Harrier behind me fire a missile – I could see the flame clearly.' The Sidewinder, fired by Frederiksen, struck the Dagger at the rear and Luna started to lose control. Instinctively he pulled on the stick to gain height before ejecting but, probably because the control surfaces on the rear of one of the wings had been damaged by the explosion, the fighter-bomber immediately lurched into a violent roll. Luna had no time to consider the matter further, he pulled the ejection-seat handle. A split second after the pilot emerged from his aircraft the Dagger smashed into the ground, and Luna could feel the blast of the impact. Immediately afterwards he was dumped on the ground hard, pieces of flaming wreckage falling around him. He had a dislocated arm and a sprained knee and so, after releasing his parachute, had to crawl clear of what, not many seconds earlier, had been a fighter-bomber.

Frederiksen saw the aircraft smash into the ground in front of him, and as it did so he came within gun range of the element leader and opened fire with his 30 mm cannon, though without seeing any hits. Meanwhile the Daggers, hugging the ground as their pilots endeavoured to avoid the cloud-covered mountains, went into a turn to the left. Frederiksen immediately pulled right, away from the fighter-bomber he had been following: if he continued his attack he knew the right-hand element of the enemy force would swing round on to his tail. Once out of the potential trap he pulled left again and loosed off the rest of his cannon shells at the right-hand element. 'I was in a high G turn at very low altitude and I wouldn't claim any hits. The last I saw of them they were continuing their turn to the left, going into cloud.' As the rest of the Daggers let down beneath cloud on the other side of the high ground it was clear one of their comrades was missing; at the time they thought Luna had flown into a hillside. Surprisingly, none of their pilots had seen the Sea Harriers. Shaken by the apparent sudden death of one of their number, the remainder pressed on grimly towards the target area.

While Frederiksen and George had been engaging the Daggers over West Falkland, a force of Skyhawks had come around the north of the island and reached Falkland Sound without interference. Six of these aircraft concentrated on HMS *Argonaut* and she was hit with two 1,000-pounders. One smashed into her hull just above the waterline between the boiler room and the engine room; it demolished several steam pipes, caused a boiler to explode, and went on to wreck part of her steering gear. The other bomb impacted below the waterline further forward and passed through a couple of fuel tanks, across the sonar compartment, and ended up in the forward Sea Cat magazine where it caused two missiles to detonate and killed two of the ship's crew. Although both bombs caused secondary explosions, neither detonated. Even so, the attack left *Argonaut* in serious trouble, moving at high speed towards Fanning Head with both engines and the steering gear out of action. Only the quick thinking of the officer of the watch saved her from even more serious damage. When he saw what was happening, Sub Lieutenant Peter Morgan grabbed a couple of men, dashed on to the exposed foredeck and released the anchor to bring the ship to a halt; for the act Morgan would later receive the Distinguished Service Cross. For the time being *Argonaut* was to remain stuck fast in an extremely exposed position outside San Carlos Water, with three hours of daylight left.

From his bridge Alan West observed the attack on *Argonaut*. But almost immediately afterwards it was *Ardent*'s turn, as the depleted Dagger formation from Grupo 6 ran out over the east coast of West Falkland. 'On the other side of the Strait of San Carlos [Falkland Sound], in Bahía Ruiz Puente [Grantham Sound], we saw a frigate close to the coast of Isla Soledad [East Falkland],' recalled Captain Robles, who was flying one of the fighter-bombers.

As the aircraft closed rapidly on their prey they were seen approaching the ship from astern, so that West had to call for full port rudder to try to bring his 4·5-inch gun to bear. 'They ran in from almost directly astern of me, but because I was turning so quickly they ended up coming in from my quarter. I waited, expecting to see a Sea Cat leave the launcher and go streaking out towards them. But for some reason it refused to go. With our 4·5-inch gun blanked off, the only weapons that could fire at the approaching aircraft were the 20 mm and the light machine-guns.'

As he ran in behind the other two Daggers, Robles watched the attack develop: 'In front of Captain Gonzalez's plane we could see the tracers flashing towards us. His flight path took him between the masts of the frigate. His bomb hit the sea about 10 metres short of it and lifted a great mass of water which practically enveloped the ship; I believe the bomb skipped and embedded itself in the hull. Then Lieutenant Bernhardt released his bombs, one of which struck the upper part of the ship. Then I arrived at the release point and let go of my bombs.'

With no effective defences to distract them, the Dagger pilots had been able to release their bombs from altitudes sufficient for them to arm in flight. West recalled: 'The first aircraft released two bombs, one of which hit us near the stern and went off. There was an enormous bang, it felt as if someone had got hold of the stern and was banging the ship up and down on the water. With the explosion a column of flash and smoke went up about 100 feet. I looked aft and saw the Sea Cat launcher about 20 feet in the air where it had been blown, and pieces of metal flying in all directions.' Other bombs came down around the ship, including one which West saw pass between the masts, but none exploded.

The bomb had struck the frigate close to the hangar; it blew off the entire roof and folded it over the starboard side, and demolished the Lynx helicopter. Several of the ship's crew were killed or injured, there was an unexploded bomb lodged aft, and she had taken severe damage; but the damage-control teams were bringing the fires under control, there was no serious flooding, and the ship's engines and steering gear were intact. HMS *Ardent* was far from finished. 'My First Lieutenant arrived on the bridge and gave me a resume of the damage. And while it was clear that it was unpleasant, there was nothing that was going to stop us for any length of time. *Argonaut* came on the radio and said she could float and fight but not move. I made a signal straight afterwards that *Ardent* could float and move but only barely could we fight: the Sea Cat launcher had been blown overboard and because of damage to the ammunition supply the 4·5-inch gun was out of action too.' West was ordered to move north-west and join the other warships, where he could receive protection from their guns and missiles.

It was 2.45 p.m. and yet more aircraft were streaking in to attack the British warships and transports. At about this time there was a strafing attack on *Brilliant*; she received twenty hits from cannon shells around her bridge and some of her crew were injured by flying splinters. Lieutenant Commander 'Sharkey' Ward and Lieutenant Steve Thomas of No. 801 Squadron were approaching the combat zone for another patrol and called the ship for instructions. Thomas recalled: 'Her controller was speaking to us, he said there was a raid coming in. Then we heard several "clonks" on the radio. There was a pause, then the controller said, "We've just been hit! ... I've lost my concentration ... Hang on a minute ... The guy next to me has been hit in the stomach and I've been hit on the arm!"' The pair of fighters moved into position over Pebble Island, ready to catch the attackers on the way out or new ones coming in.

During this phase Skyhawks entered San Carlos Water in an

attempt to hit the ships unloading there. The high ground surrounding the anchorage made life difficult for the attacking pilots, as Ensign Marcelo Moroni, who ran in to bomb with four other pilots of Grupo 5, later explained: 'The topography of the island made it difficult to see into the bay because we were too low – we were so close to the hills we could not see over them. As we topped the last hill we saw about eight or nine ships in the bay. The moment they saw us, they opened up at us with everything they had. Two of the Skyhawks went for one frigate, another two headed for another ship, and I was last of the five. Suddenly I felt a blow from my right and I thought my aircraft had been hit and damaged by enemy fire. Because of this I took no evasive action but headed straight towards my target; as soon as I dropped my bombs I continued on straight out of the bay.' All five aircraft returned safely to Rio Gallegos, only one with minor damage from small-arms fire. In fact Moroni's aircraft had come through unscathed; almost certainly the blow he felt had been caused by the slipstream of one of the aircraft in front.

Other Skyhawks of Grupo 5 ran in to attack *Ardent* as she was pulling out of Grantham Sound, and the frigate was hit again. West recalled: 'I saw another team of Skyhawks coming in, certainly three and possibly four. I imagine that with the great clouds of smoke coming from us we looked quite an inviting target, there on our own. They went down the Sound to the south of us, turned, and ran in from astern. They were in two lots, slightly angled off, and as they ran in they fired their cannon at us. We replied with our 20 mm guns and machine-guns – all we had.' Again the frigate was deluged in bombs, most of which failed to detonate. But two of those that struck her did go off, causing further serious damage around the ship's stern. *Ardent* was in a bad way. As her captain strove to assess the scale of the damage, a venomous little confrontation broke out 20 miles to the west over West Falkland.

'Sharkey' Ward and Steve Thomas were patrolling over the valley between Mount Maria and Mount Jock, through which several attacking fighter-bombers had passed during the day. The pair were at the southern end of their patrol line and were turning back on to a northerly heading, when suddenly Thomas caught sight of a pair of Daggers beneath him on their way east, the bright yellow identification markings on their wings showing up clearly. 'I barrelled in behind them, locked up a missile on the rear guy and fired. The Sidewinder hit the aircraft and took it apart. I didn't see it go in, I was busy trying to get the other one. He went into a climbing turn to starboard to try to get away. I locked up a Sidewinder and fired it. The missile followed him round the corner and went close over his port wing root. There was a bright orange flash close to the aircraft but it didn't blow up or anything.'

'Sharkey' Ward was watching Thomas engaging the Daggers, when yet another of these aircraft came past his nose going west: 'He seemed to be nothing to do with the other two, he came from a different direction. He was very low, about half a mile ahead of me and going very fast. He was doing about 500 knots [575 m.p.h.] at fiftyish feet. I just racked the Sea Harrier round hard, called Steve to say I'd got a third one, and loosed off a missile. It hit him and immediately afterwards he went into the ground. I remember seeing the leading edge of the starboard wing cartwheeling away.'

Each of the Sea Harrier pilots had seen one of the aircraft he had hit break up or crash; but Thomas would claim the second machine he had fired at only as 'possibly destroyed'. It is clear from Argentine sources, however, that this aircraft crashed shortly afterwards. For a second time, the authors are able to confirm the destruction of an aircraft claimed in this way by this pilot. With the Mirage whose destruction he caused on 1 May (another 'possibly destroyed', finished off by Argentine ground gunners at Port Stanley), Steve Thomas's score now stood at three.

Remarkably, the pilots of all three Daggers shot down by Thomas and Ward – Major Piuma, Captain Donadille and Lieutenant Senn – were able to eject safely.

While Ward and Thomas were joining up before heading back east, some 30 miles to the south of them Lieutenant Commander Alberto Philippi pulled round into Falkland Sound at the head of three Skyhawks of the 3rd Naval Fighter and Attack Escuadrilla. It was the first time this unit had gone into action during the conflict. Philippi led his aircraft up the waterway at low altitude and, shortly before reaching the entrance to San Carlos Water, caught sight of the masts of a frigate in front of him. The aircraft eased round to the east to attack against a land background, then wheeled tightly round to port to begin their bombing runs.

Twelve miles to the west, 'Sharkey' Ward was passing the coast of West Falkland when he noticed white shapes in front of him: 'At first I thought they looked like seagulls hovering over food; then I realized they were aircraft, turning tightly over the Sound.' The brilliant white gloss finish of the Argentine Navy Skyhawks made them visible for miles around. As the fighter-bombers levelled out, Ward could see they were heading for one of the frigates which was already smoking. He was helpless to prevent the imminent attack, however: his Sea Harrier was too far behind for him to engage. All he could do was broadcast a call to *Brilliant* and any other Sea Harriers in the area, to tell them what was happening.

From the bridge of the battered *Ardent*, Alan West also observed the light-coloured Skyhawks: three in line astern, wheeling round to attack him from starboard. From the leading aircraft Philippi could see the muzzle flashes of the ship's guns aiming at him and the smoke trail of a missile. 'It was my luck they did not have Sea Wolf,' he later commented. In fact it was Philippi's luck that the frigate no longer had any effective anti-aircraft defence: the muzzle flashes were from her 20 mm and light machine-guns, while the missile was an unguided chaff rocket fired in the faint hope that it might distract the attackers.

Half a mile from his target Philippi pulled up to 300 feet, lined his sight on the rapidly closing warship, and released his four 500-pound American-made 'Snakeye' bombs; as the bombs left the aircraft four drag-plates opened from the tail of each, to slow them during their fall to give the fuses time to arm and the aircraft time to get clear before impact. *Ardent* was being attacked with weapons purpose-made for low-altitude release, aimed by pilots fully trained in the anti-shipping role.

Alan West watched the string of bombs approaching his ship, then: 'There was another bloody great explosion and I was thrown into the air, hit the deck head and fell back on the deck.' The captain got up and looked out just in time to see the second Skyhawk, piloted by Lieutenant José Arca, making its attack. Just aft of the bridge Petty Officer John Leake, an ex-army man whose normal job was ship's civilian NAAFI canteen manager but who had been given a naval rank for the duration of hostilities, was leading the machine-gun team which now constituted a major part of the frigate's defence. As the Skyhawk

swept low over the ship after releasing its bombs, West saw
Leake's rounds stitch a row of holes across one of the wings.
Immediately afterwards yet another bomb exploded against the
ship's stern. The third Skyhawk, piloted by Ensign Marcelo
Marquez, ran in and made its attack without scoring further hits.

After he had completed his attack Philippi returned to low
altitude with his throttle wide open, called to his pilots '*Escapamos
por la misma* [Let's go out the way we came in],' then banked on to
a south-westerly heading down the Sound. The other two
Skyhawks followed.

Over Goose Green at 10,000 feet on the way to begin their
patrol, Lieutenant Clive Morell and Flight Lieutenant John
Leeming of No. 800 Squadron heard the radio reports of the
attack then saw bombs exploding near *Ardent*. Morell was leading
the pair: 'Having seen the bombs explode I deduced that the
attackers would probably exit going south-west down the Sound.
I looked to where I thought they would be and they appeared, lo
and behold, below a hole in the clouds. They were easy to see from
above, painted white.' Leeming saw the Skyhawks at about the
same time. The two Sea Harriers rolled over and dived at full
throttle after the attackers, running down the Sound almost in
line astern.

Marquez, in the rear Skyhawk, was the first to sense danger, as
Philippi explained: 'A couple of minutes after attacking I thought
we had escaped, when a shout from Marquez froze my heart:
"Harrier! Harrier!" I immediately ordered the tanks and bomb
racks to be jettisoned in the hope we would be able to reach the
safety of cloud ahead of us.' Almost certainly the Sea Harrier
Marquez had seen was Morell's, now gaining rapidly on Philippi
at the head of the chase. Morell locked on a Sidewinder and fired
it, and watched the weapon home in rapidly and explode just
clear of the Skyhawk's jetpipe. The first thing Philippi knew of the
missile was when he felt a powerful explosion close behind him
and the nose of his aircraft pitched up violently; even with both
hands pushing the stick he could not regain control. 'I looked out
to the right and there was a Sea Harrier 150 metres away coming
in for the kill. I called, "They've hit me, I'm going to eject, I'm
OK", then I throttled back, opened the air brakes, placed my left
hand on the lower ejection handle and pulled it.' Philippi heard
the canopy go and a powerful explosion as the seat fired; he felt a

sharp pain in his neck, then passed out.

Clive Morell was not even looking at Philippi's Skyhawk as he swept past. He knew that aircraft was finished as the rear burst into flame and pieces began to fall away. The Sea Harrier pilot was intent on trying to launch his other Sidewinder at the aircraft in front of him, Arca's, but the missile refused to budge. Morell switched to guns and emptied his magazines at the Skyhawk but did not see any hits. 'I switched back to the missile, it was locked on to him and it fired on its own accord. At first it looked as if it was guiding nicely, then it just seemed to lose interest. It got to within a length or two behind him then stopped guiding and fell away into the sea. It was one of the very few instances we had of an AIM-9L failing after launch.'

Marquez appeared to be intent on what was happening to his comrades in front and seemed not to see John Leeming bounding behind him into position for a gun attack. 'He was at about zero feet, I was at zero plus 50. Still there was no sign that he had seen me; he was heading out as fast as he could. I fired a couple of tentative bursts, then my third splattered the sea around him. He must have realized what was happening then, because about a second later he rolled hard to starboard,' Leeming remembered. 'But by then it was too late, I was within about 200 yards. Before he could start to pull round I put my sight on his cockpit, pressed the firing button, and as the first rounds struck, the aircraft exploded. I think the engine must have broken up because the aircraft just disintegrated.' Leeming was forced to pull up sharply to avoid the rapidly growing cloud of debris in front of him.

Having exhausted his missiles and cannon shells, Morell glanced back to see what was going on behind. 'To my left and behind I could see this large ball of fire going down into the sea. I thought, "I hope that's not my No. 2!" But then John called up and said, "Spag (my nickname), are you OK?" I said, "Yes, how about you?"'

Alberto Philippi regained consciousness hanging from his parachute in cloud, with drops of rain moistening his face. His helmet and oxygen mask had been torn off during the ejection. He came down in the sea about 100 yards from the shore, shed his parachute, and began swimming towards the beach.

It had indeed been a hectic few minutes: everything described in this account, from the moment 'Sharkey' Ward and Steve

Thomas had first sighted the incoming Daggers, had taken place within a space of just ten minutes – between 2.52 p.m. and 3.02 p.m. on that fateful afternoon.

The repeated attacks had crippled HMS *Ardent*. 'By now we were in quite bad order down aft; the damage was fairly localized around the stern. We were veering out of control towards one of the small islands – the engines were still running but I had no steering,' explained West. He signalled for the engines to be stopped and the frigate slid to a halt. 'There was a loud roaring sound from the fire aft, lots of smoke, and the ship was starting to list quite badly. I realized we were likely to run aground with the tidal stream so I detailed some men to slip the anchor.' A few minutes later the ship's senior engineering officer, Lieutenant Commander Terry Pendrous, came to the bridge to catalogue the more serious aspects of the damage: the tiller flat had been blown off; the after auxiliary machinery room was flooded and there was an unexploded bomb lodged there; there was a major fire raging in the after canteen area; the after part of the ship had taken so many hits that parts of it were unrecognizable, with items of equipment which had originally been on one side of the ship torn away by the blast and hurled to the other side; and, most serious of all, there was flooding aft that could not be controlled. Alan West was left to make the most difficult decision that can face a ship's captain. 'While I was pondering what to do next, the ship gave a lurch. I called for *Yarmouth* to come and stand by us. Then the ship lurched again and I gave the order to abandon. *Yarmouth* put her stern against our bow and I sent my guys off. Some of the men had been blown into the water and they were picked up by helicopters. Finally the Master at Arms came to report to me that that there was nobody else left alive on the ship, and we made our way forward to *Yarmouth*. I was the last man off *Ardent*.' Twenty-two of the ship's crew had been killed and thirty injured.

None of the naval Skyhawks which delivered the final attack on *Ardent* survived the encounter. Clive Morell and John Leeming had shot down two of them immediately afterwards; Philippi ejected but Marquez was killed. José Arca had had a narrow escape when Morell's second Sidewinder failed to home properly, but even before that his Skyhawk had suffered damage which would prevent it returning to the mainland. As the aircraft swept low over the frigate after releasing its bombs, John Leake's defiant burst of fire had punctured the wing fuel tanks, and some of Morell's 30 mm rounds had also struck the aircraft. After he shook off the Sea Harriers, Arca found he was losing fuel so rapidly that he would never make it back to Rio Grande or even one of the KC-130 Hercules tankers orbiting off the coast. The only alternative was to attempt an emergency landing at Port Stanley, but when he arrived there he found he could not extend his undercarriage. José Arca ejected from the crippled Skyhawk, which circled the town for several minutes before it crashed into the sea just off the shore. The pilot came down in the sea and was picked up by an army helicopter.

After Philippi's attack a second formation of three naval Skyhawks ran in to bomb ships in the landing area, but without scoring any hits or suffering losses. After 3.30 p.m. there were no further air attacks on San Carlos Water and the transports were allowed to continue unloading unmolested. Two by two the Sea Harriers arrived to patrol their designated areas throughout the remainder of the afternoon and early evening, without making contact with the enemy. It was dark when the final pair of Sea Harriers, flown by Neil Thomas and Mike Blissett, landed on *Hermes* at 6.25 p.m. The darkness cloaked the exit of the liner *Canberra*, now empty of combat troops, as she slipped out of San Carlos Water for the safety of South Georgia.

Meanwhile three of the pilots who had narrowly escaped death made the best of their individual situations. All three had come down within 30 miles of each other, on sparsely inhabited West Falkland.

Near Mount Maria, not far from the burnt-out wreck of his Dagger, Hector Luna inflated his rubber dinghy and used the canopy to give protection from rain as he settled down for the night; he took a pain-killer and a swig of water from his survival kit, then tried to sleep in spite of the nagging pain from his dislocated arm and sprained knee.

Some 5 miles to the south-east Jeff Glover, now a prisoner of war after ejecting from his Harrier, was lying in bed in the social club at Port Howard which Argentine soldiers had requisitioned as a field hospital. As well as a broken left arm, shoulder and collar bone, he had been severely bruised about the face when his flying helmet was torn off, and his right eye was so badly swollen he could not see out of it. The medical officer who had led his rescue, Marine Captain Santiago Llaños, took personal charge of the injured British officer and saw he was well looked after. 'The Captain and the medical orderlies treated me very kindly. I had not been able to look at myself in a mirror, but with the injuries to my face I knew I must have looked a mess. If anything, my treatment was better than that of Argentine soldiers in the hospital,' Glover remarked.

About 20 miles to the south-west of the hospital, close to where he had swum ashore after parachuting into the sea, Alberto Philippi lay shivering in the hole in the ground he had dug with his survival knife to give some protection from the wind. His back was still sore after the painful ejection, but otherwise he had escaped injury. His main problem was the cold, which made it difficult to sleep; at hourly intervals he found it necessary to get up and stamp around to warm himself.

About six hours after the last of her crewmen had left her, the battered *Ardent* finally sank. Several commentators have written that modern warships with aluminium structures are not strong enough to sustain major battle damage. The example of this particular frigate would suggest otherwise. 'I was amazed how strong she was, she had taken one hell of a hammering,' commented Alan West. Later the board of inquiry into the loss of *Ardent* would establish that she had been hit by no fewer than seven 1,000-pound and 500-pound bombs which exploded, and at least two others which lodged inside her but did not go off.

With two unexploded 1,000-pounders lodged in her hull, HMS *Argonaut* was towed into San Carlos Water; there work began to make safe and remove the bombs on her.

At the Argentine bases work was in full swing to repair the battle damage suffered by aircraft in the course of the day's fighting. Many aircraft had been hit by light machine-gun fire, but this proved relatively easy to repair. 'Most of the damage we saw was from small-arms fire, not from missiles,' commented Lieutenant Colonel Ruben Zini. 'If a plane was hit by a missile it was usually lost; only if the missile exploded some distance away would it cause minor damage, which the aircraft would survive and we could repair. Repairs were very quick: if a plane came in damaged in the evening it would normally be ready to fly again by the next morning.'

On the Royal Navy carriers, the servicing crews found damage from small-arms fire equally easy to repair. 'Some of the battle damage could be repaired on deck between sorties,' said Chief Technician Fred Welsh, serving with No. 1 Squadron. 'If it was a simple hole and nothing inside had been hit, we could cut away the rough edge and cover the hole with Speedtape – thick aluminium foil with a self-adhesive backing, rolled on by means of a special tool. We had done it all before on exercises – but the hulk on which you practise during an exercise does not have to fly!' The damaged Harrier in which Mark Hare returned that morning would be flying on operations the following day.

During 21 May more than 3,000 troops and nearly 1,000 tons of stores had been landed on the shores around San Carlos Water. Considering that an opposed amphibious landing is the most difficult of all military operations, the putting ashore of so large a force with minimal losses of troops and equipment was a remarkable feat.

By placing themselves in positions to draw the Argentine air attacks on themselves, the warships in the 'gun line' saved the vulnerable transports from a severe battering. But the cost had not been light: one frigate sunk, a frigate and a destroyer seriously damaged, twenty-four sailors killed and several wounded.

One pleasant surprise for the British forces had been the complete lack of reaction from Argentine Army units during the landings. Questioned later on this, General Menedez would state that he lacked the helicopters to fly in sufficient troops and equipment to mount an effective counter-attack. Certainly this was a major problem, and it had been aggravated that morning when Jerry Pook and Mark Hare reduced his meagre helicopter lifting capacity by about a third with the destruction of the Chinook and two Pumas near Mount Kent (the other Chinook was sitting unserviceable at Port Stanley and would remain there for the rest of the conflict).

In addition to the helicopters, the Argentine Navy and Air Force lost twelve aircraft during the day's fighting: five Skyhawks, five Daggers and two Pucarás. Nine had fallen to attack from Sea Harriers, one was shared between a Sea Harrier and small-arms fire from a ship, one fell to a ground-launched missile, and one to a ship-launched missile.

Three British aircraft had been shot down; two helicopters and Jeff Glover's Harrier GR 3, and all had fallen to ground fire. Throughout the day the Sea Harrier pilots had had things very much their own way and had suffered no losses: there was no doubt in anyone's mind who were the hunters and who the hunted. On no occasion did Argentine pilots make any serious attempt to fight back or even threaten those attacking their comrades. 'Our briefing was that if we saw an enemy aircraft at low altitude we were to go for it, with the wing man covering one's tail as best he could,' explained Flight Lieutenant Dave Morgan. 'We never took it for granted that the fighter-bombers would not bring escorts with them and we couldn't understand why they didn't.'

It is unfair to place blame on the Argentine combat pilots for the failure of their High Command to provide escorts for the raids, or to concentrate forces during the attacks from mid-afternoon once the positions of the targets were known. Even if the Mirage force was needed to protect mainland bases from possible Vulcan attacks, there was still the option of fitting some Daggers with Shafrir infra-red homing missiles to enable them to put up a fight against the Sea Harriers. In the event attacks – a total of about fifty sorties from the mainland – were launched piecemeal with forces of between three and six aircraft, separated by intervals long enough for the ships to prepare for each new attack and for Sea Harriers that had used their missiles to be replaced on the patrol lines.

It is clear, however, that the Argentine fighter-bomber pilots had little awareness of how aircraft in a formation could give each other mutual cover using their cannon armament, if enemy fighters attacked. 'We were briefed to avoid dogfights and escape at low level and alone, "Every man for himself",' commented Ruben Zini, who flew with Grupo 5. The naval Skyhawk pilots also felt outclassed by the combination of Sea Harrier and AIM-9L, so that there was no point in attempting to fight back. 'What were we briefed to do if jumped by Sea Harriers? Well, we had a lot of experience of air combat manoeuvring, but in the A-4 there was not much choice. Not only were we too slow, but we knew very well we could not outmanoeuvre the Sea Harrier. All we could do was try to escape at low level at full throttle,' commented Lieutenant Benito Rotolo of the 3rd Escuadrilla. 'We never mounted Sidewinders on our Skyhawks because our mission was always one of attack, never air-to-air combat. The Sidewinder L is a very, very effective missile and our older models could not hope to equal them.'

The British pilots considered their opponents to be good 'stick and rudder' men, but felt they had little idea of modern air fighting tactics. Flight Lieutenant Paul Barton commented: 'Their pilots were not bad. Any guy that can fly at 60 or 70 feet above the waves, picking his way between ships' masts, is a pretty skilful pilot. But basically they had not been trained sufficiently in tactical flying. Nothing their fighter or attack aircraft did struck me as being particularly clever or original. That said, however, I would give them 9½ out of 10 for sheer guts and courage.' Certainly it had come as an unpleasant surprise to the Royal Navy to discover that the Argentine pilots were prepared to run the gauntlet of Sea Harriers and the ships' missiles in order to press home attacks.

With so much going on during the day, one event of aeronautical significance was allowed to pass unnoticed both at the time and since. When Wing Commander David Emmerson and the Nimrod landed at Ascension at 9.06 a.m. (Port Stanley time), after 18 hours and 51 minutes airborne and a marathon flight to the Falklands and up the Argentine coast, they had covered a distance of 8,453 miles. It would further advance the world record they already held for the longest-distance operational reconnaissance mission ever undertaken. The record has survived to the time of writing.

As Flight Lieutenant Dave Morgan later commented, 'May 21st was a heavy day.'

6: The Logistics Battle

22-25 MAY

The more I see of war, the more I realize how it all depends on administration and transportation. . . It takes little skill or imagination to see where you would like your forces to be and when; it takes much knowledge and hard work to know where you can place your forces and whether you can maintain them there.'

Field Marshal Earl Wavell

22 MAY

By dawn on the 22nd the area around San Carlos Water was securely in British hands. Five battalions of marines and paratroops were dug in over a large area, screened against air attack by protective batteries of Blowpipe and Rapier missiles. No power at the command of the Argentinians could dislodge the troops ashore by frontal attack, though there remained one means of containing the beachhead: if sufficient of the large and vulnerable supply ships could be prevented from reaching the area or off-loading when they got there, it would be impossible for the men to advance far beyond the area they now held. Having witnessed the ferocity of the Argentine Air Forces the previous day, the troops ashore and the sailors on the ships made ready to repel a similar all-out air attack. From now on the warships would not linger outside San Carlos Water, but would remain inside it with the landing and supply ships they were to protect.

The first attack on a supply vessel that day was mounted by Sea Harriers, however. Lieutenant Commander 'Fred' Frederiksen and Lieutenant Martin Hale of No. 800 Squadron launched from *Hermes* at dawn to mount the first air patrol of the day. As they approached Goose Green on their way in, they sighted the Coast Guard patrol boat *Rio Iguazu* on its way up Choiseul Sound to deliver supplies to the Argentine garrison there. After getting permission from their control ship the pair dived on the boat, strafed it with cannon, and left it burning. Later it was seen aground, having been abandoned by its crew.

At noon Squadron Leader Jerry Pook led a strike by four Harriers of No. 1 Squadron against the airfield at Goose Green. In the target area the raiders met heavy anti-aircraft fire, but all returned undamaged.

Throughout most of the day the feared air attacks from the Argentine mainland failed to materialize: bad weather at the bases in the south prevented air operations until mid-afternoon. Only at last light did a pair of Skyhawks penetrate to the landing area; they ran through at high speed, released bombs without hitting anything, and sped clear.

Elsewhere the only real excitement was far to the north of the Falklands, where a convoy of British ships bringing reinforcements was approached by a Boeing 707 of Grupo 1 on reconnaissance. Two of the escorts, *Bristol* and *Cardiff*, engaged with Sea Dart at extreme range, and only by diving away at high speed was the aircraft able to make good its escape.

23 MAY

The first air action took place soon after first light, when four Harriers from No. 1 Squadron took off from *Hermes* to attack the airfield at Dunnose Head on West Falkland, thought to be used by Argentine transport aircraft. In fact there were no enemy troops or aircraft in the area, and one of the bombs fell close to houses, causing some damage and injuries to one of the Falklanders. (After the war Flight Lieutenant Mark Hare, one of those who had taken part in the attack, visited the settlement to apologize for the error. Jimmy Forster, the farm manager, commented drily: 'If you wanted the runway destroyed, why didn't you tell us? We'd have ploughed it up for you!')

Shortly afterwards the already depleted Argentine Army helicopter force on the islands suffered further losses. Flight Lieutenants Dave Morgan and John Leeming were flying a combat air patrol at 8,000 feet over Falkland Sound when Morgan glimpsed rotating helicopter blades close above the water at Shag Cove inlet. Earlier in his career Morgan had flown battlefield helicopters, and it was clear to him that the pilot below had made a fundamental blunder. 'If there is one thing you learn when doing nap-of-the-earth helicopter flying, that is to avoid passing over water features if you can possibly avoid it. If you do go over them, you can be seen from above for miles,' explained Morgan. The helicopter was heading north-east up the east coast of West Falkland. 'I didn't know if it was one of ours so I asked the controlling ship. He said, "Hang on, I'll find out." We were low on fuel and didn't have time to hang on, so John and I dropped down to investigate.' The Sea Harriers swept in close to the ground, and at a range of 500 yards Morgan recognized the helicopter as a Puma – and the British forces did not have any Pumas on the Falklands. 'I called it as "Hostile" to John, and he replied, "Hey, there's four of them!" Then I made out two more Pumas following the first and an Augusta 109 on the end. I went straight for the leading Puma but it was too late to engage; I turned over the top of him and was pulling up to get into a firing position, when out of the corner of my eye I saw the Puma I had flown over smash into the ground and explode in a ball of fire.' Neither pilot had fired at the Puma: either the slipstream from Morgan's Sea Harrier had sent it out of control or the pilot had lost control trying to evade (on examination of the wreckage after the war the Puma was found to have been heavily laden with mortar bombs, so there would have been little reserve of performance in hand).

In the meantime the Augusta 109 had landed and the crew were running clear. The Sea Harriers strafed the helicopter and left it burning. Morgan's account continued: 'We were just about to depart the area when John said, "There's another Puma shut down further up the valley!" The crew had obviously plonked the helicopter down on the valley floor and run away. I fired the remainder of my rounds at it, then we had to go home.' As he climbed away Morgan reported the position of the helicopter to the control ship, and soon afterwards a pair of Sea Harriers from No. 801 Squadron arrived and shot up the remaining helicopter; all four had now been destroyed.

Around the beachhead there was little Argentine air activity until shortly after midday. Now attacks were being planned in the full knowledge of where targets lay and where and how the Sea Harriers were operating: their patrol lines were in full view of the Argentine positions at Pebble Island, Port Howard and Fox Bay, and their approach and return flights were tracked by the radars at Port Stanley and Pebble Island. As a result, warnings could be broadcast of which Sea Harrier patrol areas were active at various times during the day. During the days that followed the Skyhawk units would make full use of this information; they could change route in flight, relying on the KC-130 Hercules tankers orbiting off the mainland coast to supply more fuel should they run short. 'The radars on the Malvinas gave us considerable help,' explained Lieutenant Colonel Ruben Zini. 'On several occasions we were advised on the positions of the enemy aircraft; we were told if they were to the north of the Malvinas, in the Strait of San Carlos [Falkland Sound] or to the south.' The Daggers, unable to refuel in flight, were much closer to their fuel limits and usually had sufficient for only two minutes in the target area; they would be able to make less use of the information.

Also at this time a new Argentine Air Force unit began to make an appearance near the Falklands: the Fenix Escuadron, formed from civilian executive aircraft requisitioned into service and flown by pilots given Air Force commissions for the duration of the conflict. In the main the Fenix Escuadron operated close to the mainland performing communications and search-and-rescue flights. But for the higher-performance Learjets and HS 125s there were tasks much closer to the combat area. Learjets were used to mount decoy attacks on possible targets on or near the Islands, in the hope of drawing away the Sea Harrier patrols so that attacking fighter-bombers could get to their targets unmolested; they also served as lead aircraft for attacks by Daggers, necessary because the Dagger carried limited electronic equipment and had no effective over-sea navigational capability. During attacks an HS 125 played a key role as a high-altitude communications relay aircraft, passing information on the Sea Harrier patrols from the command centre at Port Stanley to the low-flying Skyhawks and Daggers and the occasional transport aircraft.

The first attack on shipping in San Carlos Water came shortly before 2 p.m., when small formations of Skyhawks picked their way past the Sea Harriers and streaked in at low altitude to release their bombs. During one of these attacks HMS *Antelope* was singled out; Lieutenant Filipini of Grupo 5 flew over her so low after releasing his bombs that one drop tank struck the ship's after mast, causing the thin structure to collapse halfway up. Remarkably, though some published accounts have stated otherwise, the aircraft survived the collision. Filipini heard a loud bang and the Skyhawk lurched to one side; as he withdrew at high speed he made a hasty examination of his machine to gauge the extent of the damage, but everything seemed intact. (Later, on the ground at Rio Gallegos, he found that the only harm it had suffered was a deep gouge down the side of one drop tank and a fin at the rear knocked off.)

A Skyhawk of the same unit, which attacked *Antelope* shortly afterwards, was less fortunate. Almost immediately after it released its bombs it was struck by a Sea Wolf from HMS *Broadsword* and possibly a ground-launched Rapier as well. The aircraft broke up into a ball of flaming wreckage and crashed into the sea. The pilot, Lieutenant Luciano Guadagnini, was killed.

Also at this time the 3rd Escuadrilla put in an attack with three Skyhawks. The naval pilots found the Rapier batteries a disconcerting additional hazard. 'They arrived over the bay and found the ships there waiting for them,' recounted Lieutenant Benito Rotolo. 'And the surprise was that not only were there ships' missiles to contend with, but shore-based missiles as well. The pilots said they were able to see the missiles coming, however, and evade them by high-G turns. If a missile could be seen in time, it could usually be avoided.' The naval aircraft came away from the Falklands without loss. But as he was landing at Rio Grande in a strong cross-wind the formation leader, Lieutenant Commander Carlos Zubizarreta, started to drift off the runway; at the last moment he tried to eject from the aircraft but the seat failed to work properly and he was killed. Surprisingly the aircraft, though seriously damaged, was later repaired.

The attacks left *Antelope* with two bombs lodged in her hull and a smashed rear mast. Trailing steam, the frigate limped to the far end of San Carlos Water for the bombs to be made safe.

By now there were twelve Rapier firing units distributed around the slopes overlooking San Carlos Water, but their crews found it very difficult to engage the fighter-bombers as they sped through the waterways at low altitude: the same hills that gave the Argentine pilots so many problems in trying to hit the ships made the site a nightmare for those trying to guide ground-launched missiles to their targets. (In fairness, it should be pointed out that any other type of surface-to-air missile system would have suffered exactly the same problems.) From start to finish the average time enemy fighter-bombers were in sight was only about fifteen seconds; and because of the concentration of friendly helicopters in the area, and the problem of mutual interference between electronic systems on the ships and those of Rapier, part of the latter's had to be switched off or overridden. The result was that Rapier, which performed so impressively against simulated enemy aircraft flying low over the flat north German plains, was able to achieve nothing like the same success rate around San Carlos Water. During the day Rapier crews claimed the destruction of three enemy aircraft; according to the authors' research one fighter-bomber came down in the area, and it was also claimed by ships' guns and missiles.

Relative tranquillity now returned to the area for nearly two hours, then Daggers of Grupo 6 made an unsuccessful attack shortly before 4 p.m. Lieutenant Commander Andy Auld and Lieutenant Martin Hale of No. 800 Squadron were on patrol to the west when Hale caught sight of a Dagger over Pebble Island moving west at high speed. The Sea Harrier pilot immediately pulled hard right to get into a firing position, but the distance was too great. 'It soon became clear that he was running out going as fast as I was and I wasn't going to catch him. However, as I looked around the scenery I caught sight of his No. 2 trailing by something like a mile and a half. He saw me at about the same time as I saw him; we were flying about three-quarters of a mile apart on a converging course,' recalled Hale. 'As he started to out-accelerate me, I just dropped in behind him and from about half a mile I got in a shot with my starboard missile. It homed in and went right up the jetpipe. There was a tremendous explosion and the aircraft disintegrated there and then; the wreckage fell on the west side of Horseshoe Bay.'

Elsewhere over the Falklands during the day, Harriers of No. 1 Squadron flew armed reconnaissance missions in the Chartres and Port Howard areas, and during the late afternoon three aircraft carried out an attack on the airfield at Pebble Island.

While the Harrier attack on Pebble Island was in progress, a pair of Super Étendards of the 2nd Escuadrilla attempted another missile attack on British warships east of the Falklands. Again the pilots failed to find any targets, however, and the aircraft returned to Rio Grande with their Exocets.

Late that night No. 800 Squadron lost a Sea Harrier setting out on a four-aircraft strike on Port Stanley airfield. Shortly after take-off one of the machines crashed into the sea and exploded; its pilot, Lieutenant Commander Gordon Batt, was killed.

Also that night, in San Carlos Water, one of the bombs lodged in HMS *Antelope* exploded while an army bomb disposal expert was working to make it safe; one man in the team was killed and the other seriously injured. The explosion blew a hole in the ship's side from waterline to funnel and started an uncontrollable fire, which burned through to her main magazine and ignited it. Following several secondary explosions the ship burned out and she sank early next morning.

So far, of the bombs that had struck British ships, about half had failed to detonate. The Royal Navy considered it vital that this fact should be concealed as long as possible. Great was the consternation, then, when during news bulletins on the 23rd the BBC reported:

> Following the Argentine air attacks on 21 May two unexploded bombs on one warship have been successfully defused and a further one dealt with on another warship. Repairs are being carried out on the other warships, which sustained minor damage in the raid.

At the time many British servicemen in the Falklands felt the release – originating from the Ministry of Defence in London – to be an act of high treason; certainly it was a reckless piece of reporting which, at the very least, gratuitously presented Argentine forces with the information that some of their bombs were not functioning properly and that it might be prudent to try to discover why. It would remain to be seen what difference, if any, the report would make to the conduct of their future air operations.

24 MAY

Shortly after dawn two Sea Harriers of No. 800 Squadron and

four Harriers of No. 1 Squadron carried out a co-ordinated attack on Port Stanley airfield, in a further attempt to knock out the all-important runway. As had been the case on 1 May the first aircraft in, Sea Harriers piloted by Lieutenant Commanders Neil Thomas and Mike Blissett, were to toss in radar air-burst fused bombs from the north-east to distract the defences. Immediately afterwards Squadron Leader Bob Iveson led in the first pair of Harriers to attack from the north-west. 'The Sea Harriers coming from the opposite direction had the fire control radars locked on to them, but they did not go within range of the guns or missiles; they were tossing their bombs from some way out. Everything was looking in their direction,' Iveson remembered. 'We came in very low and dropped our bombs; we did not pick up much flak at all, none of the radars locked on to us until we were running out. In other words we had flown into the direction in which they were looking, rather than the other way about.'

Iveson and his No. 2, Flight Lieutenant Tony Harper, each released three parachute-retarded 1,000-pounders and sped out of the area with few problems from the defences. For the two Harriers following them into the target from almost due west, flown by Wing Commander Peter Squire and Flight Lieutenant Mark Hare, things were much more difficult as the latter commented: 'As we ran in we could see the VT [radar air-burst] fused bombs going off in the distance, each with a hugh flash and a pall of smoke, a magnificent sight and very comforting. But then things began to go wrong, because we arrived at the target about twenty seconds behind the pair of Harriers in front instead of thirty seconds – they had been delayed a bit.' Now there was a real danger that the rear pair of Harriers would suffer damage from debris thrown up by the exploding bombs of the pair in front; and it was clear why Iveson and Harper had been able to go through without being engaged by the defences: the latter were concentrating on Squire and Hare! Hare continued: 'By the time the Boss and I arrived near the airfield everyone was firing at us. Then suddenly I had to fly through the debris thrown up by Tony Harper's bombs going off in front of me.' In spite of the distractions around them the rear pair dropped their bombs on the target and got out at high speed.

This action illustrates well some of the hazards of low-altitude attacks on heavily defended targets. The approaches of aircraft running in from different directions had to be co-ordinated closely, and even relatively minor errors in timing could spell disaster. Later it would become clear that the runway had survived the attack. Two bombs inflicted damage to the edges, while others struck the runway itself but failed to detonate at the correct time to inflict damage: the Argentinians were not the only ones to have problems with bomb fusing during the conflict. Two of the Harriers returned with minor damage from small-arms fire.

About 100 miles to the west of Port Stanley, moves had been made to improve the radar early warning for those defending the San Carlos beachhead against air attack. The destroyer *Coventry* and the frigate *Broadsword* had left the main Task Group and were now patrolling to the north of West Falkland off Pebble Island. As raiding forces began to approach the landing area late that morning, the new dispositions brought their reward. Lieutenant Commander Andy Auld and Lieutenant Dave Smith of No. 800 Squadron were on combat air patrol nearby when *Broadsword*'s radar detected enemy aircraft closing from the west. The two Sea Harriers were vectored in to intercept and almost immediately Auld caught sight of the enemy formation: four Daggers of Grupo 6 running in fast and low. He pulled round behind, and fired Sidewinders at two of them; the missiles closed rapidly and impacted. An account of what happened next, written by Smith in a letter to his parents, shows well the fleeting nature of these encounters:

> No time to gawp – the second pair were breaking hard right, and I was the only one with missiles to fire. I picked up the number three and pulled hard into his turn. As my missile 'cross' [on the weapon sight] flashed across his tail, the angry growl of 'acquisition' pounded my ears. A quick press of the lock button, and the missile locked and tracked – safety catch up – and FIRE. A great flash and the Sidewinder leapt off the rails, homing straight on to the target. Another flash and a fireball. The Mirage [sic] broke up and impacted the ground in a huge burning inferno. What an incredible sight! In less than five seconds we had destroyed three enemy aircraft – but no time to reflect. The fourth was still about somewhere and as neither of us could see him he was a threat. Then suddenly I saw him under the Boss, heading

west at high speed. I turned hard, calling the Boss to break
with me to cover my tail. We followed him flat out for several
minutes, just out of missile range until, short of fuel, we had
to pull out. . .

I returned to the ship with extraordinarily mixed feelings.
Delighted at having prevented the raid from getting through
and at getting my first 'kill', but saddened and horrified at
witnessing the savage quick death of a fast jet combat at low
level.

While all of this was happening, other attacking forces were
approaching the target, also at low altitude. Piloting a Dagger of
Grupo 6, Captain Horacio Gonzalez was one of a formation of
four skirting around the south of West Falkland. 'When we
arrived at Isla Jorge [George Island] at the extreme south of Isla
Soledad [East Falkland] we altered course towards the bay, then
changed course again to go north towards San Carlos,' he
remembered. 'Four minutes before reaching our target, with the
Rivadavia Hills [Sussex Mountains] in sight, we accelerated to
550 knots [630 m.p.h.]. We hopped over the Rivadavia ridge,
which is about 300 metres [1,000 feet] high, and entered San
Carlos Bay, where we could see between ten and thirteen ships.
As soon as we passed over the Rivadavia Hills the first missiles
were fired at us from on land, then the warships in the north
joined in and everyone began firing at us with anti-aircraft
weapons of all sizes. The four of us flew in a fluid formation,
practically line abreast with about 300–500 metres [330–550
yards] between aircraft; between the leader and the No. 4 there
was an angle of 10–20 degrees, so that the Daggers could converge
on a ship and all attack before the first bomb exploded,' Gonzalez
continued. 'Between the Rivadavia Hills and the ships was only
about a mile; they were very close to the southern end of San
Carlos Bay. We had to begin our attack immediately, there
simply was no time to discuss which target we would go for. The
flight of four attacked one ship which was larger than the rest,
dropped our bombs, and began our escape, skimming the water,
passing between the ships. Since there were so many ships packed
together so closely, we could see the British had considerable
difficulty firing at our aircraft because their guns and missiles
could have hit their own ships.'

Once the Daggers were clear of San Carlos Water they swung round on to a westerly heading, but still they faced dangers. 'As we entered the Strait of San Carlos [Falkland Sound] we were jumped by a Sea Harrier which sprayed cannon fire at the No. 3 and No. 4, but without hitting them,' recalled Gonzalez. 'We fled from the Sea Harrier and continued at low altitude for about 40 miles, then began climbing to return to base.' Later examination of the Daggers on the ground would reveal that three of the four had taken hits from small-arms fire.

It is difficult to link Gonzalez's account with British reports of the attacks on shipping in San Carlos Water that day, but this is to be expected. As they swept through the waterway the attacking formations were within view of those on the ships for less than half a minute, during which all hell was let loose; and, as Gonzalez suggested, there was considerable risk of those on the ships or ashore being hit by rounds intended for aircraft coming past. The same incident looked quite different when seen from opposing sides. Sub Lieutenant Clive Rawson of No. 826 Squadron, on the supply ship *Fort Austin* anchored close to the east side of the Water, watched the attackers coming past: 'On the first raid that morning there was no warning at all; the first thing I knew was when a Rapier battery ashore opened fire. I looked round and there was an A-4 [Skyhawk] screaming down the port side of the ship. He pulled up slightly, released his bombs, and they fell about 100 yards off the port bow of *Fort Austin*. Then off he went, banking around and hugging the coastline. There were others in the raid but I don't know what happened to them,' he commented. 'The second wave came in from the south, a mixture of Mirages [i.e. Daggers] and A-4s. The Rapiers and Sea Cats engaged them. The first Mirage came past, minus bombs, along the coast. A second followed, and this time a Rapier exploded near his tail, but nothing happened. He came close past the port side of *Fort Austin*, so close we could see every detail, and our machine gunners raked him with their fire. Then he climbed, trailing a lot of smoke, perhaps because he had cut in afterburner, and we saw him disappear over the hill.'

Probably one of the attacking forces Rawson had watched was that mounted by Grupo 4 that morning; all three Skyhawks involved took hits. As the attackers withdrew to the west the pilots examined each other's machines for signs of damage. 'I looked

over the No. 3 aircraft [Lieutenant Bono's] which was flying to
my left and below; I could see he was losing fuel. Also the leader
[Lieutenant Vasquez] was losing a great deal of fuel,' recalled
Ensign Martinez, who was piloting the No. 2 aircraft. To reduce
drag Vasquez had to jettison his empty drop tanks. Over West
Falkland the aircraft began climbing to high altitude, to make the
most of the remaining fuel. 'We began our ascent and I was flying
to the right of the leader. The No. 3 man followed, a little behind
and below us; then his plane began a smooth turn to the left and,
losing altitude rapidly, fell away until it crashed into the sea. As
we saw him going down the leader and I both shouted at him to
eject, but there was no reply. Where the aircraft struck there was a
large mushroom cloud, and near it a smaller one which we
supposed might have been the canopy or the ejector seat. But we
did not see any parachute. We continued our return flight in
silence.'

As the pair of Skyhawks headed west it soon became clear that
Martinez's aircraft was losing fuel too, and great was the relief
when the pilots caught sight of the KC-130 Hercules tanker which
had come out to meet them. The aircraft quickly connected up
and began taking on fuel, each trailing a stream of the precious
liquid from their punctured tanks. The fighter-bombers remained
in position on the hoses until they were within 30 miles of their
base at Rio Gallegos, then broke away and went in to land.
During the return flight Vasquez's Skyhawk took on some 5,000
gallons of fuel through the nose probe, only to lose most of it out
the back (the aircraft's fuel tanks hold only 666 gallons!). The
operation depleted the tanker's own fuel to such an extent that it
too had to land at the fighter-bomber base to take on more. The
mission over, Martinez surrendered to his emotions: 'Once on the
ground I began to feel a very great tiredness and cramp in my
legs. Vasquez was waiting for me by his plane, and when I got out
of mine we embraced each other with eyes full of tears. It was the
first time we had reached our target, but we had lost a comrade.'
A rescue operation mounted in the area where the Skyhawk had
gone down failed to find any sign of the pilot, Lieutenant Jorge
Bono.

The only ships hit during these attacks were the landing ships
Sir Galahad, *Sir Lancelot* and *Sir Bedivere*, anchored along the
western side of San Carlos Water. *Sir Bedivere* had a bomb come

past her mast and carry away several aerials, glance off the foredeck, bounce off the sea and slam into the side of *Sir Galahad* 400 yards away. *Sir Lancelot* had a bomb smash into her starboard side and come to rest in the accommodation area near the stern. Neither bomb detonated.

After dark that evening work began to make safe the bombs lodged in the supply ships. Chief Technician 'Hank' Hankinson, a member of the RAF bomb disposal team which had arrived only that morning, went on board the abandoned *Sir Lancelot* with six men of a navy clearance diving team. The men climbed the scrambling net left against the ship's side, to be greeted by a strong smell of burning – a highly unwelcome discovery since the ship was loaded with ammunition. A hurried investigation revealed that in their understandable haste to leave the ship the cooks had left the ovens on, and the smell came from the now incinerated lunch they had been preparing. Once the ovens had been turned off Hankinson went to inspect the unexploded bomb. 'It had gone through the ship's side at an angle, there wasn't a neat round hole. After going through the starboard side it had torn through some partitions before finishing up, broadside on to the entry hole, on the floor of the entertainment film store. It had torn through water pipes, water was dripping everywhere, and the asbestos lagging was hanging down. The first I saw of the bomb was the nose, sticking out of a load of bent film cans, bits of smashed timber and asbestos lagging,' he later recalled.

The nose of the bomb was immediately recognizable to Hankinson: it was the familiar British 1,000-pounder, one of many supplied to Argentina over the years. 'That simplified things no end!' he commented. It meant that the types of fuse fitted to it would all be known to him. Careful inspection of the nose of the bomb revealed no fuse there, so it had to be in the tail. He carefully removed the pieces of debris around the tail then, lying across the bomb itself and using a piece of broken mirror taped to a wire coathanger to see round the corner, he examined the protruding end of the fuse fitted in the tail: it was of the ordinary impact type he knew well, with no possibility of delayed action or anti-handling devices. And it was clear that the bomb was in a safe condition; it could be removed as it was. Few things are simple in bomb disposal, however: even a safe 1,000-pounder represented a half-ton load in an extremely awkward place.

Before it could be lifted out by crane, holes had to be cut through each of the decks above.

Hankinson left the hard manual labour of removing the bomb to the Navy and went across to the *Sir Galahad* to see the unexploded weapon there. This time it had come to rest in the battery store, with pools of corrosive acid lying on the deck all around. Again it was a British 1,000-pounder safe to be moved, and again Hankinson handed the problem over to the Navy.

By night the skies over the Falklands belonged to nobody, and with help from ground radars on the Islands to provide warning of the occasional patrolling Sea Harrier, the lower performance Argentine Air Force types could put in an appearance. After their abortive action on 1 May the Canberras of Grupo 2 had been relegated to night operations and now flew nuisance raids against the beachhead. The elderly bombers attacked from altitudes around 500 feet, or up at 40,000 feet. Lacking bombing radars or modern navigation equipment, the Canberra crews made what amounted to area bombing attacks on San Carlos – where, compared with the area over which they were scattered, military and civilian targets were few and far between. The chances of any useful military result from such raids were extremely slender, and in the event they achieved nothing.

The other type of operation mounted by the Argentine Navy and Air Force, mainly at night though sometimes by day as well, was a good deal more successful: those by C-130 Hercules, Electra and Fellowship transports into the airfield at Port Stanley – the Argentine forces also had a logistics battle to fight. 'Sometimes we flew from Comodoro Rivadavia, sometimes from Rio Gallegos,' explained Lieutenant Colonel Alberto Vianna, a C-130 pilot with Grupo 1. 'We normally flew to the Malvinas at altitudes around 50 feet even at night, using our radar altimeters to avoid being intercepted. We did not trust autopilots when flying so low, because the wing span of our aircraft was greater than our altitude (i.e. if the autopilot put the aircraft into too steep a bank, there was a risk that one wing would strike the surface). We operated our C-130s at maximum capacity at all times, even flying with less-than-full tanks to enable us to carry as great a payload as possible,' he continued. 'Once the cargo had been off-loaded we normally turned around and took off immediately – if things were tight we didn't even shut down the engines. The bombing of the runway at Puerto Argentino never stopped our operations. Most of the bombs dropped never hit the strip, though some fell close beside it.'

Amongst the high-priority loads being flown into Port Stanley at this time were Soviet-made SA-7 Strella shoulder-launched infra-red homing missiles made available by Peru, Argentina's only fully committed ally during the conflict. After the aircraft had been unloaded, on went the wounded and pilots who had escaped from aircraft during the previous day's fighting. On this evening one was Flight Lieutenant Jeff Glover, whose Harrier had been shot down at Port Howard three days earlier. On the night of the 22nd he had been flown by helicopter to Goose Green, and on the night of the 23rd another helicopter had brought him to Port Stanley. Throughout his captivity his treatment was never less than correct, and often it was friendly. 'On the plane the shot-down pilots were not hostile in any way and some tried to strike up a conversation, but I did not want to be drawn into it,' Glover later commented. 'My big worry was that the Hercules might be intercepted by Sea Harriers and I would be shot down by my own people.' But there was no interception, and three hours later the Hercules landed at Comodoro Rivadavia.

During succeeding nights the other two pilots shot down on West Falkland on 21 May whose fortunes we have observed – Dagger pilot Hector Luna and Skyhawk pilot Alberto Philippi – linked up with Argentine forces and followed Glover along the same route to the mainland. The men followed each other one step at a time in succession, like baseball players moving from plate to plate to complete a circuit: Luna arrived at Goose Green on the 24th and would fly out from Port Stanley on the 25th; Philippi would arrive at Goose Green on the 25th and leave Port Stanley on the 28th.

25 MAY

This is Argentina's National Day, the anniversary of the beginning of the war to gain independence from Spain in 1810. Expecting this to be the occasion for further all-out air attacks against the beachhead, Vice-Admiral Woodward redisposed his forces. He moved the main body of the Task Force, including the two aircraft carriers, west to within 130 miles of the landing area so the Sea Harriers could spend a greater part of each sortie at the patrol areas. This move, coupled with the presence of *Coventry* and *Broadsword* to the north of Pebble Island to provide radar early warning of approaching raiders, promised to increase the effectiveness of the defences greatly.

During the morning clear skies over the beachhead allowed Learjet survey aircraft of Air Photographic Escuadrón I, part of Grupo 2, to fly a high-altitude reconnaissance of San Carlos at 40,000 feet. As they came past, *Coventry* attempted to engage with Sea Dart, but before missiles could be launched the targets passed out of range. The aircraft returned to the mainland with photographs showing the entire lodgement area and the positions of shipping in San Carlos Water.

During the morning and at midday small forces of Skyhawks penetrated to the landing area, but the fierce reception from the defenders with ground- and ship-launched missiles and gunfire prevented the attacks from being effective. One aircraft of Grupo 4 was shot down by a missile and crashed into San Carlos Water. The injured pilot, Lieutenant Ricardo Lucero, parachuted into the sea close to HMS *Fearless*. His rescue and subsequent medical treatment were filmed by a British television cameraman and the incident later received wide coverage. The pilot of another Skyhawk of the same unit, shot down by surface weapons, failed to eject from his aircraft. Also on this day anti-aircraft gunners at Goose Green scored another 'own goal' when they shot down a Skyhawk of Grupo 5, killing the pilot.

Around midday two separate forces of Harriers and Sea Harriers carried out toss-bombing and high-altitude attacks on the airfield at Port Stanley, but without inflicting serious damage.

Then the Argentine Air Force launched a counter-attack which was to have devastating consequences. Shortly before 2 p.m. Lieutenant Colonel Ruben Zini led six Skyhawks of Grupo 5 from Rio Gallegos to attack the warships off Pebble Island. Early on two of the aircraft aborted the mission but the others carried on towards the Islands. 'The four of us headed toward Isla Borbon [Pebble Island], and out to sea about 15 miles north of the island I caught sight of two warships, which I reported to the leader: "There to the left, the frigates!" He replied, "Yes, those are the ones!" We went straight into our attack runs: the two leading aircraft went for the frigate to the west, the other two of us went for the warship directly ahead,' recalled Ensign Jorge Nuevo.

Zini and his wing man closed rapidly on 'the frigate to the west', *Broadsword*; the latter achieved a radar lock-on and waited for the targets to come within range of her Sea Wolf missiles. At the time Lieutenant Commander Neil Thomas was leading a pair of Sea Harriers from No. 800 Squadron which had just arrived in the area on patrol. Thomas accelerated to maximum speed and was diving in to intercept when, before he could get into a firing position, he received orders to break off the chase lest he follow the enemy aircraft into the missile engagement zone. The two Sea Harriers pulled away, but at this critical moment *Broadsword*'s missile control radar tripped out and broke lock, making it impossible to launch. The ship's crew could only brace themselves for the inevitable as the two Skyhawks sped towards them and released their bombs. Three of those aimed at the frigate missed; the fourth bounced off the water before reaching the ship, struck her stern in its upward travel, emerged out of the top of the flight deck, carried away part of the nose of the Lynx helicopter, and continued on to fall back into the sea on the other side without exploding.

At the time of this attack the second pair of Skyhawks, flown by Jorge Nuevo and his leader, were about 10 miles from *Coventry* but closing at maximum speed. Again the Sea Harriers moved to intercept, again *Broadsword* achieved a lock-on with Sea Wolf, and again the fighters were ordered to break away. *Coventry* fired a Sea Dart at the approaching aircraft but it missed, as did the shots from her 4·5-inch gun. *Broadsword* was on the point of opening fire with Sea Wolf when suddenly *Coventry*, manoeuvring to make the attackers' task more difficult, cut across her bow and shielded the Skyhawks; again the missile control radar broke lock. 'As we were running towards the warship we saw it change course rapidly through 90 degrees,' Jorge Nuevo remembered. 'When I released my bombs my heading was 40 degrees off that of the ship; as we passed over it I saw three of our bombs hit. I returned to low altitude on the other side and caught up with my leader, then I saw that the other two Skyhawks had escaped successfully and we returned together.'

In war the outcome of individual actions frequently depends on luck, and on this occasion it deserted *Coventry*. The three bombs punched deep into the destroyer and exploded, blowing a great hole in her port side and causing immediate flooding, fire, and loss of all power and communications. Captain David Hart-Dyke, the ship's commander, wrote afterwards of the scene around him:

> The operations room, low down in the ship where I and some thirty men were controlling the battle, was devastated by the blast and immediately filled with very thick smoke. When I came round after being stunned, burnt and disorientated – though I was not aware of this at the time – all I could see were some people around me with their clothes alight; I could see no way out; there was nothing left of the exit through the port door; the ladder up to the bridge was gone. By this time, suffocating in the smoke, I was quite prepared to die; I was calm and death seemed unavoidable.
>
> Suddenly I found I had stumbled out through the starboard door of the operations room and was in clearer air. I then became more aware of the situation and made my way up broken and twisted ladders to the upperdeck and finally got to the port wing of the bridge. Here I collapsed on my knees to help my breathing and I turned to an officer and said: 'Get the ship going fast to the east.' I knew this was my escape route back to the Task Force. The officer replied 'Aye aye sir' and went away to do it. I had not realized at the time the ship was now severely listing to port some fifty degrees, there was no power of any sort, and the ship was on fire. We clearly weren't going to move anywhere. It was much later that I realized what a ridiculous order I had given, but it was instinctive and seemed right at the time. It shows how shocked I must have been.

Flight Lieutenant Ted Ball of No. 800 Squadron was flying one of a pair of Sea Harriers which arrived on the scene shortly afterwards, to be greeted with a sight grimly reminiscent of the loss of the *Prince of Wales* and *Repulse* almost exactly forty years earlier. 'There was *Broadsword* stopped in the water with a plume of smoke rising from her – in fact it was funnel smoke rather than from damage, but to us it looked as if she was on fire,' recounted Ball. 'Beside her was *Coventry* listing badly, surrounded by lots of little orange dinghies and with helicopters all over the place. As we watched, horrified, the huge ship rolled right over until she was upside down with only her propellers showing.'

More than a dozen Sea King and Wessex helicopters were quickly on the scene and, like so many dragonflies, hovered over the survivors and winched them one by one to safety while boats from *Broadsword* picked up others. Nineteen of *Coventry*'s crew were killed in the attack; the other 283 were saved during the rapidly mounted rescue operation.

The loss of *Coventry* was bad enough for the British Task Force, but potentially worse was in store. Even as the destroyer was being attacked, a pair of Super Étendards flown by Lieutenant Commander Roberto Curilovic and Lieutenant Julio Barraza were half way to their designated target area: the point just east of where the Harrier and Sea Harrier 'paints' disappeared off the Port Stanley radar screens, where the two British carriers had to be. The Argentine aircraft had taken off from Rio Grande an hour earlier, then headed north-east to rendezvous with a KC-130 Hercules tanker 185 miles due east of Puerto Deseado where they took on additional fuel for the long flight. As for the attack on *Sheffield*, each aircraft carried drop tanks under the fuselage and port wing and an Exocet missile under the starboard wing. Skirting 120 miles north of the Falklands to keep clear of the Sea Harriers, the Super Étendards continued until they were north-east of the Islands, then turned due south to begin their attacks. Relying on the unexpected direction and radio silence to achieve surprise, the pair continued on until Curilovic picked up the tell-tale emissions of British ships' radars on his receiving equipment. The lead pilot eased his nose round until he was heading towards them, then the pair began descending to the target approach altitude of 50 feet.

On the requisitioned container ship *Atlantic Conveyor*, RAF ground crewmen of No. 18 Squadron had been busy refitting rotor blades to two of the Chinook helicopters. The business of 'blading up' on the deck of a ship rolling on the open sea was, in the words of Sergeant Steve Hitchman, 'a swine of a job'. The men had no crane, and they had to use a fork-lift truck to hoist the blades – each 30 feet long and weighing 300 pounds – the 15 feet or more to the hubs. 'The lifting forks, to which the blades were attached by ropes, would go up or down only in a series of jerks. We had ropes tied to each end to steady them, but as we tried to move them into position the ends of the blades would flex the whole time,' Hitchman explained. 'We had a man leaning over the rotor head as the blades were manoeuvred into position, ready to push the locking bolt into place. And a couple of times he nearly lost fingers.' By the late afternoon the work on the two aircraft was complete; after engine running checks, one of the large helicopters took off to transfer supplies between ships. The helicopters were to fly to San Carlos the next day. While his comrades went to get cleaned up for supper, Hitchman descended two decks to the workshop in the hold to sharpen some knives.

Closing on the British force at their attack speed of 630 m.p.h., the Super Étendard pilots switched on their radars then eased the aircraft into the climb to begin the search for targets. Almost immediately afterwards the cluster of ships was seen, the targets were selected, and their co-ordinates were fed into the missiles; each aircraft then launched its Exocet. As the missiles sped clear the Super Étendards turned sharply and withdrew.

The first to sense impending danger was the frigate *Ambuscade* on the northern edge of the force, as her alert operators identified Super Étendard radar transmissions on their receivers. Immediately a warning was flashed to the other ships, their companies were brought to action stations, chaff rockets were fired, and each carrier scrambled its Lynx helicopter with missile decoy equipment.

On the bridge of *Hermes* Graeme Hammond, the admiral's press adviser, watched the action unfold: '*Hermes* was in the centre of the formation; ahead and slightly to the left was *Invincible*. *Atlantic Conveyor* was on our right, slightly ahead and about 2 miles away. All the ships were firing chaff rockets by this time; as ours went there would be a great "whooosh" and against the darkening sky one could see the red flames from the receding rockets.' Shortly afterwards, trailing smoke, one of the Exocets came streaking in over the waves; it smashed into the port side of *Atlantic Conveyor* and the warhead exploded. There is some evidence that the chaff or the Lynxes were successful in decoying the missiles away from the carriers, but then one Exocet seems to have re-locked on to the container ship, while the other ran to the end of its travel and fell into the sea.

In *Atlantic Conveyor*'s hold there was no loudspeaker system to give warning of the danger. The first Steve Hitchman knew of the

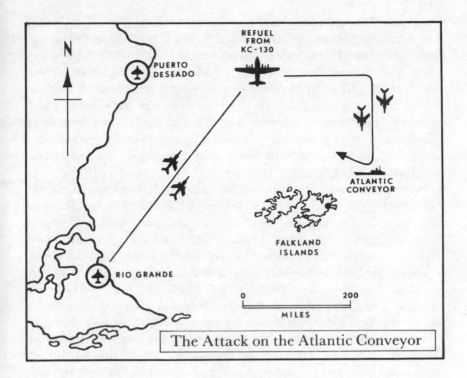

The Attack on the Atlantic Conveyor

attack was when he heard a very loud bang and saw a huge ball of fire advancing towards him. 'The blast knocked me off my feet but when I picked myself up the fireball was gone. I didn't feel any radiant heat, probably because I was wearing a lot of clothes – outside on deck it had been very cold. It was clear the ship had taken a hit, but I thought it could not have been all that bad because the explosion did not hurt my ears.' What he did not know was that the missile had exploded on the deck below his and only a minute fraction of the blast had come in his direction. The deck where the Exocet went off was packed with 4-ton trucks with full fuel tanks; these immediately caught fire and the flames spread rapidly.

The next thing Hitchman knew, acrid smoke started swirling around him from all sides. Since the loss of *Sheffield* there had been a rigidly enforced rule in the Task Force that personal gas masks would be carried at all times; the airman pulled his out of the bag and thrust it over his face. Once it was on he found he could breathe relatively easily; he has no doubt that the mask saved his life. Crawling on hands and knees on the deck where the smoke was less dense he endeavoured to retrace his steps to the upper deck. He had not gone far when, suddenly: 'The deck just ended! The plates had been blown away leaving a neat hole in front of me! I looked down through the hole into the deck below, and through the smoke I could see several large fires burning.' Hitchman groped his way aft away from the hole towards the stern, a part of the ship he had never previously visited at this level. By now the smoke was so dense that the lights in the passage could be seen only when he was immediately beneath them. He was starting to get hot, and each breath came a little harder than the last: the smoke was beginning to clog the mask's filters. 'I began to panic and clawed at the mask with my fingers, but as I did so smoke started to come in around the sides. I immediately realized the foolishness of what I was doing and stopped – a little good air was far better than a face full of smoke.' Finally Hickman was able to grope his way to a ladder, and climb it, and to his enormous relief he emerged in the open on the aft cable deck.

All around him smoke was pouring from the inside of the vessel. He looked over the stern to see the water smooth and unruffled: the propeller was no longer turning. Hickman leapt over the side and, once in the water, struggled to pull on his life-jacket and inflate it. 'Then I looked around and saw *Atlantic Conveyor* moving away from me quite slowly, in a turn to port. In her side I could see a huge hole about the size of a house, extending from just above water level almost to the weather deck. Surrounding the hole were great chunks of jagged metal sticking out around the edges.' From the time of the explosion until Steve Hitchman entered the water had been about five minutes, the longest five minutes of his life.

In the failing light helicopters were scrambled from ships in the Task Group to rescue survivors, and first to be plucked from the water was Steve Hitchman. On *Hermes* Graeme Hammond watched the stricken ship receding behind the main body of the force, with a couple of ships in attendance: 'The smoke was incredible. Even after dark you could see the thick column above the ship, with every so often orange flames emerging from the smoke column.' Twelve men died as a result of the attack, including *Atlantic Conveyor*'s master, Captain Ian North.

The Super Étendards landed at Rio Grande at 6.38 p.m., having refuelled on the outward and return flights and spent 4 hours and 10 minutes in the air during which they covered about 1,500 miles. Again the Argentine Navy pilots had to wait for a BBC bulletin to learn what they had hit. At 10.20 p.m. London time (7.20 p.m. in the Falklands and in Argentina) the news was released:

> During the last hours we have heard of further attacks on our ships. One of our ships of the Task Force has been badly damaged and early reports are that she is in difficulty. Rescue operations are in progress. I have no further details at present.

In fact the report referred to the loss of *Coventry*, bombed by Argentine Air Force aircraft earlier in the afternoon, but its vagueness led the navy pilots to believe they had hit a major British warship, perhaps even one of the aircraft carriers. The vagueness of the bulletin was also such as to cause consternation in every British family with a member on one of the Task Force ships, and has been criticized in the strongest terms since. Not until 11.45 a.m. the following morning would the name of the lost ships be revealed:

> HMS *Coventry*, a destroyer, was hit and has been lost. The *Atlantic Conveyor*, a merchant ship requisitioned to support the fleet, was also hit and has had to be abandoned. The Harrier reinforcements she was carrying for the Task Force had already been disembarked. Rescue operations to recover the crews of these two ships have continued throughout the night.

In any amphibious operation opposed by a well-equipped enemy, the loss of one or more supply ships has to be expected and even allowed for – but the destruction of *Atlantic Conveyor* and most of her remaining cargo was no less serious for that. At the time she was hit all the Harriers and Sea Harriers she had brought south had flown off, as had one Wessex and one Chinook. But after the missile detonated the smoke and fires spread so quickly that it proved impossible to fly off any of the helicopters remaining on her deck: six Wessex, three Chinooks and a Lynx. All were destroyed. Also lost were large quantities of spare parts for the aircraft she had carried, a supply of cluster bombs for the Harriers, numerous vehicles, thousands of tents, a large number of metal plates for the Harrier operating strip to be assembled ashore, and scores of other items. The fires on *Atlantic Conveyor* would burn themselves out, and for a time there were hopes that it might be possible to salvage some of her cargo, but the ship was to founder on the 30th before this could happen.

Some accounts have suggested that the loss of *Atlantic Conveyor* denied British forces a further deck from which Harriers and Sea Harriers could operate, but this is not so. From her small strengthened foredeck the aircraft had to take off vertically, and could do so only when lightly laden and when the sea was comparatively calm. There was never any intention that fixed-wing aircraft should return to the ship: *Atlantic Conveyor* was a transporter of aircraft, nothing more.

On 25 May the Argentine Naval and Air Forces demonstrated that even though they had taken serious losses, they could still hit back hard.

During the period of the heaviest air fighting, from 21 to 25 May inclusive, according to official figures which the authors accept, the Argentine Naval and Air Force Skyhawk, Dagger and Super Étendard fighter-bomber units flew a total of 180 sorties from the mainland, of which 117 reached their designated target areas. In the course of the action nineteen Skyhawks and Daggers were destroyed, a loss rate equal to one in nine of the sorties dispatched, or one in six of those which reached the target area. Comparing both sides' records, the authors believe the causes of these losses to break down as follows: twelve to action by Sea Harriers; five to surface-launched missiles and gunfire; one shared between ship's fire and a Sea Harrier; and one shot down in error by Argentine gunners. Following the withdrawal of the Mirage fighters on 1 May, and the relegation of the Canberras to night attacks only, these and previous losses reduced the effective anti-shipping force on the mainland to half its strength at the opening of the conflict.

In return the raiders had been able to sink a destroyer, two frigates and a supply ship, and inflict damage on a further destroyer, two frigates and two supply ships with hits by bombs which failed to explode.

It is now clear that the ship's missiles and the ground Rapiers inflicted fewer losses on attacking aircraft than had at first been supposed: a total of five fighter-bombers. But to judge the effectiveness of an air defence system solely on the number of aircraft it shoots down is to miss the essential point. The primary purpose of air defences is to protect targets; if in the process of securing that aim enemy aircraft are shot down, that is a bonus. By forcing aircraft to make fleeting attacks from very low altitude, the ship and shore missile systems played a vitally important role in protecting the targets; it is significant that of the bombs which struck ships in or immediately outside San Carlos Water, none detonated as intended.

In combat the effectiveness of an air arm can be measured against several different yardsticks. Of these one of the most important is the rate at which it can mount sorties against an enemy. During the critical period 21–25 May the two British aircraft carriers flew some 300 Harrier and Sea Harrier sorties with an average of thirty aircraft; during the same period the Argentine Navy and Air Force flew only 180 fighter-bomber sorties, just over half as many sorties, though they had more than twice as many aircraft. The Harriers and Sea Harriers flew an average of two sorties per day per aircraft during the five-day period, a remarkable feat which speaks volumes for the maintainability of the aircraft and the skill and sheer hard work of those who kept them flying. 'We had a good spares back-up so there was no cannibalization, there were no "hangar queens" [aircraft remaining in the hangar for want of spares, providing components for the others]. And because the aircraft serviceability was very high so was the morale of the maintainers; they were seeing their aircraft flying like hell and achieving kills, they weren't spending hours in the hangar trying to fix aircraft that would come back with the same faults after a couple of flights,' explained Lieutenant Commander Neil Thomas, who flew with No. 800 Squadron. Of course, aircraft can maintain high rates of flying if pilots can be talked into taking them up with systems inoperative; but this was not the case with the Sea Harriers. 'We weren't flying loads of rubbish,' Thomas continued. 'I never flew without a serviceable radar, and on 95 per cent of the missions my navigational equipment was running fully too. We were carrying very few unserviceabilities, and none to do with the weapons system.'

In the absence of effective radar early warning cover, the Sea Harriers' interception tactics in the defence of the San Carlos beachhead can be described as 'pre-Battle of Britain': the fighters were forced to adopt a highly inefficient system of standing patrols, with only a small proportion of their number in position at any one time, trying to catch raiders on their way to or from the target area. In the majority of cases where attackers were intercepted, the initial pick-up of enemy aircraft was visually, by the Sea Harrier pilots themselves; it was unusual to receive close control from a ship during this phase of the action (a notable exception was on the 24th, when Auld and Smith received direction from HMS *Broadsword* when they brought down three Daggers).

Certainly there would have been far more interceptions had it not been for the effective Argentine use of broadcast reports from the Falklands of the positions of the Sea Harrier patrols. The decoy attacks by requisitioned civilian aircraft of the Fenix Escuadron had little effect; although their approach in full view of the ship's radars caused great apprehension, because fuel was always tight the Sea Harriers could not allow themselves to be drawn to the west to investigate such contacts.

As the pace of events on and around the Falklands rose to a climax, work was in full swing in Britain to produce specialized items of equipment, and adapt items already in service, for use by the Task Force. Now several such projects were nearing completion after being rushed through by the departments concerned.

One of the most remarkable 'rush jobs' for the Falklands operation was a self-protection radar jammer, built into the under-fuselage gun pod of the Harrier and unofficially codenamed 'Blue Eric'. Built by staff at the Marconi Space and Defence Systems works at Stanmore in close co-operation with RAF electronic warfare experts, this jammer went from the initial discussion stage, through prototyping, testing on the ground and in the air, and production of nine converted gun pods, during a period of just two weeks between 7 and 21 May. It was a remarkable feat, and showed what could be done when it was possible to circumvent peacetime bureaucratic procedures: in normal times it would have taken at least two years to get such a piece of equipment into service from the time of the initial proposal.

'Blue Eric' was one of the new items of equipment fitted to each of four Harrier GR 3s flown to Ascension Island towards the end of May, where they were held as reserve aircraft until required by No. 1 Squadron on *Hermes*. These aircraft were also fitted with the ALE-40 cartridge dispenser system for chaff and infra-red decoys.

Another device being hastily prepared for operations by the RAF was the Shrike anti-radiation missile, an American weapon designed to home on transmissions from enemy radars. With the effective Argentine use of their radars on the Falklands, both to locate the Royal Navy carriers and also to provide warnings to enable incoming transport aircraft and fighter-bombers to avoid the Sea Harrier patrols, it became a matter of the utmost importance to destroy these radars. At Waddington Vulcan bombers were hastily modified to carry a pair of Shrikes; and at Wittering a Harrier was being adapted to carry these weapons also.

To provide the Harrier GR 3s with a precision-attack capability against targets on land, RAF Hercules transports parachuted to the Task Force kits with special noses and tails, to convert ordinary 1,000-pound bombs into Paveway laser-guided weapons. Although laser-guided bombs had been in service for some time with RAF Buccaneer units, the weapon was entirely new to the Harrier force. No. 1 Squadron would have to learn to operate the weapon during actual attacks on enemy positions.

Up till now the Nimrods had been unarmed during their lengthy and hazardous reconnaissance missions off the Argentine coast. Now, to provide the aircraft with a limited self-protection and anti-Boeing 707 capability, a few were modified with racks for two Sidewinder missiles under each wing. News of this was deliberately leaked to journalists in the hope that it would reach the Argentine Air Force, and possibly cause fighter pilots to be wary in approaching Nimrods and Boeing 707s to cease their long-range reconnaissance operations.

All these systems would become available to the British forces in the South Atlantic during the next two weeks, though in the event not all would see action.

By the evening of 25 May some 5,500 British troops and 5,000 tons of supplies and equipment had been landed at San Carlos. Now the build-up phase of the amphibious operation was complete; all was ready for the break-out from the beachhead and the advance towards Port Stanley itself.

7: To Goose Green and Beyond

26 MAY – 7 JUNE

'While the battles the British fight may differ in the widest possible ways, they have invariably two common characteristics – they are always fought uphill and always at the junction of two or more map sheets.'

Field Marshal Sir William Slim

26 MAY

On the morning of the 26th leading elements of the British commando and paratroop units began moving out of the San Carlos beachhead: the epic 'yomp' across the Falklands had begun. No. 45 Commando, Royal Marines, started towards Douglas Settlement on the north coast; 3rd Battalion the Parachute Regiment made for Teal Inlet to the west; No. 42 Commando set off in the direction of Port Stanley itself; and 2nd Battalion the Parachute Regiment moved south towards the settlements at Darwin and Goose Green.

During the day No. 1 Squadron put up seven Harrier sorties in support of the advance, but the ground troops made little contact with the enemy and the attack aircraft had difficulty finding suitable targets. The only mission to achieve any success was a pair led by Squadron Leader Jerry Pook during the early afternoon. With Flight Lieutenant Mark Hare he carried out an armed reconnaissance of the Mount Kent area and – not far from where the two pilots had destroyed three helicopters on the morning of the invasion – found a Puma on the ground. Pook despatched it with cluster bombs.

The only other event that day related to the air war occurred later that afternoon, with the arrival ashore of the sole Chinook helicopter to survive the attack on *Atlantic Conveyor*. Known to all

as 'Bravo November' after its radio callsign, the Chinook was met
by the small No. 18 Squadron ground party at Port San Carlos.
The detachment commander, Squadron Leader Dick
Langworthy, reviewed the position. He had one complex modern
helicopter, two four-man crews, nine technicians, and ten other
men to support the unit. But all spare parts, special tools and
servicing manuals had been lost on *Atlantic Conveyor*. Langworthy
resolved to get as many flights as possible out of the helicopter,
but it did not require a hardened pessimist to see that the unit's
chances of achieving anything were slim. As Chief Technician
Tom Kinsella in charge of the servicing team recalled:
'Everybody thought we would be back on board ship in a couple
of days. "Bravo November" was bound to go unserviceable, and
that would be the end of our time ashore.'

The significant point about the Chinook is its size. The next
largest helicopter type ashore was the Sea King, and at the time
there were only twelve of those from No. 846 Squadron. The Sea
King's maximum load is 4 tons, but the Chinook can carry three
times that amount. With the force ashore desperately short of
helicopter lifting capacity to sustain the advancing troops, for as
long as it could be kept flying the single Chinook would represent
a significant proportion of the whole.

27 MAY

That morning clear skies allowed Learjets of Photographic
Escuadrón I to carry out a second high-altitude reconnaissance of
the beachhead, and return with pictures of the British positions.

Meanwhile, No. 1 Squadron's main activity was to fly close air-
support missions for the paratroops advancing on Goose Green
and Darwin. Shortly after midday Squadron Leader Bob Iveson
and Flight Lieutenant Mark Hare arrived in the area to attack
reported enemy positions, but these were well camouflaged and
on the first run through neither pilot saw any target. 'On the
second pass we dropped our cluster bombs on a company position
with troops dug in, then we went out again and came back to beat
them up with our cannon,' recalled Iveson. 'After the third attack
run I was letting back down to low level, passing through about
100 feet on the way down, when there were two bangs very close
together. The whole aircraft shook and things went "pear-

shaped" very quickly after that. The controls ceased to work, the nose started to go down – and there wasn't very far to go to the ground at that point! I pulled the jet nozzle lever back to use vectored thrust to pull the nose up; in fact it didn't lift it, but at least it stopped the nose from dropping further. Then flames started to come into the cockpit so I reached down for the ejector seat handle and pulled it, thinking, "Now it's up to Martin Baker!" [the makers of the ejector seat].'

Almost certainly Iveson's aircraft had been hit by the 35 mm Oerlikon guns at Goose Green, the same weapons that had destroyed the Sea Harrier there three weeks earlier. As the ejector seat fired the pilot involuntarily closed his eyes; he felt a violent thump beneath him then a tumbling sensation. 'The tumbling stopped, I opened my eyes, and saw I was travelling horizontally not far off the ground. The aircraft must have hit the ground or exploded in the air almost immediately after I left it, because there was a big ball of fire right in front of me. Then my main parachute opened and I started to go down,' the pilot commented.

Normally a parachutist will swing round under the canopy until he is sideways on to the direction in which the wind is blowing, so that the shock of landing can be absorbed in a sideways tumble. Bob Iveson had no time for such refinements, and struck the ground immediately afterwards in the worst possible position: facing in the direction the wind was blowing him. His toes touched first, followed by his knees, stomach, chest and face. Dazed and winded, he released his parachute then felt his body to check there were no major injuries. Initially he could not focus properly, and this gave rise to an immediate problem: 'I looked up and saw a line of dots on the next hillside, about half a mile away, coming towards me. I could see only blurred images but thought they might be Argentine troops so I dropped everything, including my survival pack, and stumbled over the moorland as fast as I could in the opposite direction.' It took Iveson several minutes to regain his full sight, and when he did he saw no sign of enemy ground forces. There were a lot of sheep about, however, and in retrospect he feels sure these were the 'Argentine troops' he thought he had seen.

While Iveson was sorting himself out, Lieutenant Mariano Velasco was leading a pair of Skyhawks of Grupo 5 off the ground at Rio Gallegos, briefed to attack the equipment dump around the old refrigeration plant at Ajax Bay on the west side of San Carlos Water, photographed by the reconnaissance Learjets. The pilots picked their way past the defences and achieved complete surprise in the target area as they ran in and released their bombs.

As one of the very few empty buildings, and certainly the largest in the beachhead area, the refrigeration plant had been pressed into use by British forces as an equipment store, cookhouse and hospital complex; because of its general use and the fact that ammunition was stored around, the building bore no red cross. Chief Technician 'Hank' Hankinson of the RAF bomb disposal team was in the building when the attackers struck. 'There was an almighty great bang and we all dropped to the ground,' he recalled. Two bombs had struck the plant, one near a queue of men waiting to be fed; five were killed and twenty-six injured. 'There were dead people on the ground, an ammunition dump nearby on fire, and people milling all over the place,' he continued. While the task of extinguishing the fires went ahead, those of the wounded who could be moved were taken outside.

Velasco's Skyhawk did not long survive the attack. As the two raiders sped out of the target area gunners on the assault ships *Fearless* and *Intrepid* engaged with 40 mm Bofors, and one of the 2-pound shells struck the leader's wing. Velasco managed to cross Falkland Sound, but with his hydraulic system damaged and the rear of the aircraft on fire it was clear he would never make it to the mainland. He ejected over West Falkland between Fox Bay and Port Howard and landed with a sprained ankle.

Back at Ajax Bay a further legacy of Velasco's attack was discovered: four unexploded bombs, two lodged in the refrigeration plant and two some way from it. The bombs in the open were soon detonated with controlled explosions and caused no further problem. Those in the building were another matter, however. Members of the Royal Air Force bomb disposal team examined the weapons and identified them as 400 kg parachute-retarded bombs of French design; nobody knew what types of fuse they carried nor, in the immediate future, was there any way of finding out.

The unexploded bombs posed a painful dilemma for the commander of the bomb disposal unit, Flight Lieutenant Alan Swan, who had to decide what should be done next. Both bombs had landed close to the operating theatre, where there were wounded from both sides who could not be moved; and with major surgery in progress, the doctors and staff of the operating teams could not leave the building either. Even for the patients that could be moved there were problems, for there was no other building in which to put them; and with night temperatures outside falling below zero there was a grave risk that many of the wounded would die of exposure. One of the bombs was lodged in a steel refrigeration unit, and to expose it would have required some five hours' work with oxy-acetylene cutting equipment – which the bomb disposal team did not have. For Swan there was a stark choice: either he could order the evacuation of everyone possible from the building so that his team could try to defuse an unknown type of bomb, with all the risks of accidental detonation that implied; or the bombs could be left where they were in the hope that neither was fitted with a delayed action fuse.

Swan decided on the second course, but now had to live with it. The walls around the bombs were shored up with sandbags then, putting on a display of confidence to reassure the doctors and patients, Swan and his team agreed to bed down in the part of the hospital nearest the bombs. With the bomb disposal experts prepared to stake their own lives on the correctness of the decision, the rest of those working in the hospital resumed their normal task of tending the wounded. Each hour that passed without an explosion confirmed the rightness of the course adopted, and in fact the bombs never did go off. Afterwards, however, Swan admitted that he was a good deal less certain about his decision than he allowed others to realize at the time. 'We were not as happy about things as all that,' he later explained. 'There was always a possibility that one or both of the bombs would have gone off. After all, two of them had detonated, why shouldn't the other two?' For this and other acts of bravery during the conflict, Alan Swan later received the Queen's Gallantry Medal.

Some 15 miles to the south of Ajax Bay was Bob Iveson, trying to evade capture after ejecting from his Harrier near Goose Green. With darkness approaching he noticed the vanes of a wind-driven generator sticking above a hill in front of him, and as he breasted the rise he saw a farmhouse beside it. He was making his way towards the building when he heard the distinctive note of a helicopter coming in his direction from Goose Green, and beginning to search for him using a searchlight. Iveson hid in a patch of heather, and after a few minutes the crew gave up the hunt and returned to Goose Green. It was dark when the pilot reached the house. There was no sign of life so he tried the door, found it open, and went in. The house had been lived in but there was nobody there: there were beds and sleeping bags, even food in the larder – here was a survival kit far better than the one he had dropped when chased by 'Argentine soldiers'. From one of the upstairs windows he could see the land battle in progress as paratroops advanced on Goose Green, supported by the regular booms from guns on land and out to sea. Feeling very lonely, Iveson got into one of the beds and went to sleep.

Some 30 miles west of Iveson, Mariano Velasco had the same basic problem, though without any habitation close to hand. He too could hear the bombardment of Goose Green and, much nearer, a Royal Navy frigate shelling Argentine positions near Port Howard. Despite increasing pain from his swollen ankle, he continued walking towards Fox Bay.

28 MAY

Throughout the night of the 27th/28th, British paratroops continued their advance towards Goose Green, and by first light the leading elements were about 2 miles to the north. With the coming of dawn, however, it became clear that the paratroops were facing an enemy far stronger and better equipped than they had been led to expect. And for much of the day rain and low cloud in the area would prevent No. 1 Squadron's Harriers giving support.

The low cloud and poor visibility were less of a problem for the slower and more manoeuvrable Pucarás, and at intervals throughout the day these appeared over the battle area in twos and threes to make harassing attacks on the advancing British troops. The actions were far from one-sided, however, for the paratroops fought back with small arms and Blowpipes whenever enemy aircraft came within range. Almost all the Pucarás took hits from small-arms fire, but the Argentine pilots considered Blowpipe the real menace. 'With the gunfire our planes would return to base with holes, but the Pucará proved able to take quite heavy battle damage. We had two engines so we could return with one shot out. But a hit from a Blowpipe was another matter; it would always destroy sufficient of the aircraft to make it unable to continue flying,' commented Lieutenant Juan Micheloud of Grupo 3.

Able to make only fleeting attacks against infantrymen dispersed in the open, the Pucarás had little effect against the advancing troops. 'They did not fuss the manoeuvre companies, though clearly they were a major threat to the gun line,' commented Major Chris Keeble, who had taken command of the paratroop battalion after the death of Colonel 'H' Jones early that morning. Against helicopters, however, the Pucarás could be deadly. Throughout the day marine and army Scout helicopters had been busy supporting the battle, moving up ammunition and flying out the wounded. Late in the morning Pucarás caught a couple of these and shot down one, killing the pilot, Marine Lieutenant Richard Nunn, and his crewman. The other Scout, skilfully handled by Captain Jeffrey Niblett, evaded several attacks and was finally able to escape.

By late afternoon the paratroops' advance had ground to a halt just outside Goose Green itself. And still the Pucarás came in to attack. From his command post on Darwin Hill, just over a mile to the north of Goose Green settlement, Chris Keeble watched a couple of these aircraft sweep in and drop napalm tanks which narrowly missed forward troops. As they pulled away he saw Marine Strange stand up and, ignoring the enemy fire around him, launch a Blowpipe at one of the aircraft and guide it in to hit. The Pucará pilot, Lieutenant Hugo Argoñaraz, knew nothing of the attack before the missile impacted. 'I felt the aircraft judder, then I saw it was on fire and I knew it had been hit by a Blowpipe. Suddenly there I was, with no control over the aircraft at only 10–15 metres [30–50 feet] above the ground! I was able to eject safely.'

During the day Grupo 3 lost another Pucará near Goose Green, to small-arms fire, and its pilot was also able to eject. A third aircraft, piloted by Lieutenant Miguel Gimenez, went missing after being in action there; it may have crashed into high ground while returning to Port Stanley in cloud. A naval Macchi 339 from Port Stanley also tried to intervene and was shot down by a Blowpipe; its pilot was killed.

None of these attacks caused the paratroops casualties, but as that menace passed Major Chris Keeble had other worries to occupy his mind. 'The first problem was that as we closed on Goose Green from three directions, we had insufficient ammunition left to clear the settlement that evening. I didn't want to fight amongst houses at night,' he explained. 'The second problem was that they had at least three 35 mm anti-aircraft guns shooting at us in the direct fire role, from the tip of the peninsula. The third problem was that they had an artillery battery somewhere and we had been unable to locate it during the battle. We couldn't be accurate enough with our own artillery in the counter-battery role, because we couldn't actually see their guns and we were worried about hitting civilians in the settlement.' The answer, as Keeble saw it, was an immediate air strike, and his requests took on a new note of urgency.

Earlier in the day No. 1 Squadron had flown an armed reconnaissance of Douglas Settlement in support of the marines advancing in that direction, and a bombing mission against Argentine positions near Mount Kent. The weather around the carriers deteriorated throughout the afternoon, until by the time Keeble's urgent request arrived they were pitching in near gale-force winds under a low cloud base. Squadron Leader Peter Harris and Flight Lieutenant Tony Harper were tasked for the mission; when he heard about it Squadron Leader Jerry Pook volunteered to go as well. The three Harriers approached Goose Green from the north-north-west, descended to low altitude, and made their way down the side of Grantham Sound. The pilots were briefed on their targets over the radio by Captain Kevin Arnold, the forward air controller with Keeble's headquarters. Harris now learned of the use of the 35 mm guns against the paratroops – 'a highly unsocial act', as he later put it. The Harriers were to hit these weapons and any others seen on the distinctive promintory on the eastern side of the settlement.

The Harriers arrived to find the cloud base had lifted slightly in the target area, as they accelerated to maximum speed. 'As we ran in at 50 to 100 feet the whole area was as one would expect a battlefield to look. We could not see any people, but there was a lot of smoke and several fires burning. Target acquisition was easy because the promontory at Goose Green is such a unique feature. I could see some activity, though at high speed it was

The first encounter between British and Argentine aircraft occurred on the morning of 21 April about 1,300 miles south-southwest of Ascension Island, when Lt Simon Hargreaves, in a Sea Harrier of No. 800 Squadron, intercepted a Boeing 707 of Grupo 1 on reconnaissance. Hostilities had not yet reopened and the two sides restricted themselves to taking photographs of each other. *Above* (1), Hargreaves' picture of the Boeing. *Below* (2), view of the Sea Harrier from the Boeing, after Hargreaves had moved into close formation on it

The operation to re-take South Georgia. *Above* (3), the Victor crew of No. 55 Squadron who carried out the initial radar reconnaissance of the island: from left to right, Sqn Ldr John Elliott, captain; FO Dick Evans, co-pilot; Sqn Ldr Alistair Beedie, navigator; Sqn Ldr Mike Buxey, navigator; Flt Lt Ray Chapple, air electronics officer; and Sqn Ldr Tony Cowling, radar reconnaissance expert. *Below* (4), the crew of the Wessex helicopter from No. 737 Squadron, operating from HMS *Antrim*, who performed so notably during the rescue of the SAS men from Fortune Glacier in a blizzard and made the attack which crippled the submarine *Sante Fe*: left to right, Lt Chris Parry, observer; Lt Cdr Ian Stanley, captain; Sub-Lt Stewart Cooper, second pilot

The 'Black Buck' missions flown by Vulcans against targets in the Port Stanley area involved a round trip of 7,860 miles and were the longest range operational bombing missions ever flown. *Above* (5), Flt Lt Martin Withers of No. 50 Squadron landing at Ascension on the afternoon of 1 May after the first of these attacks. *Left* (6), Withers pictured immediately after his flight, which lasted more than fifteen and a half hours

Above (7), a fuel dump on fire at Port Stanley airfield after the 1 May Sea Harrier attack, photographed by Lt Cdr Neil Thomas of No. 800 Squadron. The only Sea Harrier damaged in the operation was that flown by Flt Lt Dave Morgan of No. 800 Squadron, *left* (8), which had a 20 mm cannon shell hit its fin. Morgan went on to become the top-scoring Sea Harrier pilot of the conflict, having destroyed two Sky-hawks and two Puma helicopters, and had a share in the destruction of an Augusta 109 helicopter

Mirages of Grupo 8 pictured at Rio Gallegos during the conflict; each carries two 375-gallon fuel tanks under the wings, which greatly restricted manoeuvrability at medium and low altitude. The aircraft *above left* (9), also carries a Matra 530 radar semi-active missile under the fuselage. The one *above right* (10), has Matra Magic infra-red homing missiles under the wings. *Left* (11), Flt Lt Paul Barton (left) and Lt Steve Thomas of No. 801 Squadron, who engaged a pair of Mirages of Grupo 8 on the afternoon of 1 May, destroying one and inflicting serious damage on the other. Thomas went on to destroy two Daggers of Grupo 6 on 21 May

Above (12), a lightly laden Skyhawk of the 3rd Naval Fighter and Attack Escuadrilla about to be catapulted off the Argentine carrier *25 de Mayo*. *Below* (13), deck crew on the *25 de Mayo* about to load 500-pound Snakeye retarded bombs on aircraft of the unit on the afternoon of 1 May, in preparation for the air strike on British warships planned for the following morning. Because of light winds over the deck the attack could not be launched, however, and the bomb in the foreground never set out for its intended destination. Note the light colouring of the Naval Skyhawks, which would make them vulnerable to attack from Sea Harriers later in the conflict.

Following the failure to launch the air strike on 2 May and the sinking of the cruiser *General Belgrano* later that day, the *25 de Mayo*, *above* (14), cruised in coastal waters for a few days then disembarked her aircraft and returned to Puerto Belgrano where she spent the rest of the conflict. In contrast, the two British aircraft-carriers operated their jet aircraft throughout the conflict almost regardless of weather conditions thanks to the flexibility conferred by the Harrier. In the picture *below* (15), *Hermes* is seen transferring fuel to the frigate *Broadsword* while steaming down-wind with her lifts lowered; even in this condition her Sea Harriers could have landed on or taken off, however.

Above (16), Super Étendard pilots of the 2nd Naval Fighter and Attack Escuadrilla, the unit which exerted a pressure on Royal Navy operations during the conflict out of all proportion to their numbers: from left to right, Lt Mariani, Lt Barraza, Lt Cdr Agotegaray, Cdr Jorge Colombo (commander), Lt Cdr Bedacarratz, Lt Cdr Curilovic, Lt Cdr Francisco, Lt Collarinco, Lt Mayora. *Below* (17), ground crew fitting an Exocet missile to a Super Étendard at Rio Grande. *Top right* (18), a Super Étendard about to leave for a mission, carrying an Exocet under the starboard wing, a 132-gallon tank under the fuselage and a 242-gallon tank under the port wing. *Right* (19), a Neptune of the 1st Naval Reconnaissance Escuadrilla, which guided the Super Étendards on to their target during the initial attack *Bottom right* (20), HMS *Sheffield* pictured shortly after the Exocet struck on 4 May

Above (21), Port Stanley airfield photographed after the attacks by the Vulcan and Sea Harriers on 1 May and the Vulcan on 4 May. The initial bomb from Flt Lt Withers' stick hit the centre of the runway; the remaining bombs cut a swathe of destruction running, south-west from that point. Sqn Ldr Reeves' bombs narrowly missed the western edge of the airfield. *Below* (22), the SAS passed this way: the airstrip on Pebble Island after the SAS attack on the night of 14–15 May. The two aircraft, a Turbo-Mentor on the left and a Pucará on the right, appear to be intact but have been made unusable by small demolition charges set off in the cockpits

Above (23), a Victor tanker of No. 57 Squadron passing fuel to a Nimrod 2; the latter type had been hastily modified for in-flight refuelling during the conflict

Above (24), Wing Cdr David Emmerson, the Nimrod detachment commander at Ascension, who flew on the record-breaking reconnaissance missions made by this aircraft. *Left* (25), Sea Harriers of No. 809 Squadron and Harrier GR 3s of No. 1 Squadron on the deck of *Atlantic Conveyor*

During the conflict there were numerous hastily introduced modifications to British aircraft. *Above* (26), an ALQ-101 jamming pod pictured after its removal from the improvised rack under the starboard wing of a Vulcan. *Below* (27), a Blue Eric radar jammer, which fitted into a modified Harrier gun pod. *Top right* (28), a Shrike radar homing missile fitted to a Vulcan. *Right* (29), and *bottom right* (30), the Sidewinder infra-red homing missile fitted to the Nimrod 2 and the Harrier GR 3

Argentine Air Force attack aircraft which took part in the conflict. *Top left* (31), Canberras of Grupo 2; the bomb in the foreground is a British 1,000-pounder. *Left* (32), a Dagger of Grupo 6. *Bottom left* (33), a Pucará of Grupo 3 at Port Stanley; the underwing pods held 2.75-inch rockets. *Above* (34), Skyhawks of Grupo 5, on their way to a target, taking on fuel from a KC-130 Hercules tanker of Grupo 1. *Below* (35), a Skyhawk of Grupo 4, carrying a British 1,000-pound bomb, taking on fuel on the way to its target

Above (36), HMS *Invincible* with Sea Harriers and Sea King anti-submarine helicopters on her deck and, amidships, a Lynx with Exocet decoy equipment at immediate readiness. *Below left* (37), Lt Cdr 'Sharkey' Ward, commander of No. 801 Squadron, who shot down a Pucará, a Dagger and a C-130 Hercules; the first two of these fell during the intensive fighting on 21 May. *Below right* (38), Lt Cdr Mike Blissett of No. 800 Squadron. *Right* (39), Blissett landing his Sea Harrier on *Hermes* on the afternoon of 21 May, after the action in which he shot down a Skyhawk of Grupo 4; note the empty starboard missile rack

Above (40), HMS *Ardent*, listing and abl
aft and with her crew abandoning ship,
following repeated hits by bombs durin;
attacks on the afternoon of 21 May. *Lef*
(41), Cdr Peter West, *Ardent's* captain

Above (42), Lt Clive Morell of No. 800 Squadron leaving his aircraft on the afternoon of 21 May, following the action in which he shot down Lt Cdr Alberto Philippi of the 3rd Naval Escuadrilla, *below left* (43). Philippi, who had led the final attack on HMS *Ardent*, ejected from his Skyhawk. *Below right* (44), Clive Morell pictured after the conflict, following his promotion to Lieutenant Commander

Harrier GR 3s of No. 1 Squadron go into action from HMS *Hermes*. *Far left* (45), three aircraft, each carrying three 1,000-pound bombs, prepare to get airborne soon after dawn on 24 May; these were part of the striking force of two Sea Harriers and four Harrier GR 3s which delivered a co-ordinated attack on Port Stanley airfield. *Above* (46), a Harrier GR 3 at readiness for an armed reconnaissance mission, carrying a reconnaissance pod under the fuselage and two BL 755 cluster bombs under the wings. *Left* (47), the weapon the Argentine troops hated: a BL 755 bomblet; 147 of these, with noses and tails folded for stowage, were housed in each bomb container

San Carlos Water – 'Bomb Alley'. *Above* (48), a Dagger of Grupo 6 sweeping through the anchorage at low altitude on the morning of 24 May, photographed by Sub-Lt Phil Dibb on the ammunition ship *Fort Austin*. In the background can be seen the supply ship *Stromness* and the bow of *Resource*. None of these ships was hit. *Below* (49), Lt Juan Arraras of Grupo 5 in his Skyhawk on the ground at Rio Gallegos after a mission. He was killed over Choiseul Sound on 8 June, when his aircraft was one of three shot down by Sea Harriers of No. 800 Squadron

Above (50), a Learjet 35A of Grupo 2, one of the aircraft which carried out a high-altitude photographic reconnaissance of San Carlos Water on 25 and 27 May. *Below* (51), blast and splinter damage to a Skyhawk of Grupo 4 which returned to Rio Gallegos, caused by a shell or missile warhead exploding nearby. Such major damage was usually repaired by cannibalizing other damaged aircraft for components

Above (52), the man who hit the *Coventry*: Ensign Jorge Neuvo of Grupo 5 pictured in the Skyhawk he was flying when he attacked the destroyer on the afternoon of 25 May. His bombs blew a large hole in the ship's port side and she capsized soon afterwards – *below* (53), a Sea King and a Wessex are picking up survivors while the frigate *Broadsword* waits nearby to receive them

Above (54), the container ship *Atlantic Conveyor* burning herself out, pictured on 26 May, the day after the Exocet missile struck her. *Below left* (55), Lt Cdr Roberto Curilovic, who led the pair of Super Étendards which attacked the British task group, leaving his aircraft at Rio Grande after his return from the mission. *Below right* (56), RAF Sgt Steve Hitchman, who was trapped below decks on the container ship and was lucky to escape with his life

Above (57), one of the twin-barrelled 35 mm Oerlikon anti-aircraft guns operated by the Argentine Army at Goose Green, pictured soon after its capture by British forces. During the conflict these particular guns shot down a Sea Harrier and a Harrier GR 3; they also probably accounted for both of the Argentine Air Force Skyhawks shot down in error in that area. *Below* (58), Sqn Ldrs Jerry Pook (left) and Bob Iveson of No. 1 Squadron. Iveson's Harrier GR 3 was shot down by these guns while he was attacking positions near Goose Green; he ejected and evaded capture. Pook took part in the textbook close air-support mission which silenced the guns after they had been used against advancing British paratroops

Above left (59), HMS *Plymouth* photographed through the gunsight of one of the Daggers of Grupo 6 which attacked her in Falkland Sound on the afternoon of 8 June. Note the cannon shells whipping up the water on the far side of the ship and the bomb hole at the rear of the funnel. *Above right* (60), damage caused by a bomb which pierced the funnel without exploding. In all, four bombs hit *Plymouth*, none of which exploded. One set off a depth charge on her flight deck, however, and this started a serious fire. *Below* (61), *Plymouth* withdrew to San Carlos Water, where her damage control teams extinguished the blaze

Above (62), a Sea Harrier getting airborne from 'Sid's Strip', the forward operating base immediately to the west of Port San Carlos. Made of aluminium matting, it was constructed in less than a week on unprepared ground with no heavy equipment by men of the Royal Engineers. *Below* (63), view of Mount Longdon taken from Flt Lt Mark Hare's Harrier GR 3, during the reconnaissance mission on the morning of 10 June. The aircraft was flying towards the right of the picture and the Argentine soldier on the left was trying, unsuccessfully, to bring his Blowpipe missile launcher to bear on the aircraft as it sped past

Above (64), a Harrier GR 3 parked on HMS *Hermes*, fitted with two Paveway laser-guided bombs. *Left* (65), Wing Cdr Peter Squire, the commander of No. 1 Squadron, who used these weapons to knock out an Argentine headquarters position on Mount Longdon on the morning of 13 June

Helicopter types which played a vitally important role supporting the British Task Force. *Top* (66), a Sea King, in this case an anti-submarine version belonging to No. 826 Squadron; other Sea Kings operated in the transport role. *Above* (67), a Lynx general-purpose helicopter, seen here carrying a Sea Skua anti-ship missile. *Below* (68), 'Bravo November', the only Chinook of No. 18 Squadron to survive the loss of the *Atlantic Conveyor* and operate on the Falklands during the conflict

Above (69), one of the Scout helicopters which, flown by Army or Marine pilots, operated in the forward areas flying in ammunition and taking back wounded. *Below*, two helicopter pilots decorated for their part in rescue operations: *left* (70), Lt Cdr Hugh Clark, the commander of No. 825 Squadron with Sea Kings, who was awarded the Distinguished Service Order for, amongst other things, his part in the *Sir Galahad* rescue operation; *right* (71), Capt. Sam Drennan, a Scout pilot with No. 656 Squadron Army Air Corps, awarded the Distinguished Flying Cross for repeatedly returning to rescue wounded troops under fire on Mount Tumbledown on the morning of 14 June

The last man back (72): Flt Lt Jeff Glover of No. 1 Squadron, who was taken prisoner after his Harrier GR 3 was shot down near Port Howard on 21 May, pictured on his return to RAF Wittering on 10 July

impossible to identify it exactly, and dropped my cluster bombs on the easternmost point,' Harris recalled. 'As I let go my bombs I saw activity to my right so I told Tony Harper to put his cluster bombs there; he just had time to re-align his attack and put his bombs to the right of mine and about 300 yards behind.' As Harper cleared the target Jerry Pook ran in from the north and fired two pods of 2-inch rockets – a total of seventy-two – at the part of the promontory not covered by the bursts of exploding cluster bomblets. The attack had come as a complete surprise to the Argentinians, and the pilots saw no return fire.

From his vantage point on Darwin Hill Chris Keeble watched the Harriers do his bidding. 'They came streaking in, one behind the other; each dropped bombs, some on the tip of the peninsula and others at the entrance of the isthmus. Then I heard the cluster bomblets going off, their explosions merging together; it looked as if some hit the sea – there was an effect like throwing gravel into water. Then came the rockets, which were most effective; they hit the tip of the peninsula where the 35 mm guns were,' he recalled. 'The attack gave a great boost to the morale of our troops. I think some of them thought the Harriers had come in a bit too close for comfort, but that is war.'

Harris's attack was a textbook example of a close air-support mission: a hard-hitting surprise attack against a target of great importance to the enemy, launched at a crucial time in the land battle, whose results were clearly seen by the ground troops – thus strengthening the resolve of those on one side and demoralizing those on the other.

Chris Keeble has no doubts about the decisiveness of the Harrier attack: 'After that there was a marked slackening in the fighting, which had gone on very fiercely the whole day. Afterwards I sat down and thought, "Where have we got to now? What is the enemy thinking?" I tried to assess the situation from his point of view. Now he was encircled and we had demonstrated that we could bring in the Harriers to attack his positions surgically. It was then I began to get the notion that their will had broken and maybe we could go for a surrender.'

After dark the fighting ceased, as the two sides broke contact to take stock of their situations. Early the next morning Keeble would open negotiations with his Argentine opposite numbers at Goose Green and later accept the surrender of the garrison there.

To the surprise of the paratroops, it turned out that the force they had outfought was more than twice as large as their own and amply supplied with ammunition and weapons.

29 MAY

During the day poor weather restricted air operations by both sides. No. 1 Squadron, now down to four Harriers, put up only four sorties during the day; two hunted unsuccessfully for radars reported to the north of Port Stanley, the other two carried out a rocket attack on positions on Mount Kent. Late in the afternoon Argentine aircraft appeared briefly over San Carlos Water but failed to inflict damage; a Dagger of Grupo 6 fell to Rapier.

Throughout the previous day Squadron Leader Bob Iveson had remained hidden in the gorse near 'his' house (Paragon House, 8 miles west of Goose Green), listening to the battle in progress to the east; at night he returned to the house and slept there. Now the firing had stopped and, ignorant of the outcome of the fighting, he decided to leave the house again on the morning of the 29th and head north to try to link up with British troops. Wrapped in a blanket to keep out the bitterly cold wind, he had not gone far when a hail shower forced him to return.

Still loose on West Falkland, Iveson's fellow ejectee Lieutenant Mariano Velasco had spent almost the entire day walking towards Fox Bay with a sprained ankle that was becoming increasingly painful. Shortly after midday on the 29th he came upon a farmhouse which, like Iveson's, had nobody in it but had recently been occupied and contained food and drink. Velasco decided to spend the night there to give his ankle a chance to recover.

On that day *Invincible* lost one of her Sea Harriers in an unusual accident. As Lieutenant Commander Mike Broadwater of No. 801 Squadron was preparing to take off in very bad weather, the ship went into a tight turn and healed over. The aircraft slid across the wet, slippery deck and fell over the side. As it was on the point of going over Broadwater ejected, and was rescued from the sea shortly afterwards. Not even the Sea Harriers could operate in such conditions with impunity.

The only other air action took place far to the north-east of the Falklands, where the 15,000-ton ship *British Wye* carrying fuel for the Task Force came under attack by a modified C-130 Hercules of Grupo 1 about 830 miles due east of Buenos Aires. The improvised bomber released eight bombs; only one struck the tanker, and it bounced off without exploding.

30 MAY

With an improvement in the weather, there was a resurgence of air activity around the Islands. No. 1 Squadron mounted six Harrier sorties against targets near Mount Kent, Mount Round and Port Stanley, and during one of these lost another aircraft. Briefed to attack enemy helicopters reported on the ground west of Port Stanley, Squadron Leader Jerry Pook and Flight Lieutenant John Rochfort were approaching from the south when they came under fire from a column of Argentine troops. Pook heard a 'clunk' as his aircraft was hit, but everything seemed all right and the Harriers continued on to the target area. There they found none of the reported helicopters, but Rochfort found an artillery position and both pilots attacked it with rockets.

As the aircraft climbed away to return to *Hermes* Rochfort noticed fuel streaming from his companion's Harrier. Initially Pook was not worried at the discovery: 'I had plenty of fuel at that stage so I could afford to lose a bit. But the leak turned out to be far more serious than I thought. At the top of climb I levelled out, and by then the fuel gauges were whistling down. I think the hit must have been on the main fuel line to the engine. I jettisoned the empty drop tanks and rocket pods, but even though it was free of this extra drag it was clear the aircraft was not going very far,' he later explained. Pook managed to get within 30 miles of the carrier before the pointers of the fuel gauges fell ominously close to zero. Mindful of the need to get out of the aircraft while he still had full control, Pook descended to 10,000 feet and ejected.

From an aircraft the sea usually appears calm, even inviting. But as Pook descended on his parachute the waves took on a quite different appearance: there was a force 5 wind, which whipped up the sea into frequent 'white horses'. As the pilot splashed into the water the wind grabbed his parachute and started to drag him across the surface; then, fortunately, he descended into a trough which collapsed the canopy and allowed him to release the harness. Pook inflated his dinghy and pulled himself into it, and no sooner was he on board than a rescue Sea King arrived to pick him up. He had been in the water for less than ten minutes and emerged from the incident with nothing worse than a stiff neck, and some very minor facial burns caused by the detonation of the explosive cord in the Harrier's canopy as he ejected.

At the same time as Jerry Pook was on his way back to *Hermes* in one helicopter, another was bringing back Bob Iveson, who had been picked up that morning. For No. 1 Squadron this was a day of thanksgiving.

Even as the two Harrier pilots were on the way back to their ship, the latter came under threat once again: carrying the remaining air-launched Exocet missile, a Super Étendard of the 2nd Escuadrilla took off from Rio Grande piloted by Lieutenant Commander Alejandro Francisco. Flying with Francisco was another Super Étendard with no missile, in case the lead aircraft suffered a radar failure; accompanying them were four Skyhawks of Grupo 4 of the Air Force, each loaded with two 500-pound bombs, which were to follow the missile's smoke trail towards the target then launch their own attack – lacking search radar, Skyhawks operating alone stood little chance of finding enemy ships in open water. On the way to the target the aircraft took fuel from a KC-130 Hercules tanker near Isla de los Estados just off the mainland, and again to the south of West Falkland. As before, the force approached at low altitude, aiming for the point just east of where the Harrier and Sea Harrier tracks disappeared off the radar at Port Stanley; on this occasion, to achieve surprise, it was planned to attack the British ships from the south-east.

Soon after 2.20 p.m. the Super Étendards picked up radar signals from British ships, turned towards their source, and ran in to attack. At about 2.30 Francisco pulled up his aircraft, acquired a target on radar, and launched his missile. The two Super Étendards then turned back for their base, leaving the four Skyhawks to follow the Exocet's smoke trail towards the target. Lieutenant Ernesto Ureta, piloting one of the Skyhawks, described what he saw next: 'The four A-4Cs went in together – Captain José Vazquez, Captain Omar Castillo, myself and Ensign Geraldo Isaac – with two 500-pound bombs on each aircraft. In the event we did not follow the Exocet far because we arrived at the target just thirty seconds after it was launched – we had been told the target was 15 miles away when it was fired.

Only two of us made it to the ship; Vazquez and Castillo were downed by missiles, probably Sea Darts,' he continued. Ureta now caught sight of what he took to be an aircraft carrier and made straight for it. 'The attack was made from about 30 degrees off the ship's stern. I released my bombs, and after flying directly over and away from the carrier I made a turn and confirmed that my bombs had hit. I can confirm that the carrier was hit by the Exocet, because I saw the thick black column of smoke rising from it. So I am sure it did hit.'

These are the grounds for the Argentine claim to have inflicted serious damage on HMS *Invincible* during this action, a claim that would be repeated by Buenos Aires several times in the months following the conflict. What really happened?

First, it is clear from British records that an Exocet attack was launched against the main Task Group that afternoon, at a time that links closely with the Argentine account. The action centred not around the aircraft carriers, however, but the destroyer *Exeter* and the frigate *Avenger*, which chanced to be some 20 miles south of the main force on their way to the Falklands to carry out a bombardment and land special forces that evening. Both ships picked up the Super Étendard's radar signals in good time and put up chaff rockets to decoy away the missile. This process was repeated throughout the Task Group. *Exeter* then engaged two aircraft flying at low altitude with Sea Dart, and shot down both. *Avenger* claimed to have engaged the Exocet missile with her 4·5-inch gun and destroyed it at a range of 8 miles; if this was the case it was a remarkable piece of shooting, with a weapon which achieved little against slower and larger aircraft targets throughout the conflict. Whether because of that or because it had been decoyed by chaff, the missile exploded clear of any British ship.

So what ship did Ureta attack and see smoking? Almost certainly it was *Avenger*, which reported having been attacked by a pair of Skyhawks whose bombs narrowly missed her. At the time visibility was not good; it would be easy for a pilot approaching at low altitude to mistake a frigate from 30 degrees off the stern, and showing her helicopter landing pad, for the aircraft carrier he expected to see. From the air ships often appear larger than they really are. The 'thick black column of smoke' Ureta saw rising from the ship would have been funnel smoke as she manoeuvred at high speed, to which would be added smoke from her chaff rockets, the 4·5-inch gun, and probably the odd Sea Cat missile. One thing is certain, however: no British ship suffered damage during the attack.

The authors have examined the evidence to suggest that Francisco had mistakenly launched his unit's last Exocet at the drifting hulk of *Atlantic Conveyor*, which sank on this day. Although some published accounts have given this story credence, it is clear that the vessel was some distance from the scene of the action when she foundered.

After the Super Étendards and the depleted force of Skyhawks landed on the mainland, their pilots could only sit and wait for the BBC to confirm the success of their attack. But the confirmation never came, and this in itself was construed as a pointer that the Royal Navy had suffered so serious a loss that it had to be kept secret.

Meanwhile, back on the Falklands, the Chinook helicopter 'Bravo November' had completed her third day of operations: now moving ammunition, 10 tons at a time, to the guns in the forward positions and Argentine prisoners, sixty at a time, from Goose Green to Port San Carlos. 'That aeroplane went on day after day with bits going unserviceable; but the engines kept going, the rotors kept turning, and she continued to do the job,' commented Squadron Leader Dick Langworthy.

That evening there was to be a more arduous task for 'Bravo November', and one which nearly resulted in her destruction. An SAS patrol had discovered that the Argentine Army had withdrawn most of its troops from Mount Kent, the important feature some 10 miles west of Port Stanley which dominates the surrounding countryside. After dark three Sea Kings of No. 846 Squadron took off from Port San Carlos and flew K Company of No. 42 Commando to take the position; then Langworthy followed in the Chinook, carrying two 105 mm guns and twenty-two men in the fuselage, with a further 105 mm gun slung underneath. In each helicopter the pilots wore night-vision glasses fixed to their flying helmets, to enable them to navigate close to the ground in the dark.

Langworthy took the heavily laden 'Bravo November' in low, keeping the ridges of Wickham Heights, Rocky Mountain and Smoko Mount on his right to lead him to his objective. The weather made flying difficult, with the occasional snow shower which reduced visibility almost to zero and forced the pilot to climb to a safe height, then let down again when he was able to see. The flight from Port San Carlos to Mount Kent took about half an hour, but it was when the Chinook arrived that the crew's problems really began.

'We had been led to believe that the ground on which we were to land would be relatively flat. Only when we arrived did we find it was on a sloping peat bog flanked on either side by stone rivers. We put down the underslung gun, no problem at all. Then we had to position the other two guns quite accurately in relation to the first; and when Dick landed the Chinook the back end sank into the peat so that we couldn't lower the ramp even with hydraulic pressure,' explained Flight Lieutenant Tom Jones, the senior crewman in the rear of the helicopter and responsible for directing the unloading operation. Langworthy raised the Chinook a few feet, the exit ramp was lowered, and the helicopter was landed again for a second attempt to get the guns out. Just as this was happening, a brisk fire-fight broke out between the SAS men covering the landing area and a company of Argentine troops to the north-east. At the same time the red dim-lighting system in the helicopter's rear cabin fused, plunging the unloading operation into darkness pierced only by the shielded beams of hand torches kept low to avoid drawing enemy fire. Under these conditions the men toiled to wheel out the 2½-ton guns, their orders shouted above the noise of the engines and turning rotor blades, and everything done to the accompaniment of tracer rounds flashing past on one side.

Finally the guns were off-loaded and Langworthy lifted the helicopter off the ground and started back for Port San Carlos, giving the developing battle a wide berth. But the worst part of the mission was still to come. As the Chinook ran out at low altitude it flew into a snow shower much thicker than any encountered earlier and, as the pilot later commented, 'The problem with night-vision goggles is that they don't work in snow.' Blinded for a few all-important seconds, Langworthy allowed the helicopter to descend, and suddenly the machine shuddered as it struck something hard. Nobody realized it at the time, but the Chinook, moving forwards at about 100 m.p.h., had hit the surface of one of the creeks to the west of Mount Kent. At the time of impact the helicopter's nose was well up, and the flat-bottomed Chinook skidded across the water like a giant surfboard. The impact threw up a cloud of spray, which flooded down the intakes of the two rear-mounted engines causing them to lose power. As this happened the hydraulic power assistance of the controls gave out, making it all the harder to control the machine.

Later Langworthy made light of what he jokingly termed 'the water-skiing trials in the Chinook', but at the time disaster was close at hand for him and his crew. 'When we hit the water it slowed us up a bit. The co-pilot jettisoned his door, then I shouted at him to come on the controls with me. We both heaved on our collective pitch levers to increase the pitch of the running-down rotor blades, and that did the trick. The helicopter lifted just clear of the water, the spray ceased, and the engines started to wind up again. I suppose we were on the water for about twelve seconds,' Langworthy recalled.

When the Chinook struck the water Tom Jones, standing in the rear cabin, was thrown to the floor and his flying helmet was torn off his head. At the same time the co-pilot's door fell clear with the result that the engine and rotor noise in the rear of the helicopter was much louder and quite different from normal. Jones thought his end had come. 'I heard the engines starting to run down, I was just waiting for the aircraft to disintegrate around me. I opened the cabin door so that I could get out quickly after the crash. I had resigned myself to death, but it seemed not to come. Then I heard a very odd noise [after the co-pilot's door had gone], which I interpreted as the helicopter starting to break up,' he recalled. 'I thought to myself, "Better jump out!" But first I glanced at the other crewman in the rear; he was down the back holding on and beckoned me to put on one of the spare flying helmets.' Jones thought that perhaps the other crewman knew something he did not; and he was right. By the time he was back on intercom Jones was shocked to learn that the helicopter from which he had been about to leap was in the climb and then passing 1,500 feet!

No longer able to navigate using ground features, in a damaged aircraft – though to what extent he had no way of knowing – Langworthy had decided to return to Port San Carlos at medium altitude. But now a further problem arose: before he could enter the missile-defended area he needed to get clearance for the change in the flight plan, but he could get no reply to his repeated radio calls. Finally Langworthy put out an emergency call and switched on all the helicopter's lights. 'We hoped people would realize that no Argentine aircraft would dare to fly into the missile zone as high as we were and lit up like that, and we had to be on their side,' Jones explained. 'We couldn't get any reply on the radio, but fortunately the people on the ground were hearing us. As we approached the airstrip at the settlement they put on the lights for us.'

It was a very subdued crew that stepped out of the Chinook after it landed at Port San Carlos. In the darkness Tom Kinsella made a careful inspection of the helicopter and found it had suffered remarkably little damage. Apart from the loss of the co-pilot's door, there was some denting of the fuselage caused by the door as it fell away and damage to the rear loading ramp caused during the scramble to get the 105 mm guns out. 'After that incident we felt nothing was going to stop "Bravo November" keeping going for the rest of the war!' commented Tom Kinsella.

31 MAY

While Dick Langworthy had been struggling to get his Chinook back to Port San Carlos, yet another Vulcan bomber was on its way to the Falklands from Ascension Island. This time the targets were the Argentine early warning radars around Port Stanley, and the aircraft carried two Shrike radiation-homing missiles under the wings. Apart from some trouble with turbulence at one of the refuelling points, Squadron Leader Neil McDougall of No. 50 Squadron reached the target area without difficulty. Like its predecessors the Vulcan approached the airfield at Port Stanley from the north-east at low altitude, then started to climb to 16,000 feet to make its attack run. Closing on the town in full view of the search radars, the bomber had a couple of Argentine gun control radars lock on to it but the aircraft was safely above the reach of their fire. Flight Lieutenant Rod Trevaskus, the air electronics officer, released a few bundles of chaff 'to keep their interest'.

McDougall and his crew had been briefed on where the long-range radars were expected to be, including one close to houses in Port Stanley itself. 'We had to be absolutely certain we did not attack the radar near Port Stanley. That one was off limits, all the others were fair game,' the pilot commented. To be certain his attack did not endanger any Falklanders, McDougall had to fly a complex pattern over the area to establish which radar he could attack. This done, he headed towards it from the north-west until he was within firing range, then dropped the Vulcan's nose, while Trevaskus in the rear fired two Shrikes four seconds apart. 'It was a moonlit night. We could see Port Stanley quite clearly, there were lights on in the town. The missiles went off – it was just like watching rockets on November 5th – then they disappeared into a patch of cloud below. We were listening to the radar beam sweeping through us, on our warning receiver,' McDougall recalled. 'Suddenly there was a flash on the ground, at the same time as the navigator who was timing the flight of the missile to impact said "Now!". And the radar signals ceased. So far as we were concerned either they had been bloody quick in switching their radar off, or we had hit it. I did not see the second missile explode, but the co-pilot thought he saw the flash as it went off beneath the cloud.'

It would appear that the Argentine operators had indeed been 'bloody quick' in switching off their radar at the last moment, because the set escaped serious damage. McDougall turned away for Ascension, and landed eight hours later without further incident.

During the day there was little Argentine air activity over the Islands. No. 1 Squadron put up seven Harrier attack sorties, concentrating on targets in the area around Port Stanley. Meanwhile, every British transport helicopter in the area was working flat out during the daylight hours, 'humping and dumping' supplies to the marine and paratroop units as they advanced eastwards.

1 JUNE

While it was dark that morning four Canberras of Grupo 2 ran in at high altitude to attack targets in the Port San Carlos area. Lieutenant McHarg of No. 800 Squadron was scrambled to intercept. He got within 4 miles of one of them before the bomber, heading west, dropping chaff and infra-red decoy flares and taking violent evasive action, managed to run the Sea Harrier short of fuel and escape.

After dawn the day was dull and overcast, and the poor

weather provided excellent cover for Argentine transport aircraft running the blockade to take in supplies to Port Stanley. On its return flight that morning a C-130 Hercules of Grupo 1 flown by Captain Ruben Martel popped up north of San Carlos Water to make a brief radar sweep of the area for British shipping. 'They were trying to find the enemy fleet to aid the attack aircraft; it was an extremely dangerous thing to do,' explained Lieutenant Colonel Alberto Vianna, who was one of Martel's commanders; the pilot carried out the search on his own initiative.

Although they were now making little contact with enemy aircraft, the Sea Harriers patrolled over the Islands almost as frequently as during the height of the fighting. As the Hercules rose above the radar horizon some 20 miles north of San Carlos Water, it was observed on the search radar of the frigate *Minerva*, which was operating as air control ship that day. Immediately Lieutenant Commander 'Sharkey' Ward and Lieutenant Steve Thomas of No. 801 Squadron, on patrol in the area, were vectored to intercept. As the fighters approached both were short on fuel; in San Carlos Water the assault ships *Fearless* and *Intrepid* were ordered to clear their helicopter decks in case the Sea Harriers needed to land on them to refuel afterwards. Thomas described the interception: 'Sharkey picked the aircraft up on radar; by then it was heading west. We thought it might be a C-130 because of its low speed. Sharkey went down through the cloud layer to engage, I stayed above it at 3,000 feet in case the aircraft had top cover. Then Sharkey called that he had a Hercules in sight at a range of about 6 miles, and I went down to join him. I emerged from cloud to see a missile leaving his aircraft, and out in front I could make out the Hercules at about 200 feet going flat out,' he recalled. Being short of fuel Ward had fired his missile at extreme range, just too far from the target as it turned out. 'The missile was about to hit the aircraft when suddenly it dropped away and fell into the water. By then Sharkey was much closer and he fired a second, which hit between the engines on the starboard wing, which immediately burst into flames. Still the aircraft kept going, so Sharkey went in closer still and emptied his guns into it. The Hercules went into a descending turn out of control to starboard, the wing struck the sea, and it cartwheeled and broke up.' Ruben Martel and the other six members of his crew were killed. Never again would Grupo 1 hazard one of its aircraft in this way.

By now, after the losses of the previous twelve days, No. 1 Squadron was down to only three Harriers, but that afternoon it received two much-needed replacements. Flight Lieutenants Murdo Macleod and Mike Beech arrived on *Hermes* after 8 hour 25 minute flights direct from Ascension Island, each supported by four Victor tankers. These were not the longest flights by the type ever made – the Harriers flown direct from England to Ascension a month earlier held that record. But the operation, conducted beyond the reach of land airfields along most of its length, was a remarkable test of both the Harrier and the Royal Air Force pilots' training. The helicopter carrier *Engadine* was positioned about halfway along the route in case one of the Harriers got into difficulties, but she was not needed. Neither pilot had landed a Harrier on a deck previously. Later Macleod said he regarded the beginning as the worst part when, in the 85°F temperature of Ascension, he had to board the aircraft wearing thick pile underwear and a rubberized immersion suit in case he was forced down in the cold waters of the South Atlantic. Once airborne Macleod found boredom the big problem, though this was relieved to some extent by playing music on the Harrier's built-in tape deck normally used to record training missions. 'My main sustenance during the trip were the Brandenburg Concertos,' he later commented. 'They came over in my earphones in glorious Lo-Fi, but it was a fairly pleasant way to pass the time.' The two Harriers put down on *Hermes* early in the afternoon; No. 800 Squadron's diarist noted: 'Two sore-arsed crabs arrived on board' (crab is the derogatory Royal Navy term for members of the RAF).

Although bad weather precluded all except one low-altitude sortie by No. 1 Squadron, the Sea Harriers continued their medium-altitude patrols over the Islands. Towards the end of the afternoon No. 801 Squadron lost one of its aircraft to ground missile fire. Flight Lieutenant Ian Mortimer was on armed reconnaissance south of Port Stanley, flying at 13,000 feet and keeping an eye open for Pucarás or transport aircraft trying to get into or out of the airstrip. He noticed movement on the ground near the runway and moved a little closer to investigate. It was an error which very nearly proved fatal. Suddenly Mortimer saw a flash on the ground and the trail of a missile: a Roland coming in his direction. At the time the Sea Harrier was over the sea about 7 miles due south of Port Stanley, and the pilot felt sure that he was beyond its reach. 'As I saw the missile coming up leaving a light grey smoke trail I turned away, put my nose up, and tried to out-run it. At no stage did I think it would hit me, I was convinced I was beyond its range and it would fall short. It passed out of my view underneath the aircraft a couple of thousand feet below, and I looked down over the nose fully expecting to see the missile reappear on the other side still below and fall away into the sea,' he recalled. 'The next thing I knew was an almighty great explosion at the rear of my aircraft. The thing I remember most was the incredible violence of it all, as the cockpit with me in it began to tumble through the sky. I pulled the handle of my ejector seat within half a second of the hit; I think I was probably upside down when I emerged from the cabin.'

The ejection seat functioned perfectly, and Mortimer had a ten-minute parachute descent before he splashed into the sea. He inflated the dinghy and climbed aboard, then released his parachute. Using his emergency radio he broadcast a brief call: 'Mayday, Mayday, Mayday, Silver Leader, shot down by Roland 5 miles due south of Stanley', and heard an answering call in English before he switched off to prevent enemy stations getting a bearing on his signals. Shortly afterwards a helicopter and a twin-engined aircraft came out from Port Stanley to look for him, concentrating their search in the area immediately underneath where the Sea Harrier had been hit. During the parachute descent the strong breeze had carried Mortimer some 5 miles east of the point of impact, however; now he could only sit quietly in his dinghy, his radio beacon off, and hope the Argentine pilots would not think of looking in his direction. When the two aircraft began moving in his direction Mortimer broadcast another brief call: 'Any Sea Harrier in the area, there are two targets at low level 5 miles south of Stanley.' This time he felt sure he had been seen: the twin-engined aircraft flew right over him and turned, and the helicopter came straight towards him. Then, almost together, the pair turned and raced back to Port Stanley, having been warned by radio of Sea Harriers approaching the area.

Again alone, Mortimer bailed the water out of his dinghy, took a couple of seasickness pills, and prepared for the night, which was now drawing on. After dark he switched on his locator beacon for two minutes each half hour, certain that the carriers would

send helicopters to look for him. Shortly after midnight he heard
the rotor beat of an approaching helicopter and switched on his
neon strobe light to mark the position. 'I was not absolutely
certain it was a British helicopter. But I was getting awfully cold;
I was at the stage where I was not too fussed who picked me up so
long as somebody did. After nine hours in the dinghy I was
beginning to envisage myself floating around in the South
Atlantic for the rest of my days – which looked like being one and
a half!' he explained. 'Within thirty seconds the helicopter had its
searchlight on and was coming towards me. I could make out the
shape of a Sea King against the dark sky, a grand sight and
getting better by the minute. The next thing I knew was this
grinning Irish face coming towards me on the end of a cable: my
mate Leading Aircrewman Mark Finucane from *Invincible*'s No.
820 Squadron.' The helicopter crew soon had Mortimer on
board, then the Sea King sped back to the carrier with the very
grateful pilot.

Also during 1 June Lieutenant Mariano Velasco, the Skyhawk
pilot shot down at the same time as Bob Iveson, was finally picked
up by Argentine troops and taken to Port Howard.

2 JUNE

There was very little flying on this day due to poor weather over
the Argentine mainland bases, the aircraft carriers, and the
Falklands. One of the few operational missions took place during
the afternoon, when airlifted paratroops advanced 30 miles in two
hops. The move began early in the afternoon when Major John
Crosland led a party of twelve paratroops, carried in three Scout
helicopters, to seize Swan Inlet House 15 miles east of Goose
Green; and from there by the simple expedient of telephoning
ahead, he was able to establish that the Argentine troops had
pulled out of Fitzroy Settlement, 15 miles to the east.

Once that had been done, preparations were made to fly in two
companies of paratroops from Goose Green to seize the high
ground overlooking Fitzroy. To lead in the Chinook and its
valuable cargo, Captain John Greenhalgh and Sergeant Dick
Kalinski flew their Scouts into the landing area first. 'We took off
ten minutes before the Chinook and flew to Fitzroy to make sure
the area was clear of enemy troops. Once there we carried out a

low-level observation and reconnaissance as a pair, leap-frogging from piece of ground to piece of ground to make sure it was clear. In this way we searched an area 5 miles by 5 miles within about ten minutes,' Greenhalgh commented.

While Greenhalgh and Kalinski were conducting their search the Chinook was following with eighty-one paratroops crammed into its fuselage. Flight Lieutenant Tom Jones, senior crewman in the helicopter, described the scene: 'The paras were doing what we euphemistically call "strap hanging" – except that there were no straps to hang from. The seats were folded against the sides of the fuselage; the men were standing up and had to carry their weapons because there was no room to put them on the floor; the troops were packed in so tightly they could hardly turn around. It was worse than a tube train in the rush hour.' By any normal criteria the helicopter was grossly overloaded, but the crew contented themselves with the knowledge that if the Chinook could lift off the ground in the hover with the huge load, it could carry it in forward flight. The only real problem was poor visibility, as Flying Officer Colin Miller, the helicopter's co-pilot and responsible for the navigation, commented: 'The weather was very bad, there was low cloud on the hills. The visibility was about 2 miles and the cloud base was down to 200 feet in places. I had to navigate using ground features, but the peaks of the hills could not be seen as they were all in cloud.' Some 5 miles to the west of Fitzroy Greenhalgh and Kalinski met the Chinook and led it to the landing area they had chosen. There Flight Lieutenant Dick Grose landed the large helicopter briefly, and within a quarter of a minute the paratroops had scrambled out and started to take up defensive positions.

Having put down his first load Grose returned to Goose Green and picked up a further seventy-five paratroops, which he also landed near Fitzroy. Now, in addition to Mount Kent, the British troops held a second important position within 10 miles of Port Stanley. In view of what would happen later, it should be pointed out that this had been a highly risky operation. Had the Chinook passed over an Argentine position on either of its flights to Fitzroy the helicopter might have been shot down with the loss of all on board – there had been no time to carry out a reconnaissance of the route. It could have resulted in the greatest loss of British lives in a single incident during the conflict. In war such risks sometimes have to be taken to shorten the fighting and prevent greater loss of life in the long run. In the event, the paratroops reached their objective safely in 'Bravo November'.

The other event of significance to the air war that day was the completion of several days' work by the Royal Engineers to construct a Harrier operating strip at Port San Carlos. The strip provided a 285-yard runway for take-offs, and a 23-yard square pad for vertical landings. Originally there was to have been parking space for a dozen Harriers, but following the loss of a large quantity of aluminium plating on *Atlantic Conveyor* the parking area was reduced to that sufficient for four aircraft. Wing Commander Fred Trowern, the senior Royal Air Force liaison officer on the Falklands, described the difficulties of building the strip: 'It was made by hand, from plates each about 10 feet long and 2 feet wide, slotted together. The helicopters flew them in, in bundles, then they had to be laid out by hand. The individual strips were damned heavy – it was as much as two men could do to lift one – and if you were not careful you could cut yourself on the edges. It was hard physical labour, carried out while the area was liable to attack from the air and the weather was very cold, wet and miserable.' The forward operating base was immediately nicknamed 'Sid's Strip' after Squadron Leader Sid Morris who commanded it. It would be a few days before the weather relented sufficiently to allow it to be used, however.

3 JUNE

Still the weather over the Falklands and the Argentine southern bases was poor and there was little flying. The sole offensive air action over the Islands was an air strike by a single Vulcan, this time carrying four Shrike missiles, in a further attempt to hit the radars around Port Stanley. Again Squadron Leader Neil McDougall approached the target from the north-east at low altitude, then popped up to 16,000 feet to begin his attack. But now the Argentine radar operators knew what to expect from an aircraft behaving in this way. 'As we got to about 9 miles from Port Stanley the radars started to switch off; and as we went past and out to sea again, they came on. We went round and round repeating that process for about 40 minutes. Then, on the final run before we had to go home, I decided to go into a descent towards the airfield to tempt them into switching on the radars to have a go at us,' McDougall commented. He eased back the throttles and the bomber started to go down. 'We got down to about 10,000 feet, heading towards Sapper Hill, and sure enough one of their radars came on. Then the guns started firing at us, I saw flashes in the sky as four shells burst below me and to the right.' Meanwhile in the rear of the Vulcan Flight Lieutenant Rod Trevaskus was able to lock on two Shrikes, and launched them one after the other at the radar. As McDougall pulled up the nose of the Vulcan to avoid going too low, he saw the flash of an explosion light up the mist just above the ground. One of the missiles had impacted close to a Skyguard fire control radar, where it caused severe damage and killed three of the operating crew.

The Vulcan pulled away from the target area and headed north, but the crew's adventures were far from over. Some four hours later they arrived at the final rendezvous with a Victor tanker off the coast of Brazil, with the shortage of fuel that had become a feature of the 'Black Buck' missions. But on this occasion, shortly after McDougall made contact with the hose trailing behind the tanker, the Vulcan's refuelling probe broke and the aircraft's windscreen was drenched in paraffin before the airflow cleared it away.

Now the Vulcan was in serious trouble. Its tanks were almost dry, there was no possibility of taking on further fuel in flight, and the nearest usable airfield was at Rio de Janeiro more than 400 miles to the west. McDougall immediately swung the nose of the Vulcan in that direction and ordered Flight Lieutenant Brian Gardner, the extra pilot on the aircraft, to collect all secret documents and target information folders and prepare to dump them. The Vulcan was still carrying the remaining two Shrike missiles, one under each wing, and McDougall had no wish to land with them still on board. He told Trevaskus to get rid of them into the sea. At the same time the co-pilot, having completed his fuel calculations, solemnly informed the crew that at the rate the bomber was burning fuel at 20,000 feet there was no way it was going to reach Rio. There was no alternative: McDougall had to climb the plane to 40,000 feet so that it could fly further in the rarefied atmosphere there.

The Vulcan had levelled out at the top of its climb by the time

Gardner had gathered the secret documents and put them in a navigator's canvas hold-all, together with a couple of hefty ground locks to ensure the bag would sink after it hit the sea. The Vulcan's cabin was depressurized, then Gardner pulled the lever to open the door on the underside of the aircraft and the bag sailed out into space. But when he tried to close the door it refused to shut properly; this meant that the cabin could not be re-pressurized. By now McDougall had declared a full Mayday emergency, but although he had radio contact with the control centre at Rio de Janeiro communication proved difficult. In the unpressurized cabin at 40,000 feet the crewmen had to breathe pure oxygen under pressure, and this had an effect on their voices similar to that experienced by saturation divers breathing oxygen and helium. 'We tried to discuss our emergency with a Brazilian but he could not understand us – which is hardly surprising, since his English was not all that good and we all sounded like Donald Ducks!' McDougall explained. Finally another controller came on the air speaking better English, at the same time as Gardner managed to close the door and the cabin was re-pressurized. Gradually their voices returned to normal.

There followed an anxious half hour as the Vulcan closed on its new destination, while the needles of the fuel gauges moved relentlessly towards the zero mark. As he neared the coast McDougall eased back the throttles to take the aircraft down to 20,000 feet, the lowest he dared go before he could commit himself to a landing. Then, he recalled, 'An American-speaking controller came up and said, "Can you see the runway ahead of you?" I said "Yes". He said, "If you're critically short of fuel you can land on that." By that time we certainly were critically short of fuel: the gauges showed about 3,000 pounds, and a Vulcan needs 2,500 pounds to do a circuit. In other words, if we missed our first approach we were going to crash, there was no doubt about it.'

At that stage the runway was about 6 miles in front of the bomber, which was flying nearly 4 miles high. Few pilots have more flying experience on the Vulcan than Neil McDougall: apart from a four-year spell as a flying instructor, he had been operating with the type since 1962. To get the aircraft safely on the ground now would require every ounce of skill and experience he had picked up during two decades of flying. McDougall pulled his throttles shut and opened the airbrakes, then wound the bomber into an almost vertical bank and took it down in a steep descending orbit. To many Brazilians who watched the impromptu performance over the outskirts of their capital, it seemed as if the bomber was about to crash. None of them can ever have seen so large an aircraft perform in so energetic a fashion. At the end of the carefully judged orbit the Vulcan was exactly where its pilot wanted it to be: about 800 feet above the ground and 1½ miles from the end of the runway. At 300 m.p.h. the aircraft's speed was too high for a landing approach, so McDougall raised the nose so that the Vulcan's huge delta wing could 'mush off' the excess speed. When he levelled out again he was at the aircraft's usual approach speed and height: 155 m.p.h. at 250 feet, three-quarters of a mile from the touchdown point. The undercarriage was lowered and from then on the landing was in every respect normal; the pilot did not even need to stream the brake parachute to bring the Vulcan to a halt on the short runway.

Afterwards McDougall would comment: 'It was not the sort of manoeuvre I would recommend anyone to use unless the situation is desperate, because if you make a mistake you are going to crash.' But the pilot did not make any mistakes; in a superb demonstration of flying skill he had saved his aircraft. For this mission McDougall would later receive the Distinguished Flying Cross.

McDougall taxied the Vulcan off the runway and shut down the engines; later he would learn there was only 2,000 pounds of fuel left in the tanks. Police immediately threw a cordon around the bomber, which was soon surrounded by a curious crowd. Leaving his crew to guard the aircraft, McDougall was taken to the Colonel who commanded the Brazilian Air Force units based at the airfield: 'We exchanged names, then he asked about the type of mission I had been flying. I said, "Sorry, Sir, I cannot tell you that until I have spoken to the British Air Attaché." He replied, "Sorry, I cannot let you speak to your Air Attaché until you tell me what you have been doing." "But I have my orders. . ." "Sorry, Squadron Leader McDougall, but I have my orders too." He said he would have to speak to higher authority, but in the meantime perhaps I would like something to drink?' The Colonel poured a couple of stiff brandies and passed one to McDougall, and the pair were exchanging pleasantries when the telephone rang. The Colonel spoke briefly in Portuguese then handed the receiver to McDougall, saying, 'It's for you!' The caller was the British Air Attaché, Wing Commander Jerry Brown, who said he would be there as soon as possible to deal with the matter.

Immediately afterwards the scene degenerated into low farce. 'As I put the phone down there was a knock on the door. The adjutant came in and spoke very quickly in Portuguese from which, even with my limited command of the language, I recognized the word "Press". Outside I could hear a commotion; the Press had arrived to interview me, en masse,' McDougall continued. 'The Colonel wanted to play the whole thing in a low key and I certainly did. He ushered me to the other door of his office and quietly we sneaked out and left the building. It was the only thing gentlemen could do in the circumstances!'

After rapid negotiations between the British Embassy and the Brazilian government, the status of the Vulcan and its crew was established. The crew could leave the country any time they wanted, but the bomber had been impounded and had to remain where it was. McDougall said he and his crew wished to remain with the aircraft, and the Colonel accepted that they had to do so. 'It was all very friendly. But if we were to stay we could not go off base because we had no passports; and we could not wander around the base because we had no uniforms. He therefore asked that we restrict our movements to the Officers' Club, the cantina and the swimming pool. If we wanted to go anywhere else we would have to be escorted (but if we asked, escorting officers were "not available"),' McDougall explained. The crew were treated well; McDougall was even able to put through a reverse-charge call to his wife Elizabeth at their home near Lincoln, to assure her that all was well. She took the news in her stride. 'It takes an awful lot to amaze my wife!' the pilot commented.

McDougall was able to insist that one of his crew be present at all times at the aircraft inside the police cordon, to prevent anyone tampering with it. Throughout, Brazilian handling of the matter was diplomatically correct, and there was no attempt to force an examination of the Vulcan's secret equipment. The Vulcan crew then settled down to make the best of things, while diplomats decided the fate of them and their aircraft.

4 JUNE

Still the weather prevented much air activity over the Falklands by either side. The sole flying over the Islands was by transport helicopters moving supplies to the ground forces. During the day a single flight-refuelled Hercules transport from Ascension dropped items of high-priority cargo by parachute beside one of the warships east of the Falklands.

5 JUNE

During the morning the cloud lifted sufficiently for the first Harriers and Sea Harriers to take off from their carriers, fly patrols, and then put down at 'Sid's Strip' at Port San Carlos to refuel. For both the fighter and the ground-attack units, the forward operating base conferred a considerable increase in operational capability. For Sea Harriers making 75-minute sorties, it meant that instead of spending 65 minutes flying to and from the operational area and 10 minutes on patrol, the aircraft now flew 33 minutes to the patrol line followed by 37 minutes on patrol – nearly four times as long as previously – followed by 5 minutes to the forward base; there they could refuel and, if they still had missiles, the process was repeated in reverse, with the Sea Harriers landing back on their carriers. In the case of No. 1 Squadron's Harriers, the pilots could wait in or beside the aircraft on the ground until the forward air controllers found suitable targets, then take off and move in at low altitude to attack; moreover, since they were now operating from a land airstrip, the Harrier GR 3s could use their inbuilt inertial navigation system to its full capability.

The first to land on 'Sid's Strip' were a pair of Sea Harriers of No. 800 Squadron piloted by Lieutenant Commander Andy Auld and Lieutenant Simon Hargreaves. Shortly afterwards they were followed by a pair of Harrier GR 3s led by Squadron Leader Bob Iveson (now back flying after ejecting from his aircraft a week earlier). That day the weather was never good, however, and No. 1 Squadron was able to mount only two two-aircraft attacks on Argentine positions.

That evening fog descended around the British aircraft carriers, making things very difficult for Lieutenant Charles

186 AIR WAR SOUTH ATLANTIC

Cantan of No. 801 Squadron when he tried to return to *Invincible* in the dark. He approached the ship using his own radar, decelerated into the hover at about 200 feet instead of the normal 70 feet, then continued on slowly towards the carrier until he saw the beam of a searchlight shining vertically from the ship; he let down through the gloom and landed with the horizontal visibility less than 50 yards. No other type of operational fixed-winged aircraft could even have attempted to land on a carrier under such conditions. As Sea Harrier pilots are fond of repeating: 'It's much easier to stop and then land on the deck than it is to land on the deck and then stop.'

6 JUNE

Once again the weather was poor, restricting air operations around the Islands. During the day a Royal Air Force C-130 Hercules delivered supplies to the Task Force. Around the British aircraft carriers the Sea Kings kept up round-the-clock anti-submarine patrols, as they had since before the fighting started. By now many of the warships had been in the combat area for more than five weeks and their crews had learned to take the attendant risks in their stride. Not so those of the warships recently arrived in the South Atlantic, which had still to overcome their initial nervousness. Vice-Admiral Woodward was heard to comment: 'Interesting to see the new arrivals like *Cardiff* reacting as we did at the beginning, producing submarine contacts every time a shrimp farts!'

7 JUNE

Finally the weather cleared to allow a full programme of sorties by the Harrier and Sea Harrier squadrons, making full use of the new airstrip at Port San Carlos. For No. 1 Squadron the main problem now was finding suitable targets; the British troops advancing on Port Stanley were having little contact with enemy forces, so the Harrier GR 3s spent much of the day on readiness at the forward base waiting for calls that never came.

The Argentine Air Force was also having problems locating suitable targets for its attack aircraft: it was eleven days since the last mission over the islands by Photographic Escuadrón I. That morning the unit's commander, Lieutenant Colonel Rudolfo De La Colina, led a high-altitude reconnaissance over the Islands by all four of his Learjets. The aircraft ran in at 40,000 feet, flying parallel tracks some miles apart to give overlapping photographic cover of the ground below. If this mission went as well as previous ones the new forward operating strip at Port San Carlos would almost certainly be detected and become a high-priority target for attack aircraft. Previous missions had not encountered Sea Dart missiles, however, and now the destroyer HMS *Exeter* was one of the warships covering San Carlos Water. Her radar operators watched the approaching reconnaissance aircraft, and when the first came within range she launched a pair of missiles.

From the Harrier operating strip Flight Sergeant Ray Cowburn, a member of the No. 1 Squadron servicing team, watched the engagement. 'There had been an Air Raid Warning Red and we were all in the slit trenches. Then there was a "swoooosh" from around the headland and we saw a couple of white smoke trails streaking upwards. One did not get very far before falling back. But the other continued on and on upwards until finally there was the puff of an explosion high in the sky. Then pieces of the flaming wreckage of an aircraft began to tumble down, fluttering like sycamore seeds.'

Captain Carlos Pena, at the controls of one of the Learjets, also watched the missile's flight: 'When it was launched there was a huge ball of fire, then we could see the missile in flight. It struck De La Colina's Learjet and exploded immediately, blowing off the entire tail section. De La Colina said on the radio very calmly, "*Me tocaron* [They've hit me]". Then the aircraft burst into flames and fell away nose first. He remained calm as the aircraft entered a spin, saying a last few words about the mission.'

Rudolfo De La Colina went to his death bravely. The Learjet had been designed as an executive jet not a combat aircraft; even had the crew had parachutes there was no way of abandoning the aircraft in flight. For nearly two agonizing minutes the remains of the aircraft with five men on board tumbled out of the sky, before the main part smashed into the ground on Pebble Island.

By the evening of 7 June British ground forces were converging on Port Stanley from the west and preparing for the final decisive actions of the conflict. During the two weeks since the Argentine successes on 25 May there had been little air activity over the

Islands from the mainland. Many considered the attacking units had shot their bolt, following the heavy losses incurred during the actions around San Carlos Water. Certainly the Argentine Naval Air Arm was able to do little more: it was down to its last two usable Skyhawks and the Super Étendard unit had expended all its Exocet missiles. But the Air Force still had a sizeable force of attack aircraft, and had been prevented from operating during the first week in June only by poor weather over its southern bases. Now, with the return of clear skies over the Falklands, the force prepared to mount further attacks in support of the beleaguered Argentine troops on the Islands.

8: The Final Actions

'Victory in war does not depend entirely upon numbers or courage; only skill and discipline will ensure it.'

Flavius Vegetius, AD 378

8 JUNE

For the second day running there were clear skies over the Islands, and the Harrier and Sea Harrier squadrons planned sorties to make full use of the forward operating strip ashore. This permitted the two British aircraft carriers to move east, out of reach of Super Étendards flying from the mainland. In fact the 2nd Escuadrilla had fired all five of its air-launched Exocet missiles and effectively disarmed itself, and Argentine attempts to purchase more of these weapons had been unsuccessful. The intelligence community was rife with rumours to the contrary, however, and prudence dictated that the air-launched Exocet still be regarded as a threat.

During the morning No. 1 Squadron sent two pairs of Harriers to operate over the Falklands; lacking suitable targets, these were ordered to land at Port San Carlos and wait at readiness there. The first three Harriers put down without difficulty. The fourth suffered a partial engine failure in the hover and struck the aluminium plating hard before it skidded to a halt. The Harrier was damaged beyond repair, and the pilot was lucky to escape with nothing worse than a severe shaking. Far more seriously the accident rendered the airstrip unusable until repairs could be carried out, and these would take several hours.

Thus a series of unrelated factors were coming together which would have decisive influence on events later in the day. Also during the morning the landing ship *Sir Galahad* arrived off Fitzroy carrying units of the Welsh Guards to reinforce the 5th Brigade, which was preparing to advance on Port Stanley. A

189

similar ship, the *Sir Tristram*, was already at anchor there off-loading ammunition. A couple of days earlier four Rapier missile firing units had been landed, but these were now disposed to protect the Brigade maintenance area near Bluff Cove three miles north of where the ships were anchored. Thus there was little protection for the ships from air attack, and the slow task of off-loading them took place in full view of the Argentine positions on the high ground a few miles away to the north-east.

Reports of the ships off-loading south of Fitzroy were passed to the Argentine command centre at Port Stanley, and from there to the mainland. Major Carlos Martinez, a Dagger pilot of Grupo 6 operating from Rio Grande, takes up the story; 'We received orders from the Comando de la Fuerza Aérea Sur [Southern Air Command] to put up six aircraft to attack troop ships at Bahía Agradable [the bay to the south of Fitzroy]. Once the order was received the ground crews began loading the aircraft with 1,000-pound bombs and pilots began planning the mission using the latest intelligence reports and information on the weather; the weather promised to be good over the mainland and in the target area.' At the same time Grupo 5 at Rio Gallegos received orders to launch eight Skyhawks in two flights against the same target.

Because they cruised at a lower speed and were to top up their tanks from a pair of KC-130 Hercules tankers on the way in, the Skyhawks were the first to take off. On this occasion the refuelling operation did not go smoothly, however. Three Skyhawks were unable to take on fuel, probably because their probes had frozen up while they were parked in the open the previous night. The designated attack leader and two other pilots were forced to turn back. Lieutenant Cachon, who had recently qualified to lead a flight but had never done so in action, was ordered to take over the lead of the Skyhawk formation. Meanwhile the Daggers of Grupo 6 had taken off and were climbing away to the east. One of their number developed an oil leak and broke away; of the initial raiding force of fourteen fighter-bombers, only ten now remained to continue the mission.

The weather forecast proved to be optimistic and the attacking forces descended to low altitude west of the Falklands to find patches of low cloud and occasional belts of rain which reduced visibility almost to zero. Cachon's first mission as formation leader was to test his skills to the utmost. 'The weight of command sent a tingle down my spine, but I calmed down when I remembered that the men with me were experienced in this type of operation and success would depend upon my leadership. The succession of check points forced me to concentrate on my navigation and as we passed Cabo Belgrano [Cape Meredith] we flew through a rain squall lasting a few seconds,' he remembered. 'Our next check point was Isla Aguila [Speedwell Island] where we passed through another belt of rain; from there we headed straight for Fitzroy. As we crossed Bahía del Laberinto [Adventure Sound] there was a downpour which lasted 30 seconds [i.e. about 4 miles across]. At the end of it I was on the point of breaking off the mission, as I feared that the rest of the island was similarly obscured. But then the rain ceased and the sky began to light up, encouraging me to continue.'

While Cachon led his force towards Fitzroy from the south-west, the five Daggers of Grupo 6 were approaching along a different route. They too had made a landfall at Cape Meredith, but from there they had headed north-east up to the western side of Falkland Sound with the intention of turning east as they passed abeam of Grantham Sound and running in to attack the target from the west. As the fighter-bombers were about to cross Falkland Sound, however, the plan went awry. Moving across the Sound and blocking their path was the frigate HMS *Plymouth*, which had just put out from San Carlos Water to bombard an Argentine position on West Falkland. The chance meeting robbed the Daggers of any possibility of surprise at their intended target and there was a hurried discussion on what to do next, as Carlos Martinez recalled: 'After seeing the frigate we accelerated so that we would have sufficient speed to penetrate any defences. Over the radio we reviewed the situation, and decided to attack the warship.'

From the bridge of *Plymouth* Captain David Pentreath had seen the fighter-bombers moving rapidly up the western side of Falkland Sound: 'They were on the deck at very low level, 2–3 miles from us. We immediately turned back towards San Carlos Water and increased to full speed. Meanwhile the aircraft went into a wide port turn at low altitude at the top end of the Sound, and came in to attack us from the port quarter.'

'We ran in to attack at 575 knots [655 m.p.h.]; the distance was less than two miles and at that speed we covered it very rapidly,'

Martinez recalled. 'As we approached the ship her anti-aircraft fire came up towards us. We replied with our 30 mm cannon but that was for psychological effect – the main thing was to get our 1,000-pound bombs on the target.' Pentreath watched the fighter-bombers closing on his ship swiftly in line astern, under fire from Sea Cat, 20 mm, and small arms but not the 4·5-inch gun – this could not be brought to bear in time. The leading aircraft released its pair of bombs, one of which smashed through the ship's funnel. 'The No. 1 scored a direct hit, the No. 2 saw the hole in the frigate,' Martinez continued. 'We didn't know whether the bomb exploded or not; we were pulling away rapidly intent on escaping.'

In all, four bombs struck *Plymouth* – and none exploded. One had gone through the funnel, causing spectacular though relatively unimportant damage; two bounced off the water before reaching the ship, smashed through the anti-submarine mortar area, continued out the side in their upward trajectories and fell back into the sea well clear; the fourth bounced off the flight deck but in passing set off a depth-charge armed in readiness for loading on the ship's helicopter. Most of the blast from the exploding depth-charge went into the air, but it started a serious fire which took some time to bring under control. Five members of the ship's crew suffered injuries during the bombing and strafing attack.

As the Daggers left the target they faced a further hazard, as Martinez recalled: 'The radar [at Port Stanley] was showing Sea Harriers 10 kilometres away, closing in to intercept. We immediately pushed up our speed to 600 knots [690 m.p.h.] to make it impossible for them to catch us. Because of cloud we climbed away individually, and rejoined formation at 35,000 feet. When we landed we found one Dagger had a gash along its drop tank, but none of the other aircraft had been damaged. This was the exception to the rule, since we lost several aircraft and very often returned with damage.' Both sides considered themselves fortunate to emerge from the encounter without more serious loss.

The Daggers sped away from Falkland Sound with a pair of Sea Harriers in futile pursuit, while Cachon's formation headed north-east along the coast of East Falkland towards the position where the enemy ships had been reported. Now there were just five Skyhawks left of the fourteen fighter-bombers that had set

out. 'We reached Puerto Fitzroy but saw nothing there. I decided
to continue on for thirty seconds, then we turned right to begin
our return flight. On the land we could see many British soldiers,
who opened fire at us,' Cachon explained. As the force was in the
turn, the leader heard a call from one of the pilots at the rear of the
formation: 'There are the ships!' Cachon glanced back toward the
shore and could make out the grey silhouettes of the landing
ships. He led the three Skyhawks at the head of the formation to
attack the *Sir Galahad* and two of the pilots saw their bombs hit.
The remaining two fighter-bombers hit the *Sir Tristram*. Freed of
the need to hug the surface or jink to avoid the accustomed hail of
anti-aircraft fire and missiles, the Argentine pilots were able to
carry out accurate attacks from high enough to give the bombs
time to arm themselves in flight. The bombs detonated and *Sir
Galahad* was immediately engulfed in flames. Troops and sailors
trapped aft began jumping into the water to get clear of the
advancing fire; others inflated rubber dinghies and boarded
them.

At the time of the attack Lieutenant Commander Hugh Clark,
a transport Sea King pilot and commander of No. 825 Squadron,
was on the ground at Fitzroy after flying in troops. He
immediately took off and made for the burning *Sir Galahad*. 'By
the time I got there the fires had started to take hold and there was
a lot of black smoke. Two of my Sea Kings were already rescuing
people from the fo'c'sle. I went to the stern and began picking
men out of the sea,' he recalled. Clark picked up two loads of
about a dozen, breaking away as soon as he had two or three
seriously injured to speed them to the shore. From start to finish it
took about a minute to winch each man up to the helicopter, so
there was no time to pull up all of those on the dinghies.

And now a new problem arose as the life rafts started to drift
back towards the blazing ship. 'There were half a dozen dinghies
packed with survivors near the stern so the immediate answer was
not to try to rescue the men from the dinghies, but rather to move
the dinghies away from the source of danger. We thought the ship
might blow up at any time; ammunition was torching off, there
were all sorts of whoomps and bangs, tracer rounds and
pyrotechnics were shooting in all directions. It really was quite
bloody awful!' Clark continued. 'So we started to blow the
dinghies away from *Sir Galahad*. We could see the rotor downwash

whipping up the surface of the sea; it was just a question of moving towards the life raft until the downwash impinged on it and started it moving, then the helicopter would follow to keep it moving.'

Much of the rescue operation involved flying through smoke and a helicopter does not, as one might suppose, clear a path for itself with its rotor; in fact the opposite is the case: the rotor disc sucks in smoke from above and draws it down past the fuselage. Unable to see the natural horizon for much of the time, the pilots had to make use of other reference points. 'The stern had the name *Sir Galahad* written on it in large letters and I used this as an artificial horizon,' Clark explained.

Everyone has seen the dramatic television film of the rescue operation around *Sir Galahad*. Gradually order was restored from chaos, the survivors were lifted from the deck of the ship or out of the water, the injured were taken from the dinghies, then the fit men were brought ashore. Even before this first phase of the rescue was complete, the second began: the helicopter shuttle to move the injured to the hospital at Ajax Bay 40 miles to the west, and from there to the hospital ship *Uganda* off the north of the Islands.

Although she would remain afloat, *Sir Galahad* was wrecked in the attack. The fire on *Sir Tristram*, though less serious, would inflict considerable damage before it was brought under control. Altogether fifty-one men were killed and forty-six injured; it was the worst single loss inflicted on British forces during the conflict. On this occasion, a calculated risk had gone disastrously wrong.

Previously published accounts have suggested that the attack on the two landing ships had been a carefully planned and executed operation, possibly co-ordinated with the attack on HMS *Plymouth* to draw away patrolling Sea Harriers and directed during the final phase from an observation post ashore or by a radar at Port Stanley. The accounts from Martinez, Cachon and other Argentine pilots make it clear that none of these suggestions is true. The meeting with the frigate in Falkland Sound had been a matter of chance; and by drawing upon herself the Daggers, *Plymouth* halved the size of the attacking force which reached Fitzroy. Far from receiving any help during their approach to the target from ground observers or radar at Port Stanley, the Skyhawk pilots had been on their own; indeed, during their initial flight past Port Fitzroy the pilots had missed seeing the ships at all. At any time the weather could have forced an abandonment of the mission and Cachon had been within an ace of calling off the attack while the raiders were still 30 miles from the target. But in spite of all of this a few of the attackers did get through, with devastating results.

The Argentine Air Force had forcibly demonstrated that it was still very much in business, but follow-up attacks on the Fitzroy area later in the day met far stronger defences and were able to achieve little. Soon after 5 p.m. Captain Cafaratti led a flight of four Skyhawks of Grupo 4 into the area, where they received a hot reception from infantrymen ashore and the re-positioned Rapier batteries. 'From the sides of the hills red fireballs came out searching for me; I thought they were going to get me. Suddenly my aircraft shuddered under the impact of what seemed like two or three hammer blows. I glanced at my temperature gauge and revolutions counter, but it seemed nothing vital had been damaged,' recalled Ensign Codrington at the rear of the formation. 'I saw no fewer than six missiles coming up towards us from the land. One exploded very close to Lieutenant Paredi's tail, another came straight for me. Instinctively I pushed on full rudder and went into a tight turn, and the missile passed under me.' All four Skyhawks had missiles explode close to them, on each occasion as the missile was at the limit of its trajectory. Codrington's and Paredi's aircraft took hits from small-arms fire and both had their tanks punctured. Very low on fuel, they managed to rendezvous with a KC-130 Hercules tanker orbiting off the mainland and plugged in; then the trio headed for Rio Gallegos with the Skyhawks taking fuel as required. Only when they had their base in sight did the fighter-bomber pilots break contact and go straight in to land.

For the remainder of the afternoon relays of Sea Harriers patrolled the skies around Fitzroy, but with the carriers far to the east and the forward operating strip temporarily out of action there were frequent gaps in the fighter cover. Dusk was fast approaching when Flight Lieutenant Dave Morgan and Lieutenant Dave Smith of No. 800 Squadron arrived in the area. As the pair flew their lengthened orbits off Choiseul Sound at 10,000 feet, columns of black smoke still rising from the burning landing ships 10 miles to the north served as a grim reminder of

the horror of war. Below the aircraft a small landing craft
emerged from the Sound; Morgan checked with his control ship
that it was friendly. The pilot then glanced back at the landing
craft, to see an aircraft low over the water some 300 yards away
streaking towards it from the south-east.

On board the landing craft, an F4 belonging to HMS *Fearless*
bound from Goose Green to Fitzroy, signalman Lance Corporal
Mark Price had just left the Land Rover in which he was
sheltering from the spray to borrow a book from one of his
comrades: 'Suddenly there was a "whoooosh" and a grey mass
came past close overhead, then a bomb exploded about 20 metres
off the stern. Then another bomb hit the craft and the next thing I
knew I was flying through the air and was thrown over one of the
trailers. That was the last thing I saw for a week.' Six men were
killed in the attack; the landing craft sank later after the survivors
had been taken off.

Morgan was already on the way down when the bombs exploded:
'I pushed my throttle forward, rolled over on my back, and went
down after him. Dave followed me. In the dive I noticed there
were two more aircraft following the first. One got a bomb on the
back end of the landing craft and it went off with a large explosion;
that made me very angry. When I was down to about 2,000 feet I
saw a fourth aircraft trailing the rest. I decided to go for him.' In
the half light Morgan thought the enemy aircraft were Mirages,
but in fact they were Skyhawks of Grupo 5. By now his Sea
Harrier was hurtling down in a power dive at just under the speed
of sound. 'I wound across and got in behind with a massive
overtaking speed. He was rapidly getting larger in my
windscreen. I locked up my missile at about 1,500 yards and fired
at 1,000 yards. My missile did a quick initial jink, then went off
after him and exploded near his tail; there was a huge fireball and
wreckage began to fall into the water,' he remembered. 'There
was no reaction at all from the others; they were in a gaggle
coming off the target, with no attempt at mutual cover.'

Still overtaking rapidly, Morgan pulled round behind a second
of the Skyhawks. Its pilot seemed to have seen either the explosion
or the Sea Harrier, because it began turning to port. Morgan
locked on his remaining Sidewinder and fired it: 'I think he saw it
coming, because he reversed his turn and broke away to
starboard. The missile reversed its turn too, cut across my nose

and went straight in and hit after he had turned through about 40 degrees. The explosion took off everything behind where the fin joined the fuselage, then the front end yawed violently and dropped into the water.'

Now there were just two left, and still the Sea Harriers were overhauling rapidly. From the rear of the stream Dave Smith observed the engagement. Later he wrote: 'I saw two bright flashes as Moggy fired his missiles. I followed the two white smoke trails and saw two huge fireballs as the Mirages [sic] disintegrated and impacted the sea. I was now in a quite dreadful situation of having several aircraft ahead and not being able positively to identify Moggy to get a clear shot. Mog then suddenly opened up on the two retreating Mirages with his cannons, and from the water kicked up by his bullets I was able to pick out one of the "bogeys".'

Having fired both missiles and all his ammunition, Morgan hauled his Sea Harrier into a vertical climb to get out of Smith's way as fast as he could; now was the rear pilot's chance: he pointed the missile he had selected at one of the aircraft in front, heard the tone in his earphones to confirm the infra-red homing head had acquired a target, then pressed the firing button. He recalled: 'There was a bright flash and a roar as the missile launched, fairly rocking my aircraft in its wake. Surely the Mirage was too low, too fast, too far away . . . I watched with a sort of helpless fascination. At that moment everything seemed to stay quite still, although in the real world my Sea Harrier was belting along at more than 10 miles a minute, a few feet above the waves. Then the darkness was lit up by another fierce flash and fireball. He must have been flying so low that the missile impact and ground impact seemed almost simultaneous.'

Flying the fourth Skyhawk, Lieutenant Hector Sanchez was a helpless spectator as his comrades went down around him; everything had happened so quickly. 'The Skyhawk behind me exploded and the No. 2 was hit squarely on the tail with an explosion that ripped the aircraft apart. The pilot ejected, but his parachute was on fire. . .' Sanchez jettisoned his fuel tanks, pushed forward his throttle and held the aircraft down to get out of the area as quickly as possible. None of the other three Skyhawk pilots survived. The Royal Navy had taken its revenge on Grupo 5, the unit whose aircraft had bombed the landing ships earlier in the day. Now very low on fuel, Morgan and Smith climbed to the east to return to their carrier. From start to finish the combat had taken less than a minute and a half.

While the brisk action was in progress, Lieutenant Commander 'Sharkey' Ward and Lieutenant Steve Thomas of No. 801 Squadron were coming from the south to join in. They saw the three fireballs in the distance as the missiles impacted but before they could close on the remaining Skyhawk HMS *Cardiff*, the control ship, warned of further enemy aircraft approaching from the west at high altitude. 'We saw them at about 30 miles, they were contrailing and they came straight for us,' Thomas explained. 'We gulped a bit at the thought of going up after those guys, we were at 20,000 feet and they were up at about 35,000. But as we got to within 10 miles they turned away; we could see their Mirage shape quite clearly.' Although Ward and Thomas did not realize it at the time, they had witnessed one of the rare appearances of air-to-air missile-armed Mirages of Grupo 8 over the Islands during this phase of the conflict; the intention was to provide fighter top cover for the attack aircraft at low level, but the high-flying Mirages remained aloof from the fighting and achieved little.

On *Hermes* No. 1 Squadron received a further two Harrier GR 3s, to restore its strength to six aircraft after the loss of one at Port San Carlos that morning. Flight Lieutenants Ross Boyens and Nick Gilchrist flew direct from Ascension Island, this time with no helicopter deck midway along the route in case they got into trouble. Boyens suffered a failure of his navigation system, but Gilchrist took over the lead and the pair reached the carrier without difficulty.

Elsewhere, the only event of note in the air war occurred well outside the exclusion zones surrounding the Falklands. The Argentine Air Force C-130 Hercules converted into a bomber by Grupo 1 went into action again, but this time with embarrassing results. The ship it attacked turned out to be a US-leased tanker, coincidentally named *Hercules*, on its way round Cape Horn in ballast. Again the bombs failed to explode, but one lodged in the ship, and she later had to be scuttled.

9 JUNE

Poor weather now returned to the Argentine mainland bases in the south, while over the Falklands the skies were clear enough to permit air operations. By first light the forward operating strip at Port San Carlos was usable again. Operating from both the strip and the carriers, No. 1 Squadron flew four sorties against enemy gun positions on Sapper Hill and Mount Longdon. In each case the positions were well defended and the Harriers faced intense fire from the ground. Flight Lieutenant Murdo Macleod's aircraft was damaged, but the seriousness of the damage did not become evident until he was about to land on *Hermes*. 'I did not know I had been hit until I was turning finals. I selected undercarriage and flaps down, but in the cockpit I did not get the usual indications that they had come down. So I went round again and asked Flyco [flying control] where everything was. He told me my wing outriggers were halfway down but the main wheels were still up. I operated the emergency system to blow the undercarriage down and landed normally,' he recalled. 'There were six or seven holes in the aircraft and the hydraulic lines in the wing and fuselage had been cut. The holes were from shell splinters mainly on the top surfaces; we had been flying very low. . .'

During this phase almost every available British transport helicopter was working flat-out to bring supplies and ammunition to support the advance on Port Stanley: the Sea Kings of Nos. 825 and 846 Squadrons, the Wessex of Nos 845, 847 and 848 Squadrons, and the lone Chinook of No. 18 Squadron. The main route was between the forward supply area at Teal Inlet Settlement and the guns and positions around Mount Kent: a 30-mile round trip, taking about forty-five minutes with loading and off-loading and made fifteen or more times per day per helicopter and crew. In the case of the Sea Kings, the main work horses, the usual load was a 2½ to 3-ton underslung pallet of ammunition. 'With the underslung loads we were operating at close to our maximum permitted all-up weight, so there was not much power margin,' explained Lieutenant Commander Hugh Clark who commanded No. 825 Squadron. 'There were some moments of excitement with the wind over the mountains – severe turbulence, down draughts, the sort of nasty things you get in those areas. If you hit a down draught with a load on you had to turn down the hill to try to get out of it. If things got really bad you would have to jettison the load, though we never had to do that.'

An ex-fighter pilot himself, Squadron Leader Dick Langworthy felt extremely vulnerable to attack from the air while flying the Chinook on these missions. 'There was nowhere to hide, we stuck out like a dog's balls. We were very worried about attack from the air, we craned our necks the whole time. In a Pucará I could have shot down any helicopter, no trouble whatsoever. Had I been the Argentine squadron commander I would have said to my guys: "Their advanced troops are here, their base is there; in between will be helicopters, go and shoot them down!" They could have had a field day against our helicopters,' he explained. 'But I never saw anything of enemy aircraft in the air; the only Pucarás I saw were lying on the ground wrecked.'

10 JUNE

Again the weather was bad over the southern mainland bases but good over the Falklands. No. 1 Squadron sent a pair of Harriers to the forward operating strip, where they waited at readiness throughout the morning, but the forward troops had little contact with the enemy and there were no requests for air strikes.

Also during the morning Wing Commander Peter Squire and Flight Lieutenant Mark Hare flew a reconnaissance in front of the advancing British forces, immediately to the west of Port Stanley. The Harriers crossed the coast near Fitzroy then split: Squire flew east, then almost due north to take him hard against the western edge of Port Stanley itself; Hare flew north-east past the important features of Two Sisters and Mount Longdon. With cameras clicking at regular intervals the aircraft took in the scene around them, though for the pilots there was little to see as they ran through at maximum speed: the Argentine static positions were very well camouflaged. 'I didn't see anything,' Hare later commented, 'When you are on photographic reconnaissance you concentrate on flying as low as you can and missing the ground by as little as possible. It was mid-morning, my heading took me almost straight into the sun. So flying was difficult, I was concentrating on the "staying alive" bit.' Bravely, Peter Squire took his Harrier past the west of Port Stanley at 300 feet, in full view of the defensive positions, to photograph them; on this occasion he was lucky, however, and his aircraft suffered no damage.

Once back on *Hermes* the films were rapidly processed; they then came under close scrutiny from the photographic interpreters. The Argentine troops had had several weeks to prepare and conceal their static positions, and had it not been for a 'give-away' many would have remained undiscovered: to keep themselves warm the conscripts lit peat fires, and the rising wisps of smoke showed up clearly when the interpreters examined the photographs under stereoscopes. The film from Hare's aircraft included a remarkable close-up shot of an Argentine surface-to-air missile team on Mount Longdon, with one man struggling unsuccessfully to bring his Blowpipe launcher to bear on the speeding Harrier. At the time the pilot had seen nothing of this threat, which was perhaps as well.

At noon a pair of Harriers launched from *Hermes* carrying 1,000-pound bombs modified for laser guidance. The intention was to attack Argentine forward positions, but on this occasion, as on some others, there was no forward air controller in position to laser-mark a worthwhile target. The aircraft returned to their ship with the valuable weapons.

Later in the afternoon Peter Squire returned to the area west of Port Stanley leading a pair of Harriers, to attack troops and vehicles photographed there earlier in the day. The aircraft came under intense fire from small arms and Murdo Macleod, flying as wing man, took a rifle-calibre round through the base of his windscreen.

11 JUNE

During this phase of the conflict the Sea Harrier squadrons continued their regular patrols over the Islands, but there was little Argentine air activity and few opportunities for combat. From time to time the Sea Harriers were able to return to the offensive. At first light that morning Lieutenant Commander Andy Auld of No. 800 Squadron led four aircraft in a low-altitude toss bombing attack on Port Stanley airfield using radar-fused air-burst bombs. One of those taking part was Lieutenant Commander Neil Thomas, who remembered the run-in to the target: 'It was quite a nice day, some showers around. At about 8 miles from Stanley I saw an orange glow on the inside of my canopy. I remember thinking, "I've not seen that reflection from the cockpit lights before." As I got closer I suddenly realized it was not a reflection, but a mass of anti-aircraft fire with the tracer curving like an umbrella over the airfield. I thought, "Blimey, they're having a good old wingding at somebody!"' Only gradually did it dawn on Thomas that the display had been laid on for the benefit of himself and his comrades. Four miles from the target and still safely out of range of the automatic fire, the Sea Harriers pulled up, released their bombs, rolled through 120 degrees, pulled around tightly, and descended close to the sea to escape. 'We tossed our bombs into the airfield and broke away,' Thomas continued. 'It was still fairly dark and I saw my three bombs explode over the target and a fire start; then I saw Clive Morell's bombs go off just to the east of mine.' The fire started by Thomas's bombs soon took hold and would be burning well half an hour later.

Most of the air action during this period was by the ground-attack Harriers, however, which encountered the enemy on almost every mission. That day No. 1 Squadron flew ten sorties against Argentine positions around Port Stanley, all involving low-altitude pentrations of the defended area and intensive return fire from the ground. More and more frequently, aircraft took hits. Late that afternoon Peter Squire and Mark Hare attacked artillery positions near Mount Longdon and Squire heard a loud bang as his aircraft was hit: a rifle-calibre bullet had gone through one side of the cockpit, narrowly missing his feet and passing out the other side. As the pair roared away from the target they were not alone. 'We were in line abreast going flat out and as low as we could, when something caught my eye. I looked around and thought "What the f— is that?" Then I realized what it was: three missiles following us!' Hare remembered. 'One fell into the ground early on, well short. Another followed us for a bit longer then it too petered out. But the third was well up and closing on us; I could not see the body of the missile, just the brightest flare I had ever seen. The missile was coming up between the two of us, high, then it started down and turned towards me,' he continued. 'As it came towards me I turned towards it and as we crossed it exploded about 100 feet above my canopy. It was a Blowpipe, going off on self-destruct at the end of its flight.'

Also that afternoon Neil McDougall's Vulcan, released by the Brazilian authorities after its enforced landing at Rio de Janeiro, returned to Ascension ten days after it had taken off.

12 JUNE

At the same time as Neil McDougall belatedly returned from his 'Black Buck' mission, Flight Lieutenant Martin Withers and his crew had been preparing for another. Early on the 12th they attacked Argentine positions south of Port Stanley airfield using air-burst bombs.

During previous days Argentine C-130 Hercules transports had flown into Port Stanley a few surface-to-surface versions of the Exocet missile, removed from a warship and modified for launching from an improved trailer. Before dawn on the 12th the defenders were able to use this weapon to hit back at one of the Royal Navy ships whose almost nightly bombardments had made life so miserable for Argentine troops. Fired over a range of about 18 miles, the Exocet struck the destroyer *Glamorgan* on the stern. Although the missile failed to detonate, it inflicted severe damage, killing thirteen members of her crew and injuring seventeen.

When it was light No. 1 Squadron flew six sorties to attack positions in the area around Sapper Hill, and again one of the Harriers returned with battle damage. Squadron Leader Peter Harris and Flight Lieutenant Murdo Macleod returned to *Hermes*, the former landing normally. As he decelerated to approach the ship Macleod had no way of knowing that a rifle-calibre bullet had pierced the pipe in the rear fuselage carrying high pressure air to the 'puffer duct', which provides control when the aircraft is in the hover. As the aircraft slowed in mid-air, resting on the downwards-pointing engine exhaust, the inside of the rear fuselage was blasted by a searing jet of air heated to 350°C (bread bakes at 230°C); immediately several items of equipment and electrical wiring in the rear compartment began to 'cook'.

From the cockpit of his Harrier safely on the deck Peter Harris watched the drama unfold: 'Flyco called, "No. 2, are you dumping fuel?" I looked over my shoulder to see what was happening, and it patently was not fuel. I called on the radio, "It's not fuel, it's smoke!" Murdo continued to decelerate. Then the

Flyco called, "You'd better land quickly, there are bits falling off your aeroplane!" In fact the "bits" were large flakes of paint blistering off the heated rear fuselage and blowing away; but I didn't know that and Murdo certainly didn't,' Harris explained. 'He brought the Harrier into an immediate hover alongside the ship, eased to the right, and landed. It wasn't a "controlled crash" on the deck, it was an immaculate vertical landing. Once on the deck he shut down the engine, and the fire crew converged on the Harrier and blanketed the rear with foam. Murdo had done extremely well to save his aeroplane.' Murdo Macleod afterwards described the incident in more modest terms, and admitted that the regularity with which his aircraft were taking hits had begun to weigh heavily: 'It was the third time on the trot my aircraft had been hit and that was getting a bit tedious. When I got back to the ready room with the rest of the pilots I said, "This is getting past a joke!"'

The regular battle damage now being inflicted on the RAF Harriers, necessitating in many cases complex repair work, posed a severe challenge to the servicing teams. Chief Technician Fred Welsh described the damaged suffered by Peter Squire's Harrier the previous day: 'The bullet came in just in front of the pilot on the port side, went behind the instrument panel, across the top of his legs missing them by about 5 inches, and out the other side. On the way it slashed through one of the cable looms, leaving torn ends that had the appearance of a shaving brush!' The ends of the wires had all to be carefully sorted out and spliced, but the aircraft was flying again within three days.

Macleod's near-disastrous incident posed more difficult problems for the repairers. 'The batteries and cable looms in the rear compartment had all started to melt,' Welsh explained. 'We repaired the bullet holes and the ducting. On the electrical side all the cables had to be spliced. Two of our radio sergeants used cables out of one of their test sets to improvise a repair.' Almost unbelievably, in view of the damage it had suffered, this aircraft would also be flying again within three days.

To many sailors on *Hermes* it seemed odd that RAF Harriers were returning so often with battle damage, while Sea Harriers were rarely hit. 'They couldn't appreciate what we meant by "going in really low", until we pinned on the wall of the Chief Petty Officer's mess a print of Mark Hare's photo of the Argentine soldiers on Mount Longdon with the Blowpipe,' Welsh continued. 'After that everyone realized that when the RAF said low, it meant LOW!'

In addition to the repair work, the No. 1 Squadron maintenance team finished modification work on one of the Harriers to enable it to carry a pair of Shrike radar-homing missiles, using a kit of parts flown from Ascension and parachuted to one of the ships in the Task Force.

One of the few Argentine missions over the Islands during the daylight hours was by Naval Lieutenant Benito Rotolo of the 3rd Escuadrilla flying a Skyhawk, briefed to attack British positions near Darwin; 'Just two minutes before beginning my bombing run, as I was about to pull up the nose of my aircraft, I caught sight of a pair of Sea Harriers against the clouds. They did not see me. Our only means of defence was to escape so I jettisoned my bombs, racks, external fuel tanks, everything, and got out of there.'

13 JUNE

By first light British forces controlled much of the high ground surrounding Port Stanley, after fierce fighting during the night. During the day preparations were in full swing for a further large-scale attack that evening.

In an attempt to stiffen the collapsing Argentine resistance, a dozen Skyhawks took off from Rio Gallegos that morning to attack British positions. Ensign Marcelo Moroni was flying one of eight aircraft of Grupo 5 which set out; soon after getting airborne one Skyhawk had to turn back with engine trouble, but the other seven took fuel from a KC-130 Hercules tanker then continued towards the Islands. The force ran over the Falklands at low altitude as far as Port Stanley, then turned about and attacked the positions on Mount Kent, flying from east to west. 'As we passed over the final hill we spotted vehicles and command positions, all camouflaged; we could see them because the terrain was light-coloured and they were much darker. There were also some helicopters on the ground. At the front of our formation were four planes, just behind them the remaining three. We aimed our bombs at the positions and the helicopters. Initially it appeared that the attack was a surprise, but then their anti-aircraft fire really opened up on us,' Moroni recalled. The attack had indeed come as a surprise, and had found the plum British target: the headquarters of the 3rd Commando Brigade on the western side of Mount Kent complete with General Moore, his staff and unit commanders assembled for a briefing on the following night's operations. One who witnessed the attack was journalist Robert Fox, who afterwards wrote in his book *Eyewitness Falklands* (Methuen 1982): 'Someone shouted, "Get down. Here they come." Charlie and I threw ourselves behind some rock, which gave little cover. I clearly saw the markings on the underside of the two olive-green Skyhawks. They seemed to swing into the side of the valley. Machine-guns opened up and there were flashes of flame from the guns, and two small bombs came gliding down with white parachutes dragging from their tails. Peat and flame erupted about fifty yards below us, and then the planes headed off down the valley towards the broad plain by Estancia House.'

Captain John Greenhalgh, a Scout pilot with No. 656 Squadron, also watched the attackers run in: 'The seven Skyhawks came through the saddle on the north side of Mount Kent; they knew what they were going for, they went straight for the headquarters. They went over the top of the headquarters and released their parachute-retarded bombs, but all missed – they had been dropped too late.' So as not to betray the position of the headquarters the helicopters had been parked in the open 500 yards away from the tents, and these drew some of the bombs. A Gazelle and a Scout suffered damage, but the soft peat ground absorbed the force of the explosions and there were no human casualties.

Meanwhile four other Skyhawks delivered a similarly unsuccessful attack on paratroops dug in west of Mount Longdon. As the fighter-bombers swept out on their way home, they came upon a lone Sea King of No. 846 Squadron piloted by Lieutenant Commander Simon Thornewill. 'I was about 120 feet above the ground,' he recalled, 'and as the first pair of Skyhawks came in I turned to face their attack. I used our standard helicopter fighter evasion tactics, flying towards them then pulling round into their turn. The first aircraft opened fire and his rounds passed to our right as I pulled to the left. The second one obviously tightened his turn before he opened fire, and there was a loud bang as a cannon shell hit one of our rotor blades. The aircraft did not handle markedly differently and I had to keep evading as the second pair were lining up for their attack. We managed to hide in a ravine, and they gave up and went away.'

As soon as the attackers had gone Thornewill landed the Sea King and the crew got out to examine the damage. The 20 mm round had punched a hole the size of a man's fist through one of the blades 8 feet from the tip, carrying away part of the main spar. 'I am surprised the blade did not fold up,' commented Thornewill. 'It speaks volumes for the strength of the aircraft.' The crew radioed for a new blade to be flown over to them; it was manhandled into place, and within a couple of hours the helicopter was flying again.

By now forward air controllers with laser target markers were in position on several of the hills overlooking the Argentine forward positions; at last No. 1 Squadron could make effective use of its newly acquired laser-guided bombs. Late that morning Wing Commander Peter Squire carried out an attack with these weapons against a company headquarters position on the side of Mount Longdon, directed by Major Mike Howles on the ground. The laser toss-bombing tactics used by the Harriers were similar to those employed by the Sea Harriers throughout the conflict: a low-altitude approach at high speed, then at a pre-calculated distance from the target the aircraft pulled up and released the bomb. 'The bomb climbs to over 3,000 feet, then comes down pretty steeply at the end – rather like a well-struck golf-drive,' Squire explained. 'The laser target marker puts a cone-shaped "basket" over the target; so long as the bomb comes down in that basket – and it will if you have pulled up at the correct distance – it will guide straight down on the target.' Prior to the Falklands conflict neither the Harrier pilots nor the forward air controllers had had experience with the laser-guided weapons, however, and they were now having to learn of their foibles 'on the job'. As a result Squire's first bomb impacted just short of its target. But in a repeat attack with his other bomb on the same target a few minutes later, he scored a direct hit.

Attacking with laser-guided bombs during the afternoon, Squadron Leader Jerry Pook hit an artillery position near Moody Brook.

Also during the afternoon there was drama at the forward operating strip at Port San Carlos, as the powerful rotor downwash from the Chinook 'Bravo November' lifted some of the aluminium plates and blew them to one side. Again the strip was temporarily out of action, at the worst possible time for Lieutenant Commander Neil Thomas of No. 800 Squadron, leading in a pair of Sea Harriers. 'We were just entering the Sound when we received a radio call, "Return to mother". There was no way we could ever have got back to our ship, fuel was down to less than ten minutes.' Hastily the flight decks of the assault ships *Fearless* and *Intrepid*, anchored in San Carlos Water, were cleared and the two fighters put down on them – Thomas on the former and Lieutenant Simon Hargreaves on the latter. Although the two ships had frequently offered their decks to Sea Harriers running short of fuel, this was the only occasion during the conflict that the offer was taken up. The fighters' fuel tanks were partially filled, to give them sufficient to reach the airstrip ashore once repairs were complete (the Sea Harrier cannot take off vertically with full tanks and a pair of missiles). Just as the strip became ready again, an Air Raid Warning Red sounded in San Carlos Water. 'From having been welcome on the ship, they said, "Buzz off!" – they wanted the deck clear for their helicopters. So I leapt into my aeroplane and took off. As I went up I thought, "What the hell do I do now if Skyhawks come over the hills?" I was not at all worried about the Skyhawks as such, but I was very worried indeed about the weight of fire that would be thrown up by the various ships in the area,' Thomas recalled. 'As I was clearing San Carlos Water the control ship came up and said it had been a false alarm. Simon Hargreaves was airborne as well; we both went to the airstrip and landed there.'

After dark that evening the final Argentine C-130 Hercules transport landed at Port Stanley, off-loaded its contents, and took on wounded and others to be flown back to the mainland; after an hour's delay due to artillery fire and the presence of Sea Harriers in the area, it took off and returned safely. During the thirty-seven days since the airlift into Port Stanley had been resumed, following the initial bombing of the runway, there had been thirty-one landings by the Hercules, which brought in more than 400 tons of equipment and flew out 264 wounded. Hercules aircraft also made two parachute supply drops to other points on the Islands. During the same period Naval Electra and Fokker F-28 transports flew a similar number of sorties into Stanley, carrying some 70 tons of equipment and 340 personnel.

Also after dark the Canberra bombers of Grupo 2 returned to the Islands for the last time, losing one of their number to a long-range high-altitude shot from HMS *Exeter*'s Sea Dart. The pilot of the aircraft, Captain Roberto Pastran, described the incident: 'After release of the bombs on Mount Kent from 40,000 feet, the missile struck our aircraft. We went into a spin and I kept calling the navigator, Captain Fernando Casado, to eject. I waited as long as I could, but after four turns I realized that for some reason he could not get out and I ejected at about 6,000 feet. Casado never did get out; I think the explosion of the missile might have caused his seat not to function.' Pastran came down in the sea, released his parachute, and boarded his dinghy. Fortunately for him there was a northerly wind, and a few hours later he was blown ashore on the north coast of East Falkland.

During the night the British commandos and paratroops resumed their advance on Port Stanley; heavy fighting broke out around Wireless Ridge in the north, Tumbledown Mountain in the centre, and Sapper Hill in the south. Although their pilots lacked night-vision binoculars, the little Scout helicopters operated continually up to the front line, flying in ammunition and pulling out the wounded. Flying between Mount Kent and Wireless Ridge, Captain John Greenhalgh of No. 656 Squadron flew four such missions. The method of identification of the forward units was simply but effective: 'I would call on the radio to say I was coming in, and the paratrooper at the regimental aid post would shine a torch to the north, the direction from which I was coming. When I sighted the torch I would confirm it was the right one by asking which colour they were shining (red, white or green). The system worked well enough.'

14 JUNE

By dawn Wireless Ridge was in British hands but fierce fighting was still in progress around Tumbledown Mountain, defended by the Argentine 5th Marine Battalion. The Scots Guards were working their way forward and Captain Sam Drennan, another Scout pilot with No. 656 Squadron, went out to pick up the wounded. During the first run he collected a Gurkah, and an injured guardsman from the middle of a minefield. The second run was somewhat more difficult. 'By then it was light and there were casualties scattered all over the mountain, including the front end. It was awful terrain, with rocky outcrops all over the place exposed to enemy shell fire,' Drennan explained. 'We approached using the standard helicopter stealth techniques, keeping a background behind us and not letting ourselves be silhouetted against the skyline. We went to the first outcrop and looked over; there were no enemy, just shells landing, and we managed to figure out where our lads were on top of the mountain. Then we just went like a bat out of Hell towards them, using the mountain as a backdrop. As we approached, one of our soldiers stood up and waved us in; we landed, quickly took on board the wounded, and scooted out.' Drennan and his crewman returned to the mountain six more times to pick up wounded, frequently drawing heavy fire. 'We learned later – we didn't know it at the time though we had a good idea – that the enemy had a good go to knock us down but by sheer luck they missed,' the pilot continued. 'At one point the Scots Guards were firing M 79 grenades over the top of my Scout, at a sniper 50 metres from us on the side of a hill. I don't know how he could have missed us – probably the grenades landing around put him off a bit.'

Afterwards, for that and other missions during the conflict, Sam Drennan received the Distinguished Flying Cross. In getting the award, he later stressed to one of the authors, he was a representative for several other army and marine helicopter pilots who performed equally brave acts to bring wounded men from front-line positions.

Later that morning helicopters had a rare opportunity to go over to the offensive. Captain John Greenhalgh in his Scout, leading two more flown by Marine crews, ran in to attack Argentine positions to the west of Port Stanley; each aircraft carried four SS 11 anti-tank missiles, wire-guided weapons with a maximum range of about 3,000 yards. 'We adopted attack formation, flying in line abreast, and moved towards the ridge in front. We had high ground behind us so we were in quite a reasonable firing position,' remembered Corporal John Gammon, Greenhalgh's crewman. 'We looked around for targets and I spotted three bunkers, then talked the others in and allocated targets. I fired one of my missiles, it went into the bunker. The Scout to my left put a missile into his bunker. The

Scout on my right launched one of his missiles, but the wire broke and it dived into the ground; his second missile scored a hit.' One of the earth bunkers contained a 105 mm gun, and the missile smashed through the wall and hurled the weapon on to its side. The impertinence of the little helicopters did not go long unanswered, however, and Argentine artillerymen began to lay a barrage of air-burst shells over them. 'We decided it was time to make a tactical withdrawal,' Gammon commented.

By noon the weather over Port Stanley had cleared sufficiently for No. 1 Squadron to resume its highly destructive attacks with laser-guided bombs. Squadron Leader Peter Harris took off from *Hermes* with a couple of these weapons, accompanied by Flight Lieutenant Nick Gilchrist, who was to deliver follow-up attacks with cluster bombs.

It was about 12.25 p.m. when the pair arrived over their target, Sapper Hill, at 30,000 feet, and established radio contact with their controller before going down to attack. As they called in Wing Commander Fred Trowern, the senior RAF liaison officer at the main headquarters on Mount Kent, received a frantic radio call: 'Brigadier Julian Thompson at 3 Brigade called me about the planned air strike. He said, "For Christ's sake hold it! The Argies are standing up on Sapper Hill and I think there's a white flag. . . Yes, there's a white flag . . . there's another white flag . . . it looks as if they're giving in. For Christ's sake stop that attack!" I told Lieutenant Commander Mike Calahan, the naval air liaison officer, to tell the pair not to attack and inform him how long they could wait over the target.'

Orbiting at 30,000 feet over Port Stanley, it seemed to Peter Harris there was something odd going on below. 'I held off, then asked, "What's happening?" Back came the controller: "We think they're giving in! At the moment we don't want to stop the rout we think is in progress. We don't want to do anything to make them stop and change their minds."' Cruising at high altitude the pair of Harriers had fuel for at least thirty minutes; but halfway through they were ordered to return to their carrier with the encouraging news: 'For your information, the people on the target you were going for have already given in; and there's a white flag over Stanley!'

Harris and Gilchrist returned to *Hermes* bearing the news. For the RAF Harriers there would be no more ground-attack missions, but the Sea Harriers continued their combat air patrols and the Sidewinders were refitted to the Harrier GR 3s which soon joined them. 'That night there were no celebrations on *Hermes*,' recalled Nick Gilchrist. 'We thought that then would be the most dangerous time. Menendes and his troops on the Falklands had had enough and were going to give in. But we thought it might be just the time for Galtieri to launch a last-ditch air strike from the mainland to show that the war was not really over. There was no victory hooley, we just drifted out of the war.'

9: Retrospect

'Almost all aspects of the art of war are "theoretical" in time of peace; they only become "practical" when the actual killing begins.'

Field Marshal Earl Haig

The South Atlantic conflict in the spring of 1982 was a 'limited war' on several different levels. In the normally accepted use of the term, the war was limited because Britain possessed nuclear weapons but chose not to use them. The area over which the conflict raged was limited to the Falkland Islands, South Georgia and the waters around them; and although both sides had the ability to expand the conflict neither did so. The conflict was of limited duration, lasting only seventy-five days from start to finish. And it was fought using only a small proportion of each side's total armed forces: those which could be transported to the area of operations and sustained there.

In the air the fighting was further limited. On the British side all aircraft based near the combat zone had to be able to land vertically on ships' decks; that limited the usable types to only thirty-four Harriers and Sea Harriers and 172 helicopters. Because of the limited number of tankers available for in-flight refuelling, no more than one operational sortie per day could be mounted into the operational area from Ascension. On the Argentine side geography limited the air forces to those which could operate from her single aircraft-carrier, those with an effective combat radius of 450 miles when delivering low-altitude attacks, those light attack aircraft and helicopters that could be based on the Falklands, and a few transport and support types; 255 in all. Really intensive air operations took place on only six days: 1, 21, 23, 24 and 25 May and 8 June.

The aerial conflict had several unique features, however. It saw

213

air operations conducted over distances greater than ever before, and was the first in which both sides made regular use of in-flight refuelling. It saw the first use in combat of short take-off and vertical landing jet aircraft, and the first ever sustained advance by a major ground force supplied almost entirely by helicopters. It also saw the first use of sea-skimming missiles against warships.

On the British side the Sea Harrier emerged from the conflict with a greatly enhanced reputation: there were never more than twenty-five of these aircraft available to the Task Force, but they took on enemy forces with more than three times as many fast jet-fighter and attack aircraft, and in air-to-air combat destroyed twenty-three aircraft for the loss of none of their own. Although the Argentine pilots made no serious attempt to engage in air-to-air combat after the initial engagements on 1 May, there is no doubt they would have done so had the Sea Harrier not demonstrated its superiority so convincingly from the very start. Because there was scarcely any fighter-versus-fighter combat, Sea Harrier pilots *never* used VIFF (thrust Vectored In Forward Flight) while engaging enemy aircraft. The Sea Harriers' success is the more remarkable if one considers that after 1 May their interception tactics can be described as 'pre-Battle of Britain': lacking radar early warning of the approach of attacking forces, pilots had to revert to standing patrols, and initial detections of the enemy were usually made visually.

Once Sea Harrier pilots had enemy aircraft in sight they usually pounced from above, closed rapidly to within missile firing range, and loosed off a Sidewinder. If the missile worked properly – and almost invariably it did – the target aircraft had little chance of escaping destruction. 'Those pilots we lost to Sea Harriers never saw the missiles being fired, though some of the other pilots did,' commented Ruben Zini of Grupo 5. 'There was generally no time to respond to a Sidewinder shot – if the pilot saw it, it was too late. In some cases other pilots called the one under attack to break [turn hard], but the missile was never outwitted.' Naval Lieutenant Benito Rotolo summed it up when he commented: 'The Sea Harrier plus the Sidewinder L was a very bad system for us, a very good system for the British.' He and his comrades found the small, light-coloured Sea Harriers 'very difficult' to see against a cloud background.

The Sea Harriers' success depended largely on the skills of the pilots who flew them, skills entirely dependent on the training they had previously received. Speaking of his own service Flight Lieutenant John Leeming, who flew Sea Harriers with No. 800 Squadron during the conflict, told one of the authors: 'In the Royal Air Force we train as hard as any air force I know. We try to make things as realistic as possible. We really go for it, we probably hurt ourselves more in training than we would be hurt in war.' His words were to prove tragically prophetic: in February 1983 John Leeming was killed when his Harrier collided with another during an air-to-air combat training flight.

According to report, twenty-six AIM-9L Sidewinders were fired during the conflict, resulting in the destruction of eighteen aircraft and contributing to the destruction of one more. On three occasions pilots fired both their missiles at the same target; on two occasions it was destroyed and on one it was not. Subtracting these from the total, we get nineteen aircraft destroyed during twenty-three missile engagements – a success rate of 82 per cent; and in each case the Sea Harrier pilots' claims to have shot down aircraft were fully confirmed by the authors' researches in Argentina, as were two claims of aircraft 'possibly destroyed'. To the surprise of many people, the AIM-9L proved as effective and reliable in combat as the brochures had said.

Using 30 mm cannon the Sea Harrier pilots destroyed two aircraft in the air, finished off one with Sidewinder damage, and contributed to the destruction of another; they also shot up three helicopters on the ground. In addition the weapon proved useful for attacking surface targets, and was a useful supplement to the fighter's missile armament.

One Puma helicopter crashed into the ground while attempting to avoid attack by a Sea Harrier; though no shots were fired, it is credited to the type.

The Royal Air Force's Harrier GR 3 also came out of the conflict well. With little or no previous training in carrier operations No. 1 Squadron's pilots flew a total of 126 attack sorties, almost all from the deck of HMS *Hermes*. Since it first entered service in 1969 the Harrier has suffered from an image problem: because the pilot can use jet thrust to provide lift the aircraft has only a small wing, and because it is somewhat smaller than comparable machines it had come to be regarded as a 'Dinky Toy' – pretty to look at but not of much practical use. The Falklands conflict has demolished that impression. In fact the small size of the Harrier has proved a positive advantage in combat: other things being equal, a small attack aircraft will take less hits from enemy gunfire than will a large one. And there are other considerations. 'The Harrier is a small aircraft, well camouflaged, and the engine is relatively smoke-free, all of which make it that much more difficult for the enemy to see it coming,' commented Wing Commander Peter Squire. Again and again the Harrier demonstrated that it was able to take battle damage and continue flying; there was no occasion when a Harrier was lost to enemy action when a comparable conventional aircraft would have survived similar damage; and there was no occasion when a Harrier returned with battle damage and repairs were not completed within three days using only the ship's resources.

As with the Sea Harrier pilots, the Harrier GR 3 pilots had to lean heavily on their previous training, especially in low flying. 'The important thing is to conceal your approach to the target; if you have to fly behind a 50-foot contour to achieve surprise, then you must do that. If you can arrive out of nowhere and hit your target, then you've won. If they get fifteen seconds' warning to line up their guns and missiles then you've blown it, you might as well crash immediately after take-off!' commented Flight Lieutenant Mark Hare. 'Unless you train to fly really low in peacetime, in war you will stand a good chance of killing yourself by flying into the ground. You must learn to concentrate your entire attention in front of you. During an approach to the target at 50 feet at 500 knots [575 m.p.h.], the ground on either side and in front to about 600 yards is just a blur.'

The conflict has shown once again that, as during the battle at Goose Green, attack aircraft can intervene with decisive effect during a ground engagement. But it has also demonstrated that there is no point in sending high-speed attack aircraft to hit camouflaged enemy positions liable to be defended by guns and missiles, if their locations are not accurately known or marked; attacking pilots will not see them in time to line up for a first-pass attack. Returning to a defended area for a second pass proved a hazardous business: two Harrier pilots lost their aircraft and nearly their lives re-learning that lesson.

If there is a criticism to be levelled at the Harrier ground-attack operations over the Falklands, it is that there were too many attempts to hit ill-defined or otherwise unsuitable targets. An old British Army maxim states: 'Time spent on reconnaissance is seldom wasted', and this is certainly true for ground-attack operations. More pure reconnaissance, as distinct from armed reconnaissance, missions should have been flown to locate suitable targets which could then have been hit in carefully prepared 'set-piece' attacks.

Quite apart from their successes against the enemy, the Harriers and Sea Harriers showed themselves to be extremely robust aircraft and relatively easy to keep serviceable. Thus during the most critical phase of the conflict immediately after the landings at San Carlos Water, between 21 and 25 May, the two British carriers, with an average of thirty of these aircraft between them, flew some 300 sorties; during the same period the Argentine Navy and Air Force fighter-bomber units on the mainland, with between two and three times as many aircraft, flew only about 180 sorties. This ability to put up a far greater number of combat sorties than his opponent, irrespective of the total numbers of aircraft available, gave a major advantage to the British Task Force Commander.

The jump-jets have added an entirely new dimension to carrier air operations. During the conflict these aircraft flew combat missions under conditions in which no other naval jet aircraft could have operated, *regardless of the size of their carrier*. One has only to consider the difficulties faced by the pilots on *25 de Mayo* (which is 50 feet shorter than *Hermes* but 16 feet longer than *Invincible*) during her abortive attempt to intervene in the conflict, to appreciate that there has been a fundamental change in what is now possible. The Argentine Skyhawks could not take off with a full load unless the ship was sailing straight into a moderate breeze, and they could not land if the ship was not going into the wind, if the deck was pitching beyond certain limits, if it was night, or if visibility was poor. In contrast, the Harriers and Sea Harriers were able to take off in wind speeds ranging between zero and the maximum in which the deck crew could work without risk of being blown over the side; they could land regardless of the ship's direction with respect to the wind or the amount the deck was pitching, at night, and in appallingly low visibility. Ashore on the Falklands these aircraft were able to operate off the 285-yard airstrip constructed on ungraded ground in a week by army engineers with no heavy equipment.

Although on the British side the Harriers and Sea Harriers were the stars of the show, several other aircraft types made valuable though less spectacular contributions during the conflict: the diminutive Scout and Gazelle helicopters flown by army and marine pilots, flitting to and from the front line taking in ammunition and evacuating wounded; the Chinook, Sea King and Wessex transports, which made possible the ground forces' advance on Port Stanley; the Sea King anti-submarine helicopters, which mounted patrols throughout the entire conflict to prevent enemy submarines reaching firing positions; the Victor tankers, which mounted the radar reconnaissance in support of the landings on South Georgia and which made possible the flights by all other aircraft which went into the operational area from Ascension Island; the Vulcan bombers, whose difficult ultra-long-range attacks forced the Argentine air commander to re-position his Mirage fighters to meet possible attacks on the mainland; the Nimrod reconnaissance aircraft which confirmed that the Argentine fleet was keeping clear of the fighting; and the Hercules transports which brought south mail and other high-priority items required by the Task Force.

The hastily improvised modifications introduced into British aircraft before they were sent south had varying degrees of success in combat. Those which had the greatest effect were the carrier-operating modifications to the Harrier GR 3, the fitting of in-flight refuelling probes to the Nimrods and Hercules, and the installation of Omega and Carousel navigation systems to the Vulcans and Victors. Without these modifications, the aircraft could not have operated in the main combat area. Other modifications had little direct effect on the air war, though they certainly increased the pressure on Argentine forces and might have played a more important part had the conflict continued longer: for example, the fitting of laser-guided bombs to the Harrier GR 3 and Shrike missiles to the Vulcan. Yet other modifications were not used in combat at all, but conferred a capability which might have been useful: the 'Blue Eric' radar jamming pod and the Shrike missile installation on the Harrier GR 3, and the installation of Sidewinder missiles on this aircraft and the Nimrod. Finally there were modifications which, though rushed through with commendable speed, were completed just too late to see use before the conflict ended: the fitting out of the C-130 Hercules as a tanker; the installation of airborne early warning radar on the Sea King helicopter; of 190-gallon combat tanks and launchers to carry four Sidewinders on the Sea Harrier; and of the Harpoon long-range anti-shipping missile on the Nimrod. The conflict has underlined the huge advantage in times of national crisis of having a strong indigenous defence industry.

Although electronic warfare did play a significant part in the conflict, its impact was less than might have been expected in a conflict involving a major power in the 1980s. The most important use of electronic warfare on the British side was to counter the air-launched Exocet missiles: it is likely that the three missiles which failed to score hits were decoyed away by chaff or helicopter-borne electronic systems. Reportedly the Exocet which struck *Atlantic Conveyor* had already been decoyed away from another warship, and it was bad luck that the container ship happened to be on the other side of the chaff cloud or helicopter-borne decoy it went for.

The ALQ-101 jamming pod fitted to the Vulcan bombers during the first two 'Black Buck' missions against Port Stanley airfield seems to have provided useful protection against the defending gun and missile control radars; so did the chaff released by the Harriers and Sea Harriers. A number of items of electronic equipment were hastily built and deployed to counter Argentine weapon control radars but security considerations permit only one, the 'Blue Eric' jamming pod for the Harrier, to be mentioned in this account. For various reasons, however, none of these systems made any great impact on the fighting before the conflict ended. Although resolutely flown, the Vulcan missions with Shrike radiation-homing missiles failed to knock out the Argentine early warning radars at Port Stanley.

There has been considerable press speculation about the advance warning received by the Task Force of air attacks from the mainland, and the part played by possible SAS intelligence teams keeping watch on movements from the airfields there. The authors have evidence that on several occasions ships did receive warning when aircraft took off from Rio Gallegos and Rio Grande, the main Argentine bases during the conflict. Whether this information came from SAS patrols or less unconventional sources – for example, submarines off the coast observing approaching aircraft on radar before they descended to low altitude to approach the Falklands – the authors have no way of knowing. What is certain is that this information, while it may have been useful in providing a general warning that attacks were imminent, did not play any significant part in the direction of the Sea Harriers: even if the approximate times of raids were sometimes known in advance, the attackers' routes were not known, so fighter patrols could not be positioned to meet them. Throughout the period of the most intense air fighting, between 21 and 25 May inclusive, the great majority of Sea Harrier patrols were launched at pre-planned times throughout the day; scarcely ever were fighters scrambled from the deck to meet incoming attacks. The statement in some published accounts, that the early warning of air attack improved steadily throughout the conflict, hardly squares with the fact that during the final three weeks – apart from the single hectic action on 8 June – numerous sorties by Sea Harriers failed to intercept a single Argentine fighter-bomber. For these reasons the authors take the view that while the Task Force did have advance information on the approach of attacking aircraft, it is an overstatement to say that it had any great effect on British air operations or the success of the defences.

A detailed list of British aircraft losses, with causes, is given in Appendix 8. Altogether thirty-four aircraft were lost of which eleven, or just under one-third, were destroyed in operational accidents, in many cases during flying in very bad weather; four Sea Harriers, a Harrier GR 3, four Sea Kings and two Wessex were lost for this reason. A further thirteen aircraft, all helicopters, were lost on board the ships *Ardent, Coventry, Atlantic Conveyor* and *Glamorgan* when they were hit in action. Nine aircraft were shot down by enemy fire: two Sea Harriers, three Harrier GR 3s, three Gazelles, and a Scout. One Harrier and a Sea Harrier were lost probably to 35 mm anti-aircraft fire at Goose Green; two Harriers were lost to automatic fire from 20 mm or smaller weapons at Port Howard and near Port Stanley; and one Sea Harrier was lost after being hit by a Roland missile near Port Stanley. Of the helicopters two were shot down by small-arms fire from the ground near Port San Carlos, one was shot down by a Pucará near Goose Green, and the cause of the remaining loss is not clear. The loss of the Sea King helicopter near Punta Arenas in Chile is in a category by itself; it was probably abandoned after a deliberate one-way mission.

On the Argentine side the air unit which performed most impressively was undoubtedly the 2nd Naval Fighter and Attack Escuadrilla, although its four usable Super Étendards flew only twelve operational sorties during the conflict; of the five Exocet missiles fired two scored hits, and of those only one warhead detonated. For all that, the unit caused the destruction of the destroyer *Sheffield* and the container ship *Atlantic Conveyor*, and exerted a powerful influence on British naval operations that continued long after the last of its missiles had been expended. Because of the risk of Exocet attack the British aircraft carriers spent most of their time well to the east of the Falklands, with the result that Sea Harriers had to fly combat air patrols at ranges close to the operational limit, with correspondingly short times in position to block attacks. The unit thus contributed indirectly to the destruction wrought by all other Argentine air units throughout the conflict.

Also impressive were the missions into Port Stanley flown by C-130 Hercules, Electra and Fokker Fellowship transports of Grupo 1 and the 1st and 2nd Naval Logistics Escuadrillas, respectively. These aircraft flew some sixty fights into the Falklands *after* the airfield was hit on 1 May, often at night and under appalling weather conditions, and with the continual risk of interception by Sea Harriers. In the event only one of these aircraft, a C-130 Hercules, was lost, and that was because its crew climbed above the radar horizon to conduct a brief search for British ships during their return flight. As well as helping sustain the sagging morale of the Argentine garrison on the Falklands, the aircraft transported in several important cargoes, including 155 mm guns to defend Port Stanley against bombarding warships and, later, surface-launched Exocet missiles, one of which inflicted serious damage on HMS *Glamorgan*.

Throughout the fighting the American-built TPS-43 and TPS-44 early warning and fighter control radars at Port Stanley played an important role. They provided information on the positions of patrolling Sea Harriers and, by tracking aircraft moving to and from the carriers, also gave a useful indication of the whereabouts of the main Task Group. The radars thus contributed directly to the sinking of *Atlantic Conveyor* and the success of the Argentine aerial resupply operations, and made it possible for many of the attacking fighter-bombers to avoid areas patrolled by Sea Harriers. The siting of the radars close to civilian housing in Port Stanley restricted their area of coverage on low-flying aircraft, but prevented their being attacked from the air and enabled them to continue operating until the surrender.

The Argentine fighter-bomber units gave a salutary demonstration that brave pilots flying near-obsolete or unsuitable aircraft can penetrate modern missile defences and inflict major and even fatal damage on warships with 'iron' bombs. Although the men showed they were competent flyers, their combat tactics were often poor and units suffered heavily as a result. The unit with proportionately the heaviest losses was Grupo 4: it started with twenty A-4C Skyhawks, and lost nine aircraft and eight pilots; two were lost in an accident, two were shot down by Sea Harriers, and the rest by surface-to-air missiles and guns. The unit which suffered most from the depradations of the Sea Harrier was Grupo 6, which lost eleven of its thirty-four Daggers in action: nine to Sea Harriers' Sidewinder missiles, and two to surface-to-air missiles. Because Sidewinders homed on the plume of infra-red energy emitted from the rear of the aircraft, the explosions of these missiles frequently shattered the rear ends of fighter-bombers but left the noses intact for long enough for their pilots to eject; six Dagger pilots parachuted to safety after their aircraft were destroyed.

The most successful Argentine unit against shipping was Grupo 5, whose A-4B Skyhawks inflicted the death blows on *Coventry* and *Sir Galahad*, probably dropped the bomb which caused the loss of *Antelope*, scored hits on *Ardent*, and inflicted damage on *Glasgow* and *Sir Tristram*. In action the unit lost ten aircraft and nine pilots: three to attack by Sea Harriers, two to 'own goals' by Argentine anti-aircraft gunners, and the remainder to surface-to-air missiles or guns.

During the conflict there was considerable over-claiming about the number of British ships sunk and damaged, though the authors believe most claims by Argentine pilots were made in good faith. HMS *Ardent* was attacked and seriously damaged three times on 21 May, but each raiding force claimed to have sunk or seriously damaged a separate frigate. Similarly *Antelope* was claimed twice, after being hit in two separate attacks on 23 May. On several occasions attacking pilots saw their comrades' bombs strike British ships and, quite reasonably, these were later claimed as seriously damaged; only much later would they learn that most of the bombs failed to detonate. The claim to have inflicted serious damage on the aircraft carrier *Invincible* during the combined Exocet and Skyhawk attack on 30 May was also honestly made by the pilots involved, though it is clear they were mistaken. In a quite different category are the propaganda efforts of the Argentine government, of which the most notable was the spurious claim to have inflicted serious damage on HMS *Hermes* early in the conflict; this originated entirely in Buenos Aires, much to the disgust of Argentine Air Force pilots interviewed.

The Pucará, Turbo-Mentor and Macchi 339 light attack aircraft based on the Falklands appear to have achieved little apart from the shooting down of a single Scout helicopter and inflicting minor damage and wounds on three crewmen on HMS *Argonaut*. The authors have found no occasion where they caused casualties during attacks on British ground troops. All thirty-four of these aircraft sent to the Islands were lost. Likewise the attacks by the obsolete Canberra bombers of Grupo 2 appear to have been completely ineffective, causing no damage or casualties; the unit lost two of its six bombers.

By the close of the conflict several Argentine Daggers, Skyhawks and Canberras were fitted with chaff-dispensing systems, and some Skyhawks and Canberras carried infra-red decoys as well. The authors have found no occasion where the use of such counter-measures was successful in decoying a missile once it had been launched, however.

The authors estimate that approximately three-quarters of the bombs dropped by Argentine aircraft during the conflict failed to detonate. Even after the BBC news release on 23 May mentioning unexploded bombs, there is little evidence that the problems of bomb fusing were resolved: during the attack on HMS *Plymouth* on 8 June there were four hits by bombs, none of which exploded. Where ships were hit by bombs which functioned correctly – during the attacks on *Ardent*, *Coventry*, *Sir Galahad* and *Sir Tristram* – the significant common factor in each case was that there was no effective defensive fire; as a result attacking pilots were able to release their bombs from altitudes high enough to allow the bombs to arm themselves before impact. Although aircraft could avoid the surface-to-air missile and gun defences by approaching targets at ultra-low level, the bombs would not function effectively unless they were released from altitudes greater than 200 feet.

The authors give comprehensive details of the Argentine aircraft lost in the conflict in Appendix 4; with listing by type in Appendix 5 and by causes of loss in Appendix 6. Appendix 7 compares the authors' figures on Argentine losses with those published in the British Government White Paper 'The Falklands Campaign: The Lessons' (Cmnd 8758). The reason for all this detail is that the authors' figures differ in major respects from those in the White Paper and the authors wish to present the strongest possible case to support their contention that there are errors in the official British Government figures.

The authors' figures indicate that the Argentine forces lost a total of 102 aircraft during the conflict: sixty-three from the Air Force, thirteen from the Navy, three from the Coast Guard, twenty-two from the Army, and one that had belonged to the British governor of the Falklands. There is also evidence that six Daggers and a similar number of Skyhawks were written off after the conflict as 'damaged beyond repair', probably because they were cannibalized to provide spares or because pilots had overstressed them while evading British missiles. Taking only those aircraft lost during the conflict, the authors believe thirty-two were destroyed by Harrier GR 3s or Sea Harriers in the air or on the ground; twenty were destroyed by surface-to-air missiles, guns and small-arms fire; eighteen were destroyed during the SAS attack on Pebble Island, on the *General Belgrano*, and in operational accidents; and thirty-two aircraft of all types were captured in varying states on the ground.

The main area of contention between the authors and the White Paper centres around the claims for the surface-to-air missile and gun systems: the authors' figures, based on information from official and unofficial British and Argentine sources, indicate that there were twenty losses to this cause; the White Paper states that there were fifty-two. The authors are able to confirm the following claims by British surface weapons:

	Author's Figures	Figure in White Paper
Sea Dart	5	8
Sea Wolf	3	5
Sea Cat	1	8
Rapier	1	14
Blowpipe	2	9
Stinger	1	1
Guns (including small arms)	3	7
Multiple weapons (including Rapier)	4	–
	20	52

The five losses in the 'multiple weapons' column went down in the area around San Carlos Water on 23, 24 and 25 May, and in each case the authors have reason to believe that more than one weapons system laid claim to the aircraft destroyed. The authors' evidence overwhelmingly supports the case that thirty-two of the aircraft 'confirmed' in the White Paper as having been shot down, did not in fact go down; the aircraft overclaimed were thirty-one Skyhawks and Mirage/Daggers, and one Macchi 339.

There are well-established historical precedents for over-claiming by surface-to-air weapons systems. One relevant to this account occurred during the Second World War, when it was found that British coastal anti-aircraft gun batteries appeared to be shooting down many more enemy aircraft per engagement than were those inland. For a time the reason seemed to defy analysis: both types of battery used the same equipment, and there were no significant differences in training or operational methods. Then a civilian operational research team was called in to examine the problem and found the answer quite quickly: to get their claims confirmed the inland batteries had to be able to point to a wrecked aircraft on the ground, while the 'confirmation' of claims from coastal batteries did not suffer from this constraint. In fact, the coastal gun batteries were claiming considerably more aircraft than they were shooting down.

If we consider this example in relation to the actions around San Carlos Water, there is more than a hint that history has repeated itself. During the period between 21 and 27 May, the surface-to-air missiles and guns claimed and had 'confirmed' a total of thirty-one Skyhawks and Mirage/Daggers in that immediate area. To meet the official confirmation criteria aircraft claimed destroyed had to be seen to break up or crash, so all should have come down within, say, 7 miles of the system that hit them. In a circle of radius 10 miles centred on San Carlos Water, about half the area is sea and half land, so in any random distribution of crashes it would be reasonable to expect the wrecks of about fifteen fighter-bombers to be littering the land area. The authors understand no official count has been made of wrecks to substantiate the victory claims, but have been told unofficially that there are scarcely any wrecked aircraft on the ground in that area. Moreover, had so large a number of fighter-bombers been shot down in the area, one would expect at least a few pilots to have ejected and been taken prisoner; in fact there was only one. It is of course just possible that every disputed aircraft did crash into the sea and not one of their pilots ejected, but statistically this is unlikely in the extreme. The authors believe the true figure for Argentine fighter-bomber losses to these causes was *six*.

It is *not* the authors' case that the surface-to-air missile and gun crews claimed recklessly, nor that those charged with confirming their claims did not rigorously apply the officially approved criteria (involving independent corroboration from other units in the area). It *is* the authors' case, however, that history has shown that the accurate confirmation of victory claims, especially by surface-to-air weapons, is extremely difficult; and in the heat of action it will frequently happen that men will report seeing aircraft appear to crash, when in fact they do not.

In compiling their list of Argentine aircraft losses the authors have carefully correlated information from both British and Argentine sources. Many people have poured scorn on the information on the conflict coming out of Argentina – and with good reason, for much of it has been clumsy propaganda unlikely to fool anyone. During his visits to Argentine Naval and Air Force bases, however, co-author Jeffrey Ethell personally interviewed a large number of pilots; several spoke extremely frankly, even going to the point of refuting official statements on the conflict originating from higher up. Each unit provided lists of the names of the pilots and aircrew it lost during the conflict, in most cases with information on how the aircraft were lost. Significantly, in every case where the bodies of Argentine aircrew were found and identified by British forces on the Falklands, the men's names had previously been given to the authors; this points strongly to the authors' list being complete or nearly complete.

On being shown these findings, some have darkly suggested that the authors may have been victims of an elaborate hoax by the Argentine forces aimed at discrediting the official British figures. If there was a hoax, it must certainly have been elaborate: with several Argentine aircrew officers apparently speaking their own minds and refuting official statements previously made, but really following a carefully scripted line of disinformation; with the admission of losses not claimed by the British to give that line credibility; with the release of names of aircrew killed in action only in cases where their bodies were likely to be found by British forces and identified; with the confirmation of all the Sea Harriers' claims plus two 'possibles' – merely to cast doubts on the claims made for the surface missile and gun systems. Some may find it plausible that the Argentine forces would go to so much trouble to achieve so little; the authors do not.

Any event, once it has happened, can be made to seem inevitable by a competent historian. The Falklands conflict became inevitable only because each of the contestants felt the other had pushed matters to the point where the only way out was to resort to armed force. During the three weeks following the Argentine landings each side stood its ground while moving ahead with military preparations, fully expecting the other to back down at any moment. Neither believed that two civilized nations would go to war over an issue so minor, but ended up in a position where fighting became inevitable.

If there is hope for the future of the Falklands, it is that neither side can now doubt that the other feels strongly enough about the issues to resort to armed force. Once that is accepted fully it becomes clear that the solution, as in every previous war in history that has reached a conclusion, must come from the diplomats.

Appendix 1
Comparative Ranks

Note: In the text, most Argentine ranks have been translated very literally (as shown here in brackets), in order to make them easier to follow for English-speaking readers.

Royal Navy	Armada Argentina
——	Teniente de corbeta (Ensign)
Sub Lieutenant	Teniente de fragata (Lieutenant)
Lieutenant	Teniente de navío
Lieutenant Commander	Capitán de corbeta
Commander	Capitán de fragata
Captain	Capitán de navío
Commodore	Contralmirante
Rear-Admiral	Vicealmirante
Vice-Admiral	Almirante
Admiral	——
Admiral of the Fleet	——

Royal Air Force	Fuerza Aérea Argentina
——	Alférez (Ensign)
Pilot Officer	Teniente (Lieutenant)
Flying Officer	1er Teniente (Lieutenant)
Flight Lieutenant	Capitán (Captain)
Squadron Leader	Mayor (Major)
Wing Commander	Vicecomodoro (Lieutenant Colonel)
Group Captain	Comodoro (Colonel)
Air Commodore	Brigadier
Air-Vice Marshal	Brigadier Mayor
Air Marshal	Brigadier General (General)
Air Chief Marshal	——

Appendix 2
Argentine Combat Air Units

ORDER OF BATTLE FOR FALKLANDS OPERATIONS, 1 MAY 1982
(figures based on best available information)

Air Force (Fuerza Aérea Argentina)

GRUPO 1
Bases: El Palomar (main); Comodoro Rivadavia (operational)
Aircraft: 2 Boeing 707s (used for transport and long-range reconnaissance); 7 C-130 Hercules (used for transport; one used as an improvised bomber); 2 KC-130 Hercules tankers

GRUPO 2
Bases: Paraná (main); Trelew, Rio Gallegos (operational)
Aircraft: 6 Canberra B 62s (also 2 trainers, probably non-operational); 4 Learjet 35As (used for photographic and radar reconnaissance)

GRUPO 3
Bases: Reconquista (main); Port Stanley, Goose Green, Pebble Island (operational)
Aircraft: 25 Pucarás (number deployed to the Falklands)

GRUPO 4
Bases: Mendoza (main); Rio Gallegos (operational)
Aircraft: 20 A-4C skyhawks

GRUPO 5
Bases: Villa Reynolds (main); Santa Cruz, Rio Gallegos (operational)
Aircraft: 26 A-4B Skyhawks

GRUPO 6
Bases: Tandil (main); San Julian, Rio Gallegos, Rio Grande (operational)
Aircraft: 34 IAI Daggers; 3 two-seater trainers (probably non-operational)
On or about 10 June some 10 Mirage 5 aircraft reached the unit from Peru, but these played no part in the conflict

GRUPO 8
Bases: Morón (main); Comodoro Rivadavia, Rio Gallegos (operational)
Aircraft: 11 Mirage IIIs (plus 4 believed on overhaul or in reserve); 2 two-seater trainers (believed non-operational)

SEARCH AND RESCUE AT PORT STANLEY
Aircraft: 2 Bell 212s (UH-1N)

Naval Air Arm (Aeronaval Argentina)
2ND NAVAL FIGHTER AND ATTACK ESCUADRILLA
Bases: Espora (main); Rio Grande (operational)

Aircraft: 4 Super Étendards (1 further aircraft on strength, used to provide spares for others)

3RD NAVAL FIGHTER AND ATTACK ESCUADRILLA
Bases: Espora (main); *25 de Mayo* (operational; they later flew from Rio Grande)
Aircraft: 11 A-4Q Skyhawks (8 of these were on the *25 de Mayo*)

1ST NAVAL ATTACK ESCUADRILLA
Bases: Punta del Indio (main); Port Stanley (operational)
Aircraft: 5 Macchi 339s (number operational on the Falklands)

4TH NAVAL ATTACK ESCUADRILLA
Bases: Punta del Indio (main); Pebble Island (operational)
Aircraft: 4 Beech T-34C Turbo-Mentors (number operational on the Falklands. All destroyed during SAS attack on the night of 14–15 May)

1ST NAVAL RECONNAISSANCE ESCUADRILLA
Bases: Espora (main); Rio Grande (operational)
Aircraft: 2 SP-2H Neptunes (serviceability poor; withdrawn from operations after 15 May)

1ST NAVAL ANTI-SUBMARINE ESCUADRILLA
Bases: Espora (main); *25 de Mayo* (operational)
Aircraft: 6 S-2E Trackers

1ST NAVAL HELICOPTER ESCUADRILLA
Bases: Various warships
Aircraft: 7 Alouettes; 2 Lynx

2ND NAVAL HELICOPTER ESCUADRILLA
Bases: Espora (main); *25 de Mayo* (operational)
Aircraft: 4 SH-3D Sea Kings

1ST NAVAL LOGISTICS ESCUADRILLA
Bases: Buenos Aires (main); Comodoro Rivadavia (operational)
Aircraft: 3 Electras

2ND NAVAL LOGISTICS ESCUADRILLA
Bases: Buenos Aires (main); Comodoro Rivadavia (operational)
Aircraft: 3 Fokker F-28s

Army (Ejercito Argentino)
601 COMBAT AVIATION BATTALION
Aircraft deployed to the Falklands: 2 Chinooks; 5 Pumas; 3 Augusta 109s; 9 Bell UH-1H Iroquois; 6 others (approximate figure)

Coast Guard (Prefectura Naval Argentina)
Aircraft: 5 Skyvans; 3 Pumas

LADE (State Airline)
Aircraft: 12 Fokker F-27s; 6 Fokker F-28s

Fenix Escuadron
Bases: Various
Aircraft: 10 Learjets; 1 HS 125

These were all requisitioned civil aircraft; they served as formation leaders, decoys, and radio relay aircraft

TOTALS (1 MAY)

MEDIUM-RANGE FIGHTER, FIGHTER-BOMBER AND BOMBER AIRCRAFT	*Air Force*	97
	Navy	15
		112
SHORT-RANGE ATTACK AIRCRAFT, BASED ON FALKLANDS	*Air Force*	25
	Navy	9
		34
RECONNAISSANCE AIRCRAFT	*Air Force*	6
	Navy	8
		14
TRANSPORTS, HELICOPTERS, SUPPORT AIRCRAFT	*Air Force*	15
	Fenix Escuadrón	11
	Navy	19
	Army	25
	LADE	18
	Coast Guard	8
		96
	Grand Total	**256**

Appendix 3
British Combat Air Units

ORDER OF BATTLE IN SOUTH ATLANTIC, 1 MAY 1982
(unless otherwise stated)

Royal Navy

737 SQUADRON
Bases: HMS *Glamorgan*, HMS *Antrim*
Aircraft: 2 Wessex

800 SQUADRON
Base: HMS *Hermes*
Aircraft: 12 Sea Harriers

801 SQUADRON
Base: HMS *Invincible*
Aircraft: 8 Sea Harriers (includes some aircraft from 899 Squadron)

809 SQUADRON
Arrived south on 18 May with 8 Sea Harriers; gave up 4 aircraft each to 800 and 801
Squadrons

815/702 SQUADRONS
Bases: Various warships
Aircraft: 9 Lynx (a further 15 arrived south during the course of the conflict)

820 SQUADRON
Base: HMS *Invincible*
Aircraft: 9 Sea Kings (anti-submarine)

824 SQUADRON
Bases: RFA *Fort Grange*, RFA *Olmeda*
Aircraft: 7 Sea Kings (anti-submarine)

825 SQUADRON
Arrived on the Falklands on 28 May with 10 Sea King transport helicopters

826 SQUADRON
Base: HMS *Hermes*
Aircraft: 9 Sea Kings (anti-submarine)

829 SQUADRON
Bases: Various warships
Aircraft: 4 Wasps (8 more arrived later)

845, 847 AND 848 SQUADRONS
Arrived after 21 May with 45 Wessex helicopters; a further 6 were lost with the
Atlantic Conveyor

846 SQUADRON
Bases: HMS *Hermes*, HMS *Fearless*
Aircraft: 13 Sea Kings (transport)

899 SQUADRON
Base: HMS *Hermes*
Aircraft: 5 Sea Harriers (During operations this unit's aircraft and pilots were
integrated with those of No. 800 Squadron, and are described as belonging to the
latter in the main text)

Royal Marines

3RD COMMANDO BRIGADE AIR SQUADRON
Arrived on the Falklands on 21 May with 12 Gazelles and 6 Scouts

Army Air Corps

656 SQUADRON
Arrived on the Falklands on 21 May with 6 Gazelles and 6 Scouts

Royal Air Force

I SQUADRON
6 Harrier GR 3s arrived south on the *Atlantic Conveyor* on 18 May and transferred to *Hermes*; 2 reinforcement aircraft were flown direct from Ascension on 1 June, 2 more on 8 June

18 SQUADRON
1 Chinook arrived on the Falklands on 26 May, 3 others were lost on the *Atlantic Conveyor* the previous day

Based on Ascension Island
(Due to the immense distances involved and the need for extensive tanker support, only one aircraft could be sent to the operational area on any one day)

55 AND 57 SQUADRONS
Aircraft: Victors (used as tankers and for radar reconnaissance, from 20 April)

44, 50 AND 101 SQUADRONS
Aircraft: Vulcans (used as bombers, from 1 May)

120, 201 AND 206 SQUADRONS
Aircraft: Nimrods (used for maritime reconnaissance, from 15 May)

47 SQUADRON
Aircraft: C-130 Hercules (used as transports, from 16 May)

TOTALS (1 MAY)

SEA HARRIERS	20
ANTI-SUBMARINE HELICOPTERS	25
TRANSPORT HELICOPTERS	13
GENERAL-PURPOSE HELICOPTERS	15
LONG-RANGE AIRCRAFT AND OPERATING FROM ASCENSION: MAXIMUM IN OPERATIONAL AREA ON ANY ONE DAY	1

Grand Total   74

Appendix 4
Argentine Aircraft Losses
(based on best available information)

	Date	Time (local)	Type and unit	Location
1	3 April	morning	Puma (Army)	Grytviken, S. Georgia
2	1 May	08.15	Islander	Port Stanley
3	1 May	08.20	Pucará (Grupo 3)	Goose Green
4	1 May	16.30	Mirage (Grupo 8)	N. of W. Falkland
5	1 May	16.31	Mirage (Grupo 8)	Falkland Is.
6	1 May	16.41	Dagger (Grupo 6)	W. Falkland
7	1 May	16.45	Canberra (Grupo 2)	N.W. of Falklands
8	2 May	17.00	Alouette (1st Naval Helo. Rec. Esc.)	S.W. of Falklands
9	3 May	——	Macchi 339 (1st Naval Attack Esc.)	Nr Cape Pembroke
10–11	9 May	——	2 Skyhawks (Grupo 4)	S. Jason I.

Cause	Details
Small-arms fire	Shot down by Royal Marines during the landings on South Georgia
Sea Harrier (cluster bomb)	Destroyed on the ground during attack by No. 800 Sqn on airfield
Sea Harrier (cluster bomb)	Destroyed on the ground during attack by No. 800 Sqn on airfield. Aircraft was about to take off; the pilot, Lt Jukic, was killed
Sea Harrier (Sidewinder)	Shot down by Flt Lt Barton, No. 801 Sqn. The pilot, Lt Perona, ejected
Sea Harrier (Sidewinder)	Severely damaged by missile fired by Lt Thomas, No. 801 Sqn. Attempting an emergency landing at Port Stanley, it was shot down by ground defences. The pilot, Capt. Cuerva, was killed. Credited to Lt Thomas because, even had it landed, it would probably never have been able to take off again
Sea Harrier (Sidewinder)	Shot down by Flt Lt Penfold, No. 800 Sqn. The pilot, Lt Ardiles, is listed as killed
Sea Harrier (Sidewinder)	Shot down by Lt Curtiss, No. 801 Sqn. Lt Gonzales and Lt Ibañez both ejected but could not be rescued from the sea
submarine attack	Went down with the cruiser *General Belgrano*
operational accident	Crashed into the ground returning to Port Stanley in bad weather. The pilot, Lt Benitez, was killed
operational accident	Crashed into cliff when approaching W. Falkland in bad weather to attack British warships. The pilots, Lt Casco and Lt Farias, were killed

	Date	Time (local)	Type and unit	Location
12	9 May	——	Puma (Army)	Nr Port Stanley
13–15	12 May	14.00	3 Skyhawks (Grupo 5)	E. of Falklands
16	12 May	14.15	Skyhawk (Grupo 5)	Goose Green
17–22	15 May	morning	6 Pucarás (Grupo 3)	Pebble I.
23–6	15 May	morning	4 Turbo-Mentors (4th Naval Attack Esc.)	Pebble I.
27	15 May	morning	Skyvan (Coast Guard)	Pebble I.
28	21 May	08.15	Chinook (Army)	M. Kent
29	21 May	08.15	Puma (Army)	M. Kent
30	21 May	08.15	Puma (Army)	M. Kent
31	21 May	09.30	Pucará (Grupo 3)	Sussex Mts
32	21 May	10.16	Dagger (Grupo 6)	Nr Fanning Hd, Falkland Sound
33	21 May	12.10	Pucará (Grupo 3)	Nr Darwin
34–5	21 May	13.04	2 Skyhawks (Grupo 4)	Nr Chartres, W. Falkland
36	21 May	14.20	Dagger (Grupo 6)	S.E. of Mt Robinson, W. Falkland
37–9	21 May	14.53	3 Daggers (Grupo 6)	N. of Port Howard, W. Falkland

Cause	Details
HMS *Coventry* (Sea Dart)	——
HMS *Brilliant* (Sea Wolf)	Two were shot down by missiles, the third crashed into the sea while attempting to evade an approaching missile. All credited to Sea Wolf. The pilots, Lt Bustos, Lt Nivoli, and Lt Ibarlucea, were all killed
operational accident	Shot down by Argentine AA gunners. The pilot, Lt Gavazzi, was killed
ground action	Destroyed on the ground during attack by SAS
ground action	As above
ground action	As above
Harrier GR 3 (30 mm cannon)	Destroyed on the ground by Flt Lt Hare, No. 1 Sqn
Harrier GR 3 (30 mm cannon)	As above
Harrier GR 3 (30 mm cannon)	Destroyed on the ground by above and Sqn Ldr Pook, No. 1 Sqn
Stinger	Shot down by missile fired by SAS. The pilot, Capt Benitz, ejected
Sea Cat	Engaged by missiles from *Argonaut* and *Plymouth*, it crashed into the sea. The pilot, Lt Bean, was killed
Sea Harrier (30 mm cannon)	Attacked by Lt Cdr Ward, Lt Cdr Craig, and Lt Thomas, No. 801 Sqn. Credited to Ward. The pilot, Major Tomba, ejected
Sea Harrier (Sidewinder)	Shot down by Lt Cdr Blissett and Lt Cdr Thomas, No. 800 Sqn. The pilots, Lt Lopez and Lt Manzotti, were both killed
Sea Harrier (Sidewinder)	Shot down by Lt Cdr Frederiksen, No. 800 Sqn. The pilot, Lt Luna, ejected with injuries
Sea Harrier (Sidewinder)	Two were shot down by Lt Thomas, one by Lt Ward, No. 801 Sqn. Maj. Piuma, Capt Donadille and Lt Senn all ejected

	Date	Time (local)	Type and unit	Location
40	21 May	15.11	Skyhawk (3rd Naval Ftr & Attack Esc.)	Falkland Sound
41	21 May	15.11	Skyhawk (as above)	Falkland Sound
42	21 May	15.21	Skyhawk (as above)	Falkland Sound, Port Stanley
43	23 May	10.15	Puma (Army)	Nr Shag Cove, W. Falkland
44	23 May	10.15	Augusta 109 (Army)	as above
45	23 May	10.16	Puma (Army)	as above
46	23 May	10.25	Puma (Army)	as above
47	23 May	——	Skyhawk (Grupo 5)	San Carlos Water
48	23 May	16.00	Dagger (Grupo 6)	Pebble I.
49–51	24 May	11.00	3 Daggers (Grupo 6)	Pebble I.
52	24 May	——	Skyhawk (Grupo 4)	San Carlos Water, W. of W. Falkland

Cause	Details
Sea Harrier (Sidewinder)	Shot down by Lt Morell, No. 800 Sqn. The Pilot, Lt Cdr Philippi, ejected
Sea Harrier (30 mm cannon)	Shot down by Flt Lt Leeming, No. 800 Sqn. The pilot, Lt Márquez, was killed
HMS *Ardent* (small-arms fire) and Sea Harrier (30 mm cannon)	Damaged by small-arms fire while attacking *Ardent*; suffered further damage from cannon fire from Sea Harrier flown by Lt Morrell, No. 800 Sqn. Tried to make emergency landing at Port Stanley but undercarriage could not be lowered. The pilot, Lt Arca, ejected
Sea Harrier	Flew into the ground while attempting to evade attack by Flt Lt Morgan, No. 800 Sqn. Credited to Sea Harrier
Sea Harrier (30 mm cannon)	Shot up on the ground by Flt Lts Morgan and Leeming, No. 800 Sqn.
Sea Harrier (30 mm cannon)	Shot up on the ground by Flt Lt Morgan, No. 800 Sqn.
Sea Harrier (30 mm cannon)	Shot up on the ground by Lt Cdr Gedge and Lt Cdr Braithwaite, No. 801 Sqn
multiple weapons	Believed shot down by combined fire from several weapons. Claims in area on this day: *Broadsword*, one with Sea Wolf and one with 40 mm Bofors; *Antelope*, one with Sea Cat; Rapier claimed three; Blowpipe missile operators also claimed. The pilot, Lt Guadagnini, was killed
Sea Harrier (Sidewinder)	Shot down by Lt Hale, No. 800 Sqn. The pilot, Lt Volponi, was killed
Sea Harrier (Sidewinder)	Two were shot down by Lt Cdr Auld, one by Lt Smith, No. 800 Sqn. Lt Castillo was killed. Maj. Puga and Capt Diaz ejected
multiple weapons	Crashed into sea on return flight after being damaged when engaged by multiple weapons. Lt Bono was killed. Claims in area on this day: *Argonaut*, one with Sea Cat and one with 40 mm Bofors; *Fearless*, one with Sea Cat; Rapier claimed three; Blowpipe missile operators also claimed

	Date	Time (local)	Type and unit	Location
53	25 May	12.30	Skyhawk (Grupo 4)	San Carlos Water
54	25 May	——	Skyhawk (Grupo 4)	San Carlos Water
55	25 May	——	Skyhawk (Grupo 5)	Nr Goose Green
56	26 May	15.10	Puma (Army)	M Kent
57	27 May	17.00	Skyhawk (Grupo 5)	San Carlos Water, W. Falkland
58	28 May	——	Macchi 339 (1st Naval Attack Esc.)	Goose Green
59–60	28 May	——	2 Pucarás (Grupo 3)	Goose Green
61	28 May	——	Pucará (Grupo 3)	not known
62	29 May	——	Dagger (Grupo 6)	San Carlos Water
63–4	30 May	14.31	2 Skyhawks (Grupo 4)	E. of Falklands
65	1 June	10.50	Hercules (Grupo 1)	50 miles N. of Pebble I.
66	7 June	09.17	Learjet (Grupo 2)	Pebble I.
67–9	8 June	16.47	3 Skyhawks (Grupo 5)	Choiseul Sound

Cause	Details
multiple weapons	**53** (Lt Lucero, ejected) and **54** (Lt Garcia, killed) both shot down by combined fire from several weapons. Claims in the area
multiple weapons	on this day: *Yarmouth*, one with Sea Cat; Rapier claimed three; Blowpipe missile operators also claimed
operational accident	Shot down by Argentine AA gunners. The pilot, Lt Palava, was killed
Harrier GR 3 (cluster bomb)	Destroyed on the ground by Sqn Ldr Pook, No. 1 Sqn
Bofors 40 mm	Hit by fire from *Fearless* or *Intrepid* while attacking target at Ajax Bay. The pilot, Lt Velasco, ejected from the severely damaged aircraft over W. Falkland
Blowpipe	Shot down by Royal Marine. The pilot, Lt Miguel, was killed
Blowpipe and small-arms fire	Shot down while attempting to attack British ground troops. Lt Cruzado and Lt Argañaraz both ejected
operational accident	Believed to have crashed into high ground while returning to Port Stanley from Goose Green in bad weather. Lt Gimenez missing, believed killed
Rapier	Lt Bernhardt killed.
HMS *Exeter* (Sea Dart)	Shot down during combined Skyhawk and Super Étendard attack on the British Task Group. Lt Vasquez and Lt Castillo were both killed
Sea Harrier (Sidewinder and 30 mm cannon)	Shot down by Lt Cdr Ward, No 801 Sqn. The pilot, Capt. Krause, and six crew were killed
HMS *Exeter* (Sea Dart)	Shot down during a high-altitude photographic reconnaissance mission. The pilot, Lt Col De La Colina, and four crew were killed
Sea Harrier (Sidewinder)	Two were shot down by Flt Lt Morgan, one by Lt Smith, No. 800 Sqn. The pilots, Lt Arraras, Lt Bolzan and Ensign Vazquez, were all killed

	Date	Time (local)	Type and unit	Location
70	13 June	22.25	Canberra (Grupo 2)	N. of Port Stanley

Aircraft captured after the surrender on 14 June, in various states, in addition to those above:

AIR FORCE
71–2   2 Pucarás (at Goose Green)
73–83   11 Pucarás (at Port Stanley)
84–5   2 Bell 212s (at Port Stanley)

NAVY
86–8   3 Macchi 339s (at Port Stanley)

COAST GUARD
89–90   1 Puma (at Port Stanley)
            1 Skyvan (at Port Stanley)

ARMY
91   1 Chinook (at Port Stanley)
92–3   2 Augusta 109s (at Port Stanley)
94–102 9 Bell UH-1Hs (at Port Stanley)

Cause   **Details**

HMS *Exeter* (Sea Dart)   Shot down during high-altitude night attack.
                             The pilot, Capt. Pastran, ejected; the
                             navigator, Capt. Casado, was killed

Appendix 5
Argentine Aircraft Losses by Type

Air Force

MAINLAND-BASED
    11 Daggers
    19 Skyhawks
    2 Canberras
    1 Learjet
    1 C-130 Hercules
    2 Mirage IIIs
FALKLANDS-BASED
    25 Pucarás
    2 Bell 212s   AIR FORCE TOTAL   **63**

Navy

MAINLAND-BASED
    3 Skyhawks
SHIP-BASED
    1 Alouette (*General Belgrano*)
FALKLANDS-BASED
    5 Macchi 339s
    4 Turbo-Mentors   NAVY TOTAL   **13**

Coast Guard

FALKLANDS-BASED
    2 Skyvans
    1 Puma   COAST GUARD TOTAL   **3**

Army

FALKLANDS AND SOUTH GEORGIA
    2 Chinooks
    8 Pumas
    9 Bell UH-1Hs
    3 Augusta 109s   ARMY TOTAL   **22**

Captured from British
    1 Islander   **1**

                                  Grand Total   **102**

Appendix 6
Argentine Aircraft Losses by Cause

Harrier Action
SEA HARRIER (IN THE AIR AND ON THE GROUND)

Sidewinder	18		
30 mm cannon	5		
Sidewinder and cannon	1		
Cluster bombs	2		
Crashed evading 30 mm, and small-arms fire	1		

HARRIER GR 3 (ALL ON THE GROUND)

30 mm cannon	3		
Cluster bombs	1	HARRIER TOTAL	32

Surface-launched Missiles, Guns, Small Arms

Sea Cat	1		
Sea Dart	5		
Sea Wolf	3		
Bofors 40 mm	1		
Blowpipe, Stinger, Small Arms	5		
Rapier	1		
Multiple weapons (San Carlos Water)	4	SURFACE WEAPONS TOTAL	20

Miscellaneous Losses

SAS attack, Pebble I.	11		
With ship	1		
Operational accident	6	MISCELLANEOUS LOSSES TOTAL	18

Captured on Ground
(This includes aircraft which suffered cumulative damage on the ground during attacks by Sea Harriers, Harrier GR 3s, naval bombardment, etc., where the exact cause of the damage which rendered the aircraft beyond repair cannot be determind)

Air Force	15		
Navy	3		
Coast Guard	2		
Army	12	CAPTURED TOTAL	32

	Grand Total	**102**

Appendix 7
The Number of Argentine Aircraft Lost During the Falklands Conflict: Comparison of the Authors' Figures with Those Issued by the British Government

One problem the authors have had to face during the preparation of this book has been that of evaluating the mass of sometimes conflicting information and figures originating from London and Buenos Aires on the number of aircraft the Argentine forces lost during the conflict. At first sight the differences between the authors' total figure (102 aircraft of all types lost) and those in the British Government White Paper 'The Falklands Campaign: The Lessons' (Cmnd 8758) (72 aircraft destroyed and 14 probably destroyed in the air; 31 destroyed on the ground) might seem insignificant. However, the authors' figure includes and the White Paper figure omits the five light attack aircraft and 13 helicopters captured more or less intact around Port Stanley after the conflict; also the authors have discovered 15 cases where Argentine sources mention aircraft that were lost which do not appear in the White Paper figure (in Appendix 4 these are Nos 2, 3, 5, 8, 9, 10, 11, 15 [Skyhawk which crashed evading missile], 16, 29, 39, 46, 55, 61 and 88). In the table that follows the losses are broken down by aircraft type, and it can be seen that the authors' figures and those in the White Paper differ in some important respects.

When the two sets of figures which relate to the same aircraft are considered – setting aside those losses in the authors' total which are not mentioned in the White Paper – there is a difference of 30; the 'confirmed' White Paper figure, plus those aircraft captured in various states after the conflict, being 118, while the authors' total is only 87. With the majority of aircraft types there is complete or almost complete agreement between the authors' and the White Paper figures. The only major discrepancies centre around the claims for Skyhawks and Mirage/Daggers destroyed: the authors' information substantiates only 27 of the 60 such aircraft whose claims are 'confirmed' in the White Paper. The divergence becomes even more marked if the claims of the Sea Harriers for Skyhawks and Mirage/Daggers are removed from the two figures: the White Paper confirms 16 such aircraft destroyed by Sea Harriers, and the authors agree with every one of these. For the surface-to-air missile and gun systems the White Paper 'confirms' 43 claims, for which the authors are able to find information to support only 12. It is the authors' belief that the remaining 31 Skyhawks and Mirage/Daggers were claimed in error and these aircraft were not shot down.

	Authors' Figures AIRCRAFT LOST (figures in brackets indicate aircraft not mentioned in the White Paper)	Believed Breakdown of White Paper Figures		
		CONFIRMED	PROBABLY DESTROYED	CAPTURED
Skyhawk	22(6)	37	8	—
Mirage/Dagger	13(2)	23	4	—
Pucará	25(2)	21	—	2
Macchi 339	5(2)	3	—	1
Turbo-Mentor	4	4	—	—
Canberra	2	2	1	—
Skyvan	2	2	—	—
Islander	1(1)	—	—	—
C-130 Hercules	1	1	—	—
Learjet	1	1	—	—
Puma	9(2)	6	—	1
Chinook	2	2	—	—
smaller helicopters	15	2	1	12
Totals	**102(15)**	**103**	**14**	**15**

Appendix 8
British Aircraft Losses

	Date	Time (local)	Type and unit	Location
1–2	22 April	morning	2 Wessex (845 Sqn)	S. Georgia
3	23 April	evening	Sea King (846 Sqn)	S. of Ascension
4	4 May	morning	Sea Harrier (800 Sqn)	Goose Green
5–6	6 May	09.00	2 Sea Harriers (801 Sqn)	E. of Falklands
7	12 May	14.35	Sea King	E. of Falklands
8	17 May	21.30	Sea King	E. of Falklands
9	19 May	19.15	Sea King (846 Sqn)	E. of Falklands
10	20 May	morning	Sea King (846 Sqn)	Nr Punta Arenas, Chile
11–12	21 May	morning	2 Gazelles (RM)	Port San Carlos
13	21 May	09.00	Harrier GR 3 (1 Sqn)	Port Howard
14	21 May	14.48	Lynx (815 Sqn)	Falkland Sound
15	24 May	20.00	Sea Harrier (800 Sqn)	E. of Falklands
16	25 May	15.25	Lynx (815 Sqn)	Off Pebble I.
17–26	25 May	16.40	1 Lynx, 6 Wessex and 3 Chinooks	N.E. of Falklands
27	27 May	13.30	Harrier GR 3 (1 Sqn)	Goose Green
28	28 May	——	Scout (RM)	Goose Green

Cause	Details
operational accident	Crashed in very bad weather on Fortune Glacier, during operation to rescue SAS patrol
operational accident	
ground anti-aircraft fire	Probably shot down by 35 mm Oerlikon. Lt Taylor was killed
operational accident	Probably collided in poor visibility. Lt Cdr Eyton-Jones and Lt Curtiss were killed
operational accident	Ditched
operational accident	Ditched
operational accident	Tail rotor struck large sea bird and the helicopter crashed. Twenty-two on board were killed
abandoned	Aircraft lost in circumstances which are still secret
small arms	Shot down during initial landings
ground anti-aircraft fire	Probably shot down by 20 mm fire. Flt Lt Glover ejected and was taken prisoner
air attack	Destroyed during bombing attack on HMS *Ardent*
operational accident	Crashed into sea shortly after taking off from HMS *Hermes*. Lt Cdr Batt was killed
air attack	Went down with HMS *Coventry*
Exocet	Lost on the *Atlantic Conveyor*
ground anti-aircraft fire	Probably shot down by 35 mm Oerlikon. Sqn Ldr Iveson ejected and evaded capture
air combat	Shot down by Pucará of Grupo 3. Lt Nunn was killed

	Date	Time (local)	Type and unit	Location
29	29 May	——	Sea Harrier (801 Sqn)	E. of Falklands
30	30 May	12.15	Harrier GR 3 (1 Sqn)	Nr Port Stanley
31	1 June	15.00	Sea Harrier (801 Sqn)	S. of Port Stanley
32	6 June	——	Gazelle (656 Sqn)	W. of Fitzroy
33	8 June	09.30	Harrier GR 3 (1 Sqn)	Port San Carlos
34	12 June	03.30	Wessex (737 Sqn)	Off Port Stanley

Cause	Details
operational accident	Slid off the deck of HMS *Invincible* while she was turning in very bad weather. Lt Cdr Broadwater ejected as the aircraft went over the side, and was rescued
small-arms fire	Hit in its fuel system, the aircraft was unable to regain its carrier. Sqn Ldr Pook ejected and was rescued from sea
Roland	Hit by missile. Flt Lt Mortimer ejected, and and was rescued from the sea after eight hours in a dinghy
missile	Shot down by missile, type not certain
operational accident	Suffered partial engine failure in hover while coming in to land at Port San Carlos airstrip and was damaged beyond repair. Pilot unhurt
Exocet	Wrecked when missile hit HMS *Glamorgan*

Appendix 9
Argentine Ships Lost or Damaged

25 APRIL

Santa Fe (submarine), seriously damaged by depth charges from a Wessex of No. 737 Squadron from HMS *Antrim*, off Grytviken, South Georgia, early in the morning. Later attacked by a Wasp of No. 829 Squadron from *Endurance* and hit by an AS 12 missile which damaged the conning tower. She was run ashore and the crew abandoned her

2 MAY

General Belgrano (cruiser), torpedoed by the nuclear submarine HMS *Conqueror* south-west of the Falklands at 4 p.m. Sank with heavy loss of life

3 MAY

Alférez Sobral (patrol boat), seriously damaged after being hit by Sea Skua missiles fired by a Lynx of No. 815 Squadron from HMS *Coventry* soon after midnight

Comodoro Somellera (patrol boat), sunk after being hit by Sea Skua missiles fired by a Lynx of No. 815 Squadron from HMS *Glasgow* soon after midnight

9 MAY

Narwal (a stern trawler operating under Argentine Navy orders), bombed and strafed by Sea Harriers of No. 800 Squadron north of Port Stanley in the morning. Her crew abandoned her and a Royal Navy boarding party took possession, but she sank under tow on the following day

16 MAY

Bahía Buen Suceso (freighter), strafed by Sea Harriers of No. 800 Squadron alongside the jetty at Fox Bay on West Falkland in the morning. Her crew abandoned her. Later she broke adrift during a gale and was blown aground

Rio Carcaraña (freighter), bombed and strafed by Sea Harriers of No. 800 Squadron in Falkland Sound in the morning. Abandoned by crew

22 MAY

Rio Iguazu (Coast Guard patrol boat), strafed by Sea Harriers of No. 800 Squadron in Choiseul Sound east of Goose Green at 8.30 a.m. Damaged and run aground

Appendix 10
British Ships Lost or Damaged

I MAY

HMS *Arrow* (frigate) and HMS *Glamorgan* (destroyer), suffered minor damage during an attack by Daggers of Grupo 6 off Port Stanley at 4.40 p.m.

4 MAY

HMS *Sheffield* (destroyer), hit by an Exocet missile from a Super Étendard of the 2nd Naval Fighter and Attack Escuadrilla 100 miles south of Port Stanley at 11.02 a.m. The missile failed to explode, but started an uncontrollable fire and the ship had to be abandoned. Sank on 10 May

12 MAY

HMS *Glasgow* (destroyer), suffered moderate damage during an attack by Skyhawks of Grupo 5 off Port Stanley at 2 p.m. A 1,000-pound bomb passed right through the ship, but did not explode until it was well clear

21 MAY

HMS *Argonaut* (frigate), suffered minor damage during an attack by a Macchi 339 of 1st Naval Attack Escuadrilla off San Carlos Water at 10.36 a.m. In a later attack by Skyhawks at 2.30 p.m. she was hit twice by 1,000-pound bombs which failed to detonate. Seriously damaged

HMS *Antrim* (destroyer), suffered serious damage when attacked by Dagger of Grupo 6 off San Carlos Water at 11 a.m.; she was hit on stern by a 1,000-pound bomb which failed to detonate

HMS *Broadsword* (frigate), suffered minor damage during a strafing attack by Daggers of Grupo 6 off San Carlos Water at 11 a.m. In a later attack at 2.40 p.m. she suffered further minor damage

HMS *Ardent* (frigate), suffered serious damage when hit by a 1,000-pound bomb during an attack by Daggers of Grupo 6 in Grantham Sound at 2.30 p.m. Suffered further heavy damage during an attack by Skyhawks of Grupo 5 at 2.45 p.m., and yet more serious damage during an attack by Skyhawks of the 3rd Naval Fighter and Attack Escuadrilla at 3.01 p.m. Ship later abandoned and sank

HMS *Brilliant* (frigate), suffered minor damage during strafing attack off San Carlos Water at about 2.45 p.m.

23 MAY

HMS *Antelope* (frigate), suffered damage when hit by two bombs which failed to explode, during attacks by Skyhawks of Grupo 5 and the 3rd Naval Fighter and Attack Escuadrilla in San Carlos Water at 2.09 p.m. During later operations to defuse the bombs one exploded and the ship burnt out and sank

24 MAY
Royal Fleet Auxiliaries *Sir Galahad* and *Sir Lancelot* suffered moderate damage, and
  Sir Bedivere minor damage, when hit by 1,000-pound bombs which failed to
  explode, in San Carlos Water at 11.14 a.m.

25 MAY
HMS *Broadsword* (frigate), suffered moderate damage when hit by a 1,000-pound
  bomb which failed to explode, during an attack by Skyhawks of Grupo 5 off
  Pebble Island at 3.24 p.m.
HMS *Coventry* (destroyer), capsized after being hit by three 1,000-pound bombs
  during an attack by Skyhawks of Grupo 5 off Pebble Island at 3.25 p.m.
Atlantic Conveyor (container ship), hit by an Exocet missile from a Super Étendard of
  the 2nd Naval Fighter and Attack Escuadrilla 100 miles north-east of Port
  Stanley at 4.41 p.m. Ship burned out; sank on 30 May

8 JUNE
HMS *Plymouth* (frigate), suffered serious damage during an attack by Daggers of
  Grupo 6 off San Carlos Water at 2.02 p.m. Hit by four 1,000-pound bombs; none
  of them detonated but one set off a depth charge on the flight deck which started a
  severe fire
Royal Fleet Auxiliaries *Sir Galahad* and *Sir Tristram* were severely damaged during
  attacks by Skyhawks of Grupo 5 off Fitzroy at 2.10 p.m. The former was later
  scuttled, and the latter relegated to use as accommodation ship

12 JUNE
HMS *Glamorgan* (destroyer), hit by a land-launched Exocet missile off Port Stanley
  at 3.30 a.m. The missile failed to explode but caused serious damage

Appendix 11
Brief Details of the Main
Aircraft Types Used by the
Argentine Forces

Note: The versions described are those used by the Argentine forces; the war loads
are those carried by aircraft during the conflict.

Dassault Mirage III Single-seater French-built interceptor fighter, capable of
Mach 2.2 at high altitude carrying no underwing stores. During operations,
carrying missiles and two 375-gallon drop tanks and sometimes flying below 20,000

feet, the aircraft was considerably less manoeuvrable and only slightly faster than the subsonic Sea Harrier. Built-in armament: two 30 mm cannon. Normal missile load: one Matra 530 semi-active radar homing missile under the fuselage and/or two Matra 550 Magic infra-red homing missiles under the wings. Although this type could carry bombs, it never did so during the conflict.

Israel Aircraft Industries Dagger Unlicensed copy of the Mirage V, the ground-attack version of the aircraft above, with simpler avionics and a slightly greater internal fuel tankage. Like the Mirage III this aircraft is capable of supersonic speed at high altitude, but not at low altitude carrying the normal load of drop tanks and bombs. Built-in armament: two 30 mm cannon. Normal bomb load: two 1,000-pound or four 500-pound bombs. On a few occasions Daggers flew high-altitude escort missions carrying two Shafrir infra-red homing missiles under the wings.

Douglas Skyhawk Single-seater American-built naval attack aircraft. Maximum speed about 575 m.p.h. at low altitude carrying bombs and fuel tanks. Modified for in-flight refuelling. Built-in armament: two 20 mm cannon. Normal bomb load: up to two 1,000-pound or four 500-pound bombs. The Argentine Navy version could carry two early-model Sidewinner missiles, but never did so during the conflict.

Dassault Super Étendard Single-seater French-built naval attack aircraft. Maximum speed 630 m.p.h. at low altitude with normal war load. Able to refuel in flight. Built-in armament: two 30 mm cannon. Normal war load: Exocet active radar-homing anti-ship missile under the starboard wing, drop tanks under the port wing and fuselage. Although it was ordered for operations from the aircraft carrier *25 de Mayo*, at the time of the conflict the necessary modifications to the ship had not been completed.

British Aerospace Canberra B 62 Two-seater British-built twin-jet bomber. Maximum speed 515 m.p.h. at low altitude or 540 m.p.h. at 40,000 feet. Normal bomb load: six 1,000-pound bombs.

FMA Pucará Two-seater Argentine-built twin turbo-prop light attack aircraft; on operations normally flew with only one pilot. Maximum speed at low altitude with normal military load, less than 300 m.p.h. Built-in armament: two 20 mm cannon, four 7.62 mm machine guns. Normal war load: two napalm tanks or two pods each with nineteen 2.75-inch unguided rockets.

Macchi 339 Two-seater Italian-built jet trainer and light attack aircraft; on operations normally flew with only one pilot. Maximum speed at low altitude with normal military load, less than 500 m.p.h. Normal war load: two 30 mm gun pods and four 5-inch unguided rockets.

Gates Learjet 35A Five-seater American-built twin-jet executive aircraft. Some fitted with aerial cameras for use as high-altitude survey and photographic reconnaissance aircraft. Maximum cruising speed 525 m.p.h. at 41,000 feet.

Appendix 12
Brief Details of the Main Aircraft Types Used by the British Forces

Note: The aircraft described are in the configurations used, and carrying the war loads employed, during the conflict.

British Aerospace Sea Harrier FRS 1 Short take-off and vertical landing naval single-seat fighter, reconnaissance and anti-ship strike aircraft, with a secondary ground-attack role. Maximum speed about 690 m.p.h. at low altitude. Can be fitted for in-flight refuelling. Normal war load two 30 mm gun pods, plus: two AIM-9L Sidewinder infra-red homing air-to-air missiles, or three 1,000-pound bombs of normal configuration or with parachute retardation tails or with radar air-burst fusing; or two BL 755 cluster bombs each containing 147 bomblets.

British Aerospace Harrier GR 3 Short take-off and vertical landing single-seat attack and reconnaissance aircraft, modified for operation from aircraft carriers and with a secondary air-to-air combat role. Maximum speed about 690 m.p.h. at low altitude. Can be fitted for in-flight refuelling. Normal war load two 30 mm gun pods, plus: bombs as Sea Harrier; or two Paveway laser-guided bombs; or two Strike radar-homing missiles; or two pods each with thirty-six 2-inch rockets. Can be fitted to carry a reconnaissance pod under the fuselage carrying five cameras to give horizon-to-horizon coverage. For the air-to-air combat role can be fitted to carry two AIM-9G Sidewinder missiles.

British Aerospace Vulcan B2 Four-jet long-range bomber, fitted for in-flight refuelling. Maximum speeds 400 m.p.h. at 10,000 feet, 610 m.p.h. at 40,000 feet. Crew of six carried during extended-range operations. War load: twenty-one 1,000-pound bombs of normal configuration or with radar air burst fusing; or two or four Shrike radar-homing missiles.

British Aerospace Nimrod MR 2 Four-jet long-range maritime reconnaissance aircraft, modified for in-flight refuelling. Normal speeds on patrol about 400 m.p.h. at 8,000 feet, 500 m.p.h. at 30,000 feet. Crew of up to eighteen carried during extended-range operations. During operations aircraft carried a mixed war load of 1,000-pound bombs and Stingray anti-submarine homing torpedoes. Later some aircraft were fitted to carry four AIM-9G Sidewinner missiles under the wings.

Westland Lynx HAS 2 Three-seater general-purpose naval helicopter. Maximum speed 167 m.p.h. In the anti-ship role this aircraft carried two Sea Skua semi-active radar-homing missiles.

Index

257

259